Academic Freedom in a

Palgrave Critical University Studies

Series Editor:
John Smyth, University of Huddersfield, UK

Titles include:

Joanna Williams
ACADEMIC FREEDOM IN AN AGE OF CONFORMITY
Confronting the Fear of Knowledge

Forthcoming titles include:

James Arvanitakis and David Hornsby (*editors*)
UNIVERSITIES, THE CITIZEN SCHOLAR AND THE FUTURE OF HIGHER EDUCATION

Suman Gupta, Jernej Habjan and Hrvoje Tutek (*editors*)
ACADEMIC LABOUR AND UNEMPLOYMENT IN GLOBAL HIGHER EDUCATION
Neoliberal Policies of Funding and Management

Palgrave Critical University Studies
Series Standing Order ISBN 978–1–137–56429–0 Hardback
978–1–137–56430–6 Paperback
(*outside North America only*)

You can receive future titles in this series as they are published by placing a standing order. Please contact your bookseller or, in case of difficulty, write to us at the address below with your name and address, the title of the series and the ISBN quoted above.

Customer Services Department, Macmillan Distribution Ltd, Houndmills, Basingstoke, Hampshire RG21 6XS, England

Academic Freedom in an Age of Conformity

Confronting the Fear of Knowledge

Joanna Williams
University of Kent, UK

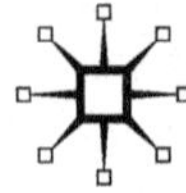

First published 2016 by
PALGRAVE MACMILLAN

Palgrave Macmillan in the UK is an imprint of Macmillan Publishers Limited, registered in England, company number 785998, of Houndmills, Basingstoke, Hampshire RG21 6XS.

Palgrave Macmillan in the US is a division of St Martin's Press LLC, 175 Fifth Avenue, New York, NY 10010.

Palgrave Macmillan is the global academic imprint of the above companies and has companies and representatives throughout the world.

Palgrave® and Macmillan® are registered trademarks in the United States, the United Kingdom, Europe and other countries.

ISBN 978-1-137-51478-3 ISBN 978-1-137-51479-0 (eBook)
DOI 10.1057/9781137514790

This book is printed on paper suitable for recycling and made from fully managed and sustained forest sources. Logging, pulping and manufacturing processes are expected to conform to the environmental regulations of the country of origin.

A catalogue record for this book is available from the British Library.

A catalog record for this book is available from the Library of Congress.

Contents

Acknowledgements

I could not have written this book without help from many different people I am fortunate enough to know. My University of Kent colleagues (especially those who are also my students) put up with me testing out new ideas and prevented me from lapsing into intellectual complacency. The inspirational online magazine *Spiked* has given me a forum to rehearse arguments for academic freedom. I am grateful to all the team at *Spiked*, especially Brendan O'Neill, Tim Black, Viv Regan and Tom Slater, for creating a space where free speech is not only discussed as a principle but consistently exercised in practice. Ella Whelan did a fantastic job of providing me with examples, references and encouragement. Jennie Bristow is not only a superb editor but also a wonderful friend – this book benefits enormously from her insights. My husband, Jim Butcher, and my children, George, Harry and Florence, remind me not only of the crucial importance of arguing for liberty, but also of the need for a life away from the university.

Introduction

Current debates about free speech on campus, and arguments over the limits to academic freedom, extend beyond the confines of higher education. Discernible public unease over the emergence of a new generation of censorious students sits alongside discussion about the role universities should play in preventing terrorism, or the place of academic freedom in a marketized higher education sector where commercial interests often dominate. It is important that such questions are being asked, even more so when academic freedom is considered in the broader context of the purpose of a university.

However, such debates often present threats to academic freedom as arising entirely outside of academia. This ignores the pressures on scholars to self-censor and the re-evaluation and re-definition of academic freedom that is taking place within higher education itself. This book explores the historical importance of academic freedom to the pursuit of knowledge and asks what becomes of this project when concepts such as truth and objectivity are considered increasingly problematic.

All around the world, national governments are imposing restrictions on academic freedom. In the UK, there has been disquiet over the duty that the government's proposed counterterrorism and security legislation will place upon universities to prevent students from being 'radicalized' into joining extremist groups. While some in government think it incumbent on academics to police the behaviour of students, monitor their whereabouts and report anything suspicious to the police, academics and the public are less convinced (Travis, 12/01/15).

The proposed legislation builds upon the UK's Prevent strategy, which was introduced by the then Labour government in the mid-2000s as an attempt to eradicate violent extremism. As a result of Prevent, universities have, over the past ten years, implemented a plethora of rules to regulate student societies and invitations to external speakers. The latest proposals will go further in preventing 'radical' ideas from being heard on campus. Anyone with strongly held religious or political views will be banned outright, while for others, the time and energy needed to comply with bureaucratic checking mechanisms will surely act as a deterrent.

The Canadian government is likewise proposing anti-terror legislation that would criminalize 'advocating terrorism' within higher education. In the wake of the terrorist attacks of September 11, 2001, American researchers perceived an increase in restrictions on academic freedom stemming from federal government. The Patriot Act, re-authorized in 2006, allows federal government officials to request 'business records' of booksellers and librarians, thereby revealing academics' reading material (Streb, 2006, p. 9). In addition, research funders are reported to be increasingly selective in the work they will support; the Ford Foundation, for example, refuses to fund activity that 'promotes violence, terrorism, bigotry, or the destruction of any state' (Butler, 2006a, p. 132). There are concerns that academic freedom in Hong Kong is being restricted by the government in Beijing.

That such issues attract public attention shows that, rhetorically at least, the concept of academic freedom has historic resonance, and that challenges to it pose a threat to a dearly held value. For defenders of academic freedom, it is reassuring to see the indignation that threats to its existence attracts.

It is easy to identify threats to academic freedom that originate from outside of the academy. They are normally politically motivated and carry the weight of legislation. More frequent and insidious, however, are threats to academic freedom that occur within universities. Such threats can often go unnoticed or are even welcomed as the value, meaning and purpose of academic freedom are increasingly called into question. When threats to academic freedom from within universities do hit the headlines, stories often focus around particular individuals who somehow cause dissent within their institution. In 2014, the names of three academics in particular made the headlines, not just in the national higher education trade press, but in the international mainstream media.

The most high-profile case was that of the American academic Steven Salaita who, in the summer of 2014, was appointed Professor of American Indian Studies at the University of Illinois at Urbana–Champaign. This tenured position was subsequently rescinded before Salaita had formally arrived on campus. It was initially suggested that Salaita's appointment was overruled by senior managers once they became aware of the forthright nature of his comments on social media criticizing the state of Israel and defending the Palestinian cause (Wilson, 08/08/14). Since then, it has been reported that the University of Illinois received petitions from institutional financial backers who were supporters of Israel and wanted the appointment suspended (Adler, 09/11/14). Salaita contested his dismissal and was granted $5,000 by the American Association of University Professors (AAUP) for his involvement in an academic freedom controversy (Toensing, 17/10/14). In December 2014, an internal investigation criticized the University of Illinois for 'the use of civility as a standard in making hiring decisions' (Jaschik, 02/01/15).

In the UK, Thomas Docherty, Professor of English and Comparative Literature and a renowned critic of government higher education policy, was suspended from his post at Warwick University for nine months over allegations of insubordination towards his head of department (Matthews, 24/07/14). He stood accused of employing sarcasm and inappropriately sighing in job interviews. He has since been reinstated and although faced with a hefty legal bill, all charges against him have been dropped (Morgan, 30/10/14).

In Australia, Barry Spurr, Professor of Poetry and Poetics at the University of Sydney, was suspended for sending emails that contained racist and sexist content. Although Spurr had used his university email account, his inflammatory messages were sent privately to around a dozen senior academics and officials within the university. These emails, considered especially newsworthy because of Spurr's appointment as a consultant to the federal government's national English curriculum review, were published on the Australian website *New Matilda* (Graham, 19/10/14). Students began a campaign to have Spurr removed from the university, which went on to garner national support (Jabour, 23/10/14).

There are numerous other cases, which attract less media attention. At the University of Leeds in the UK, Carole McCartney, Reader in Law, was reprimanded for sending political tweets in which she questioned the policies of the government's then home secretary, Theresa May (Parr, 21/08/14). At the University of Kansas in the US, Journalism Professor David Guth was placed on indefinite paid leave for tweets he sent vehemently criticizing the National Rifle Association following a shooting in a navy yard (Staff Reporter, 21/09/13). Mark Walcott, the Head of Performing Arts at Newham College in East London, was immediately suspended from his post after a colleague secretly recorded him making a homophobic 'staffroom rant' (Jeory, 27/11/13).

This recent spate of high-profile battles between individual academics and university managers can make it appear as if academic freedom is an issue just for certain individuals, particularly those with a fondness for using social media, rather than something of broader concern to the collective and public goals of higher education. For many within universities, academic freedom is taken for granted until a defence against draconian management decisions is sought; then it is called upon as a last-ditch insurance policy, the alibi of those unwise enough to have 'misspoken' and made comments considered beyond the pale by the right-thinking majority.

The focus on national government policies on the one hand and individual cases on the other reflect and exacerbate a confusion about the meaning of academic freedom. While academic freedom is needed to defend universities and academics from national government edicts or heavy-handed institutional managers, much of the day-to-day undermining of academic freedom comes from more well-meaning fellow colleagues or even students. There is little discussion of the significance of academic freedom to the act of scholarship.

In today's marketized and consumer-driven higher education sector, many students have come to expect freedom *from* speech (Lukianoff, 2014). They argue the university campus should be a 'safe space', free from emotional harm or potential offence. Lecturers are often all too ready to self-censor so as to satisfy rather than cause upset. Managers and administrators enforce speech codes (Lukianoff, 2012), anti-harassment policies and equality and diversity initiatives, all of which are well intentioned but have the effect of privileging intellectual safety and comfort over academic freedom. The urge in lecturers to conform and keep focused on their career at a time of growing concern over job security runs deep. This means that restrictions upon academic freedom may rarely be felt, and those who do find their freedom curtailed may find it increasingly difficult to locate the source of the threat.

What is often forgotten in today's discussions is that the principles of academic freedom are fundamentally important to the pursuit of knowledge. Freedom to propose the outrageous and challenge the ordinary is as essential for individual liberty as it is for society's collective knowledge and understanding of the world to advance. This understanding – that personal freedom is a prerequisite for both a critique of conventional knowledge and the search for the new – was established over two centuries ago. In 1784, the philosopher Immanuel Kant defined enlightenment, or people's awakening from their self-imposed immaturity, as requiring nothing but freedom. For people to take control of their own lives, Kant argued, they needed the 'freedom to make public use of one's reason in all matters' (2009, p. 3). Kant proposed the motto of enlightenment to be *Sapere Aude!* or *Dare to Know!* John Stuart Mill, writing in *On Liberty* some 80 years later, was also adamant that freedom was essential for intellectual accomplishment: 'Genius can only breathe freely in an atmosphere of freedom' (2005, p. 82).

Individual freedom in the private sphere is necessary for received orthodoxies to be ruthlessly criticized and new ways of seeing the world to be tested; in the public domain, freedom makes collective acts of judgement possible. Intellectual freedom is essential for making a 'marketplace of ideas', a metaphor that draws upon concepts discussed in Mill's *On Liberty*, a reality. The term 'marketplace of ideas' was first used by H. G. Wells in his 1918 novel *Joan and Peter: The Story of an Education* (Kissel, 08/09/14) and later by US Justice Oliver Wendell Holmes in 1919. It compares the free exchange of ideas to the free exchange of goods within a market economy. Just as it is assumed that rational consumers freely choose the best product having considered issues of price, quality and relevance to their needs, so it is assumed that rational, intellectually autonomous individuals can choose from a range of ideas those they consider to be the best (Gordon, 1997, p. 235). In this way, the metaphor of the marketplace of ideas refers to the notion that truth will emerge if ideas are set in competition with one another.

The significance of academic freedom, as both Kant and Mill were acutely aware, lies in the fact that it enables scholars to challenge the dominant orthodoxies of the day. In order for society's collective understanding of the world to progress, knowledge needs to be contestable and open to being superseded when intellectual advances are made. This does not mean that there is no truth or objectivity in knowledge. On the contrary, Kant repeatedly argues that truth is integral to the exercise of scholarship: 'truth (the essential and first condition of learning in general) is the main thing' (1979, p. 45). The role of philosophers, Kant claims, is to critique existing knowledge 'in order to test its truth' (1979, p. 45). Therefore, for understanding to advance, academics need the freedom to test existing truth claims, disprove fallacies and propose new truth claims, knowing that these too may be tested and superseded. In sum, discovering truth is the goal of advancing knowledge, and academic freedom is essential to this process.

Academics and students alike have long recognized the importance of freedom to any truly scholarly or intellectual pursuit; yet universities, as institutions whose very purpose is entwined with the pursuit and transmission of knowledge, have rarely been havens of unfettered liberty for those who work or study within them. From the emergence of the European university in the medieval period, through to the challenge posed to the church by scientific thought, and from the impact of McCarthyism in the USA in the 1950s to today's market-driven focus on institutional reputation and image management, the history of higher education can be read as the struggle for academic freedom. This began as the struggle for universities to gain autonomy from church or state, and later became a fight for individual scholars to secure intellectual freedom from and within the university to teach, research and engage with the public as they deemed best.

New threats to academic freedom

Today there is little collective agreement over either the definition or significance of academic freedom, and this makes recognizing and responding to attacks on intellectual liberty more difficult. In the following chapter, I present a schematic view of the history of academic freedom, primarily from the perspective of the British and

American higher education sectors. I draw out the main trends and developments and how definitions have changed over time. While this selective history does not account for some of the more subtle twists or contradictions that have occurred, it does allow general themes to emerge. It is notable that many trends that today appear to restrict academic freedom or enforce a culture of conformity in universities began as progressive attempts to expand knowledge into new areas and utilize new methods. Today such radical ideas often tend to shape the pursuit of knowledge in a more partial and stifling direction than the traditional approaches they critiqued.

The concept of academic freedom I draw upon throughout this book is deliberately broad and general: academics should have all the same rights to free speech enshrined within law as other citizens. Obviously this proviso puts in place many limitations on academic freedom. In the UK, for example, libel laws have long impinged upon the publication of research (Corbyn, 10/12/09). Germany outlaws Holocaust denial (Staff Reporter, 15/01/07), and hate speech is a crime in Australia (Liptak, 11/06/08). In one respect, academic freedom simply asserts the importance of free speech, as a foundational right of everyone in society, to scholars in particular.

Beyond this, academics need additional employment protection denied to other workers because they may need to challenge views held by senior colleagues within their own disciplinary area, the nature of higher education more broadly or their own institution in particular. This does not provide protection for lecturers who are somehow incompetent or otherwise in breach of their contract of employment, but it does guarantee a freedom to speak out and provide a critical voice on issues within, and importantly beyond, the individual's field of expertise. I suggest this extra job security comes with a moral obligation upon scholars not to curtail the speech of people outside the academy. As far as possible, academics, as public intellectuals, should open up debates to include wider society.

Today it can often seem that academics are as likely to be involved in calls to restrict free speech as they are to defend such points of principle. Certain issues, for example rape and climate change, are held up as requiring specialist knowledge that can only come from years of research. Too often academics fear dangerous consequences from allowing people without this knowledge to engage in debate;

they worry people may reach the 'wrong' conclusions and that some discussions must therefore be held away from the public.

In October 2013, a public event held at the London School of Economics (LSE) entitled *Is Rape Different?* had as one of its speakers Helen Reece, Associate Professor of Law and author of 'Rape myths: Is elite opinion right and public opinion wrong?', published in the esteemed *Oxford Journal of Legal Studies*. In this article, Reece argues that the regressiveness of current public attitudes towards rape has been overstated. At the LSE event, Reece, along with her fellow panellist, the barrister Barbara Hewson, argued that the assumption that rape myths are widespread serves to close down rather than open up debate, as all discussion can be said to perpetrate such myths and therefore contribute to a climate whereby women feel responsible for their own rape and do not report crimes.

As if to illustrate her point, a group of feminist critical lawyers based at the University of Kent published a response to the debate in which they argued, 'We deplore LSE Law's decision to give a platform to Reece and Hewson's dangerous and unsupported views and its failure to engage responsibly with the public on such an important and sensitive issue as rape' (Editors, 2013). The published response acted as a petition calling for the LSE to 'ensure that the ideas disseminated [at the debate] do not feed dangerous stereotypes about women being responsible for the sexual violence perpetuated against them'.

This episode revealed a call from one group of academics to restrict the freedom of a fellow academic to participate in a debate, on the assumption that a free discussion of the issue of rape, particularly one that involves members of the public, is somehow dangerous. We see that, however well intentioned, the threat to academic freedom in this instance comes not from national government or university managers, but from fellow colleagues.

A further argument, again made by academics seeking to restrict discussion of rape more broadly and the publicity around the LSE debate in particular, was that the freedom afforded to a few individuals in positions of power (academics) served to undermine the more general free speech rights of rape survivors who perhaps lacked the confidence or security to discuss their situation openly (Cooper, 2013). The argument was made that only by restricting dominant opposing voices could the free speech of the more vulnerable hope to be safeguarded.

However, as soon as rights to free speech are set in opposition to one another in this way, then an individual or a group is left responsible for deciding who gets to speak – based, presumably, on the proposed content of the arguments or the identity of the speaker. Free speech for some becomes free speech for none, as all are expected to comply with the moral framework dictated by an unelected clique. Which voices get heard, in keeping with more general free speech principles, has never been determined on the basis of social justice. While this may be unfair, and is certainly not always nice, it is only through a clash of competing views that new ideas can challenge and, based on the validity of the arguments proposed, perhaps even supersede previously held orthodoxies. For this reason, it is always in the interests of under-represented groups for there to be more free speech rather than less.

A similar attempt to keep debate away from the general public and restrict it to academic experts can be seen with the issue of climate change. There is a pervasive view among academics that the science is now settled and the existence of man-made global warming proven beyond reasonable doubt. The Australian Prime Minister Tony Abbott was roundly criticized for providing government funding for the 'climate change contrarian' Bjorn Lomborg to establish a research centre at the University of Western Australia (Readfearn, 23/04/15). Claims that the science of climate change is beyond dispute have been interpreted by Professor Brian Cox, physicist and television presenter, as meaning that public debate on the issue is unhelpful. Cox said, 'I always regret it when knowledge becomes controversial. It's clearly a bad thing, for knowledge to be controversial' (Mathiesen, 03/09/14). His argument is that scientific knowledge can only properly be challenged by fellow experts, and although the public should be allowed to question what decisions are made as a consequence of this knowledge, only scientists should be able to question the knowledge itself.

Arguing that the current science of climate change is beyond public contestation is not only antithetical to academic freedom; it also calls into question the basic principles of a centuries-old scientific method. Physicist David Deutsch recognizes this and argues that 'conjecture and refutation is the only way, in principle, that knowledge can be acquired' (Pinker, 2014). In a liberal democratic society, the right to refute cannot be restricted according to a citizen's level of academic qualification or their profession. Knowledge must be open for everyone to challenge. The advantage of a marketplace of ideas is that the best, least refutable, ideas will win out no matter how often they are contested or by whom. The assumption that some knowledge is incontestable contributes towards a culture of conformity in universities.

Academic freedom has not always been so misunderstood or lightly held. In America in 1915, the then recently formed AAUP published its *Declaration of Principles of Academic Freedom* following investigations into the plight of scholars who had lost their livelihoods after expressing views which offended the political or religious sensibilities of their institution's trustees. The signatories to the *Declaration* demanded freedom of inquiry and research; freedom of teaching within the university or college; and freedom of extramural utterance and action. These three elements remain at the heart of today's definitions of academic freedom. Then, as now, it is 'the right of university teachers to express their opinions freely outside the university or to engage in political activities in their capacity as citizens' that appeared most immediately pressing in the effort to secure intellectual liberty.

Fifty years later, the battle for free speech in higher education fell to students. In September 1964, students at the University of California, Berkeley, began an unprecedented campaign against the restrictions preventing them from taking part in political debates and activity on campus. In what later became known as the Free Speech Movement, thousands of students and some professors were involved in months of protests demanding the same First Amendment rights to agitate, discuss, fundraise and recruit people to their chosen political causes as other citizens. Eventually the university management had little choice but to lift institutional *in loco parentis* legislation and meet the students' demands (Slater, 26/09/14). Removing stifling restrictions on political discussion allowed everyone at the university to think more freely.

Both the AAUP *Declaration* and the Berkeley student protests played an important role in defining and confirming the importance of academic freedom, not in a restricted and technical sense but in a far broader relationship to freedom of speech and of conscience.

Today, far from championing academic freedom, we see examples of scholars seeking to keep debates away from the public or to censor views which they personally find politically objectionable. The often self-imposed restrictions on speech appear to stand in contrast to the spirit of the 1960s, when many students and radical lecturers at universities across Europe and the USA challenged the censoriousness of university managers and their infantilizing imposition of moralistic rules governing personal behaviour. Even then however, demands for free speech often sat alongside campaigns to bar military recruiters and officer training schemes from US campuses, as well as the refusal to allow right-wing political groups a base from which to speak. 'No Platform for Fascists' was a popular slogan among students on both sides of the Atlantic. This trend for students and political radicals to be at the forefront of outlawing that which they perceive to be politically objectionable continues today.

Although such calls to limit debate are normally focused upon single issues, campaigners for academic Boycott, Divestment and Sanctions (BDS) against Israel effectively seek to curtail the intellectual freedom of individual scholars in every university in an entire country. BDS proponents urge academics to 'boycott Israeli institutions and government-sponsored projects until the Israeli state abides by international law' (Maira, 09/04/14). BDS campaigns began in the UK in 2005 but rapidly spread to the USA, culminating in December 2013 with the American Studies Association (ASA) voting in favour of an academic boycott of Israeli universities. As former AAUP President Cary Nelson suggests, this promotes the view that 'ideas should be judged not by their quality but by a political assessment based on national origin' (2015, p. 62).

A boycott means that Israeli scholars are prevented from collaborating in research projects, attending conferences (unless they have private finance) and engaging in other forms of pursuing and disseminating knowledge that involve liaison with an academic community reaching beyond their own national borders. For the most part, these restrictions occur irrespective of the intellectual field or specific content in which scholars are engaged. Some BDS campaigners argue Israeli scholars who issue statements condemning the actions of their government should not have their intellectual liberty curtailed. However, this sets in place a qualification upon academic freedom whereby its exercise for some becomes dependent upon their public expression of personal political beliefs which are then subjected to formal approval processes. This is an unjust, undemocratic and selective imposition that degrades any notion of academic freedom.

The debate surrounding campaigns for an academic boycott of Israeli universities demonstrates how academic freedom is being redefined today. Steven Salaita (2014b), a leading BDS advocate, argues that 'boycott is not a contravention of academic freedom but an expression of it'. His fellow campaigner Sunaina Maira (09/04/14) similarly suggests that 'the boycott enlarges academic freedom for all'. The assumption is that Palestinians, or those arguing for their cause, have their freedom of speech restricted by Israelis or their lobbyists in the West and so a boycott of Israeli academics helps an oppressed group gain a voice. This is an argument for academic justice similar to that propounded by those wanting to restrict debate on rape. Essentially its proponents suggest that in order to allow some (usually those labelled as vulnerable or oppressed) to have academic freedom, others must be denied it.

The redefinition of academic freedom as a matter of justice has the unfortunate effect of killing academic freedom in order to save it (Nelson, 2015, p. 71). Ironically, as we can see with the case of Salaita, academics who undermine academic freedom in one sphere then look to draw upon those very same principles when they find themselves to be under attack. Current demands from feminists or BDS campaigners to promote justice through regulating academic freedom help foster a culture of conformity in higher education, because instead of encouraging criticality and debate, the terrain of discussion is limited to politically acceptable, uncontroversial, safely established parameters. Meanwhile, dissenters are told 'you can't say that', or resort to self-censorship.

A political divide

As the above examples illustrate, a trend has emerged whereby some within universities see the Enlightenment origins of academic freedom as tainting it with an elitism that serves only to further the interests of already dominant voices. This leads to academic freedom being rejected as 'one of the pillars upon which academic liberalism builds its edifice' (Chatterjee and Maira, 2014, p. 35). Instead, it is argued, the time has come to abandon, or at least redefine academic freedom and to focus on justice and inclusion, a point that will be explored more fully in Chapter 7.

Presenting intellectual liberty and social justice as antithetical leads to discussions of academic freedom becoming unhelpfully, and often falsely, presented as divided along political lines. Championing the cause of academic freedom has, in the popular imagination, come to be associated with the libertarian 'right'. David Horowitz, for example, argues that significant numbers of 'left-wing' lecturers oppose academic freedom and its emphasis on debate. Instead, he suggests, they abuse their power in the classroom to indoctrinate students into their favoured political causes (2007, p. 43). Although caricatured as libertarian, Horowitz campaigns for academics to exercise 'the restraint of disciplined and professional standards of inquiry and expression' (2007, p. 16). This is far more in keeping with Stanley Fish's view of academic freedom as teaching and research in accordance with the standards of the discipline (2014, p. 10). Such a limited view of academic freedom makes no allowances for scholars to engage in public debate beyond their particular area of professional expertise.

Meanwhile, 'left-wing' critics argue that academic freedom is an elitist principle used to promulgate further the views of the already powerful, and that building a progressive ethos into the concept necessitates thinking about academic freedom in a deeper way to encompass questions of access, affordability and campus democracy. Chatterjee and Maira argue the university campus must be 'reimagined as a site of solidarity with those engaged in struggles against neoliberal capitalism' (2014, p. 20). This would necessitate a commitment to particular forms of action and a rejection of any sense that academic freedom can be a politically neutral right designed to further goals of scholarship.

It is true that academic freedom is an elitist principle but it is an elitism that privileges ideas based on their intellectual merit rather than their social origins. Academic freedom, like more general free speech rights, permits ideas to be raised and orthodoxies to be challenged, but it says nothing whatsoever about the merit of such ideas or the reception they must receive. Academic freedom does not decree that all knowledge is equally valid or even equally as worthy of attention: precisely the opposite is the case. In the process of being ruthlessly exposed in the metaphorical public square, some ideas win out over others. This gets to the heart of why some scholars researching rape or climate change, or those campaigning in support of Palestine, seek to redefine academic freedom. They want, in the name of justice, to give some ideas a privileged status based upon the particular content expressed or the identity of the proposer. Academic freedom allows for no such privileges.

Critics of academic freedom argue that in a marketplace of ideas, the knowledge of dominant social groups will triumph over that of less powerful sections of society, irrespective of the intellectual merit of the ideas proposed. Obviously not everyone has equal access to the media or other channels to promote their views. Some ideas, and some people, are more readily heard, more sympathetically received and more enthusiastically publicized. However, the fact that some individuals or groups of academics experience difficulty in getting their voices heard means the argument must be made repeatedly for more academic freedom, not less. It also means that debates need to be opened up to as wide an audience as possible so as to circumvent the tendency for people to confirm that with which they already feel comfortable.

Furthermore, the assumption that ideas of dominant social groups triumph is an argument for ever more vigilance against judging ideas based on the identity of the proposer. Rather, knowledge should be evaluated solely on the basis of intellectual merit. The modern-day stigma of elitism tarnishes principles of free speech that, although often applied pragmatically, are universal in nature.

Contemporary critics reject academic freedom in favour of political identification with those whose causes they consider worthy of support. Despite the appeal to democracy, the formal privileging of some ideas over others and some social groups over others is dependent upon the political biases of an unappointed academic elite. Academics have no special rights to determine the values that have weight in society, however much they may believe they have justice on their side. Exposing ideas to critical scrutiny, which is the liberal project that academic freedom supports, allows for some ideas to be discredited and better ideas to win out. Circumventing this intellectual process curtails both freedom and justice.

Since first formalized as a concept at the end of the nineteenth century, academic freedom has been linked to the pursuit of knowledge as a search for truth. This was not a search for an ultimate truth for all time, but a contestable truth that could be countered and superseded when new and better knowledge was proposed. The rejection of academic freedom in favour of justice represents a growing tendency among scholars to view knowledge itself as problematic. Knowledge is increasingly viewed not as objective or politically neutral so much as ideologically loaded and representative of the perspectives of a dominant ruling elite. The pursuit of knowledge as a search for truth has been widely disparaged. Instead, knowledge is often reduced to particular viewpoints representing a multitude of 'truths', each dependent upon the social group or individual identity of the knower. Pursuing and imparting knowledge becomes increasingly problematic.

When arriving at truth is deemed neither possible nor desirable and socially constructed knowledge is dependent upon viewpoints, new ideas present little challenge to the status quo and simply represent an additional perspective. The chief purpose of academic freedom, to enable scholars to critique existing orthodoxies and propose new understandings, becomes redundant. The aim of higher education becomes reduced to inculcating a suspicion of knowledge and a rejection of truth claims. A hollowed-out concept of academic freedom is reduced to providing an insurance policy for beleaguered individuals because there is no longer any sense of its necessity in relation to broader collective goals of knowledge and truth.

The aim of this book is to provide a defence of academic freedom, particularly in the humanities and social sciences, at a time when the concept of disciplinary knowledge is under threat from an intellectual relativism and a desire to curtail debate. Knowledge provides an objective basis for critique and judgement and, in turn, new knowledge emerges from processes of contestation and discussion. Restricting the terrain of discussion, placing some topics beyond challenge, presenting knowledge as simply individual perspectives and blurring knowledge, beliefs and values all contribute towards the creation of a culture of conformity in academia. Such enforced consensus is the antithesis of academic freedom. A challenge to the culture of conformity, alongside a defence of academic freedom, is needed for critique to be possible and for the intellectual project of evaluating existing knowledge and proposing new knowledge to be meaningful. Safeguarding individual liberty requires constant vigilance: and in the decades since the 1960s' Free Speech Movement, complacency about academic freedom has crept into higher education.

Students as censors

When scholars encourage the abandonment of truth, question the possibility of knowledge and seek to redefine academic freedom, it should come as little surprise to see students endorse this mission. Stories of campus censorship emanating from students who have learnt to find offence and respond with calls for restrictions at the feet of academics appear in the mainstream media with some regularity. British students have waged a long-running and ongoing campaign against a national tabloid newspaper, *The Sun*, on the grounds that the newspaper's iconic Page 3 pictures of topless models promote misogyny and rape culture. In 2014, students from 30 universities voted to stop the sale of the newspaper from all campus shops (Tilbury, 18/03/14). In the previous few months, similar arguments were employed by student leaders at more than 20 UK universities to ban Robin Thicke's hit song *Blurred Lines* being played at campus venues (*Guardian Music*, 12/11/13). In November 2014, students at the University of East Anglia successfully campaigned to have a prospective member of parliament for the UK Independence Party banned from taking part in a campus debate, 'in order to protect students who feel intimidated or degraded by the party' (Sherriff, 28/11/14).

The assumption behind such calls for censorship is that some ideas, words or images are either too dangerous for free circulation or inherently offensive (Shukman, 04/11/14). In the USA in September 2014, students at a New York art college mounted a petition to have a picture, 'Dolphin Rape Cave', removed from a campus exhibition of student art work (Such, 24/09/14). The picture illustrated the internet meme that dolphins engage in acts of rape to make a point that people are also 'animalistic' in nature; the petitioners argued the work could 'trigger' students who had experienced sexual assault. Similar arguments had been raised at Wellesley College earlier the same year over an art installation showing a man sleepwalking in his underwear. Students argued it should be removed because 'We'd rather avoid looking at a creepy, potentially triggering sculpture on our way to class' (Mahmood, 02/06/14).

The use of the word 'triggering' in both instances is no coincidence. In March 2014, students from the University of California, Santa Barbara, demanded that lecturers provide trigger warnings, or advance alerts, if the content to be covered on the syllabus was likely to include material some may find distressing, thereby allowing concerned students to miss particular classes. Academics at universities throughout America are increasingly providing students with such alerts either verbally or in handouts or emails. One college advised faculty members to 'be aware of racism, classism, sexism, heterosexism, cissexism, ableism, and other issues of privilege and oppression' and recommended material likely to trigger distress be made an optional component of programmes of study (Jarvie, 03/03/14). Such advice is based on the erroneous assumption that universities have a responsibility to protect students from controversial or potentially sensitive material.

In reality, this is impossible to implement. Any colour or smell may act as a reminder of past traumatic events and, followed to its logical conclusion, the entire canon of English literature could contain warnings as to the emotional nature of the content and the issues covered. More problematically, demands for trigger warnings and closing down debates suggest that the university should be a safe space rather than an intellectual challenge for students (Lowe, 24/10/14). For real learning to take place, students need to be pushed beyond their comfort zone. The use of trigger warnings in a higher education context that privileges student satisfaction above nearly all other considerations encourages lecturers and students alike to self-censor and remove troublesome material from the curriculum or the debating chamber before it even becomes an issue.

There are already examples of lecturers or university administrators pre-empting claims of offence and self-censoring. The new art museum at Kennesaw State University removed an art installation based on the homestead of prominent author Corra Harris (1869–1935). In an 1899 magazine article ostensibly critical of lynching, Harris used racist language and traced the practice to the dangers she said were posed by black men. The university had earlier faced controversy when it accepted her homestead as a gift. Although many elements of Harris' life provided the context for the 2014 exhibition and her views on race were covered, the work was still removed prior to the launch (Jaschik, 03/03/14).

Students take their cue from such discussions and, far from their 1960s counterparts who argued for free speech, ask to be monitored and protected from words they find offensive.

At Colgate University in New York, more than 300 students were involved in an occupation intended to raise awareness of the 'micro-aggressions' experienced by black students at the university's predominantly white campus. It was prompted by reports of racist remarks being made to students on public transport and the anonymous posting of racist comments on the social networking app Yik Yak. In an online petition to garner support for the sit-in, protesters argued that 'Colgate University, at this moment, has insufficient methods to address equity and inclusivity' (*Colgate for All*, 2015). They demanded that university managers intervene in campus life and monitor all aspects of staff and student interactions. One call was for 'cameras with audio' to be introduced on the university's shuttle-bus service, the Colgate Cruiser: 'This initiative responds to reported instances of racism, aggression, and micro-aggression that take place on the cruiser.' Calls for private conversations to be monitored, when done in the name of inclusivity and anti-racism, received widespread support from students, lecturers and administrators.

Such calls for censorship infringe upon more than just the lifestyle choices of some students: they curtail the free discussion of ideas. In November 2014, a group of students at Oxford University successfully closed down a debate organized by an anti-abortion group, *Oxford Students for Life*. Campaigners objected to the male speakers expressing views on something they could never personally experience and argued the debate would therefore threaten the 'mental safety' of the university's students. They declared their intention to bring 'instruments' to disrupt the debate; this threat alone ensured the college administrators closed down an event by then considered to raise 'security and welfare issues' (O'Neill, 22/11/14). One student demanding the debate be called off argued: 'The idea that in a free society absolutely everything should be open to debate has a detrimental effect on marginalised groups' (McIntyre, 18/11/14). Her statement recalls verbatim the arguments of lecturers who seek to restrict discussion around rape or to enforce boycotts against Israeli academics.

Reappraising academic freedom

It seems that tabloid newspapers, idiosyncratic academics and emotionally complex issues are not welcome in higher education nowadays. As the examples in this chapter suggest, today's demands for censorship and speech codes, as well as the promotion of particular values, come less from fusty managers and more from well-intentioned academics, feminist and environmental activists, students' union officials and equality and diversity officers. Such restrictions on free debate in higher education are rarely challenged as they occur within a climate dominated by political consensus.

Too often, groupthink comes to replace criticality and the rigorous questioning of subject knowledge. New moral orthodoxies have emerged on a range of issues such as protecting the environment, gender equality, the dangers of neo-liberalism and the need to promote cultural diversity. Lecturers and students alike are encouraged to police their language, monitor their behaviour and self-censor. Outlawing the offensive and protecting the vulnerable are often considered more important than defending a seemingly abstract concept such as academic freedom which comes to be portrayed as an outdated tool designed to maintain the privilege of a social elite while curbing the voices of those on the margins of academia. Consequently, a commitment to academic freedom is quietly dropped, reduced to mere rhetoric or redefined to encompass broader social and political priorities.

The focus of this book is not the demand for campus censorship emanating from students so much as the threat to academic freedom posed by their lecturers. However, there are obviously some important points of connection between the two. Students and lecturers consider themselves and each other to be increasingly sensitive to the impact of inappropriate language and images. In the lecture theatre, student bar and campus shuttle bus, some topics are considered beyond discussion. In some cases, such as climate change, this is because the science is presented as settled; other issues, such as rape, are off limits because they may trigger psychological problems in vulnerable students. Universities, where in the interests of the pursuit of knowledge, discussion needs to be as free as possible, are rapidly becoming places where academic freedom and critical thought are curtailed and replaced by a culture of self-monitoring and censoriousness. Speech codes and anti-harassment policies, designed to promote the university campus as an inclusive and emotionally safe environment, dictate the acceptable language of academic discourse and enforce a culture of conformity. A number of factors come together to make this limiting of scholarly debate possible: most fundamentally the problematizing of knowledge, the disparaging of truth and the rejection or redefinition of academic freedom.

Despite a rhetoric of commitment to academic freedom today, it remains ill-defined, poorly understood and readily jettisoned by national governments, universities and scholars alike. A reappraisal of academic freedom a centenary on from the AAUP *Declaration of the Principles of Academic Freedom* is badly needed. The 1915 document is necessarily of its era: the Second World War, the disparaging of Enlightenment values and the rise of post-modernism could not have been foreseen. Likewise, when AAUP members argued for the right of university teachers to express their opinions freely outside the university, they could not have possibly imagined the advent of Twitter and other forms of social media. Yet in many ways this old statement appears more necessary now than ever.

Academic freedom at the heart of the university

Academic freedom must be about more than defending the rights of individuals to send controversial tweets, although this in and of itself is undoubtedly important. What is all too often missing today is a sense of academic freedom as lying at the heart of the university, as integral to the collective enterprise to critique and advance knowledge. The aim of this book is to make the case for academic freedom as foundational to the idea of a university.

Part I traces the history and development of academic freedom; its importance in relation to the purpose of higher education; and the principal challenges to academic freedom today. Chapter 1 traces the history and development of the concept of academic freedom, and Chapter 2 considers the tendency for academics to self-censor today and the blurring of the boundaries between knowledge, beliefs and values which threatens the potential for genuinely critical thought.

Part II considers the role of academic disciplines in providing a basis for the critique of existing knowledge and the pursuit of new knowledge. Chapter 3 explores the origins of academic disciplines and their importance to knowledge, criticality and the exercise of academic freedom. Chapter 4 argues that the questioning of the rules associated with academic disciplines, and the increasingly blurred boundaries between subjects, can be seen as a challenge to the objectivity of knowledge and leaves scholars without a structured framework for criticality.

Part III considers the impact of recent political and academic trends within social science and humanities disciplines upon knowledge, criticality and the exercise of academic freedom. Chapter 5 explores how Critical Theory, with its assertion that interpretations are multiple and lie in the reception of a text by the reader rather than in the intention of the author, has created a culture of relativism whereby anything can count as an object of study and all responses are equally valid. Chapter 6 considers the impact of academic feminism having moved from arguing that female and male students should have equal access to knowledge to declaring that the traditional curriculum is oppressive, patriarchal and elitist, representing only the concerns of those who are 'pale, male and stale'. Chapter 7 further explores the impact of trends such as identity politics in bringing about a supposedly radical shift from academic freedom to academic justice.

Throughout, this book locates current discussions of academic freedom in the context of changed understandings of the role and purpose of higher education, criticality and knowledge. The liberal pursuit of knowledge and the practice of intellectual criticism are dependent upon academic freedom, but for this freedom to be meaningful it needs to be more than an abstract proposition. Academic freedom needs to be exercised and its practice depends upon new knowledge, ideas and interpretations being pitched against existing views in a marketplace of ideas. This is what a university should be for.

Part I

Academic Freedom Then and Now

1
Free to Be Critical

While the rhetoric of academic freedom continues to be upheld in higher education, discerning particular principles that lie behind the words can often be difficult. It can sometimes seem as if a lightly held but frequent recantation of the mantra of academic freedom is no more than a necessary rite for legitimate entry into the scholarly community. In practice, academic freedom is often misunderstood, rejected as elitist or redefined beyond all recognition, until the point at which individual scholars seek a defence of their own position.

Academic freedom has not always been held in such low regard. This chapter recalls the importance of academic freedom to those working in higher education in the past, not just as a personal insurance policy or an abstract belief, but as a fundamental tenet of scholarly work, central to intellectual and social goals which connected advancing knowledge to the pursuit of truth.

The role of universities in conserving, curating and pursuing knowledge was, until recently, based upon principles of truth and rationality which could be traced back to ideas of scholarship associated with the Enlightenment. Academic freedom was essential for allowing scholars both to critique existing understandings and to propose new ideas. The rejection and redefinition of academic freedom that has taken place over the course of at least the past three decades represents a significant challenge to the liberal academic project. This chapter considers the historical development of academic freedom as context to current debates within higher education.

Back to first principles

One of the first formal definitions of academic freedom appears in the 1915 *Declaration of Principles of Academic Freedom and Academic Tenure* produced by the newly established American Association of University Professors (AAUP). The AAUP was not conceived with the primary goal of defending academic freedom, but rather to 'further the professionalization of the professoriate' (Tiede, 2014, p. 1) and to provide a voice for scholars within rapidly changing universities. Founding members of the AAUP, in particular Arthur Lovejoy, James McKeen Cattell and E. R. A. Seligman, only latterly pushed for a focus on academic freedom as one element of the demand that authority in the university should lie with scholars rather than administrators. They argued that the principle of tenure and the professional autonomy for scholars to teach, research and manage their own affairs as they saw best, was essential for maintaining academic standards.

The establishment of the AAUP, and its subsequent focus upon academic freedom, largely arose from a pragmatic response to a number of high-profile incidents in which professors had either resigned or been dismissed from their universities for espousing views that contradicted the teaching of the church or the beliefs of their institution's financial sponsors. Throughout the 1890s, large-scale dismissals from American universities occurred following changes in the electoral fortunes of the political party controlling the state legislature. In 1895, Edward Bemis, a Professor of Economics and History, was dismissed from the University of Chicago after his sympathy with the cause of striking workers was reported in the press. The President of Brown University, E. Benjamin Andrews, resigned his post in 1897 in response to requests from the university's trustees that he should 'exercise forbearance in expressing his views' (in Tiede, 2014, p. 22). The business magnate and philanthropist, Rockefeller, had been expected to make a large donation to Brown following his son's graduation. When no such donation appeared, the trustees of the university placed the blame upon Andrews, a vocal advocate for the monetization of national debt. Andrews resigned, claiming he would not be able to carry out the wishes of the trustees 'without surrendering that reasonable liberty of utterance [...] in the absence of which the most ample endowment for an educational institution would have little worth' (in Tiede, 2014, p. 22).

In the previous year, 1896, the sociologist Edward Ross was dismissed from Stanford University for expressing views in his teaching which were critical of the institution's sole benefactor, Jane Leland Stanford. As a result of the dismissal of Edward Ross, several other professors either resigned or were dismissed from their posts. This conflict between academics and benefactor prompted the publication, five years later, of the American Economic Association's first report on academic freedom violations in the US. Arthur Lovejoy, one of the professors to resign from Stanford in response to the Ross case, took up a post at Johns Hopkins University where he issued 'the Hopkins call' to establish an association 'to create means for the authoritative expression of the public opinion of college and university teachers; to make collective action possible; and to maintain and advance the standards of the profession' (in Tiede, 2014, p. 22).

This association, which would later become the AAUP, convened on January 1st 1915 in New York and elected the philosopher and educationalist John Dewey as its inaugural president. The first AAUP committee, the Committee on Academic Freedom and Tenure, was led by Seligman and its immediate task was to respond to one particular incident, the dismissal of four professors (and the subsequent resignation of 15 others) at the University of Utah. The investigation into this incident led to the publication of the *Declaration of Principles of Academic Freedom*. However pragmatic in origin, this *Declaration* has stood for a century as a cornerstone in debates around academic freedom. One reason for this longevity is the intrinsic relationship that was drawn between academic freedom and the fulfilment of the scholarly 'calling' which Dewey described as 'none other than the discovery and diffusion of truth' (in Haskell, 1996, p. 68).

As noted in the previous chapter, the 1915 *Declaration* presents academic freedom as comprising three core elements: 'freedom of inquiry and research; freedom of teaching within the university or college; and freedom of extramural utterance and action'. Fundamental to this concept of academic freedom was the recognition that working in academia was unlike other forms of employment in private business, and that scholars served a social role in relation to knowledge which lent them a duty to 'impart the results of their own and of their fellow-specialists' investigations and reflection, both to students and to the general public'. In order for them to carry out this role they needed to work 'without fear or favor' so that:

> in the interest of society at large, that what purport to be the conclusions of men trained for, and dedicated to, the quest for truth, shall in fact be the conclusions of such men, and not echoes of the opinions of the lay public, or of the individuals who endow or manage universities.

As will be explored later in this chapter, the AAUP *Declaration* was necessarily of its time. It is steeped in the aspiration to take knowledge out of the hands of amateurs and to professionalize its pursuit within the academy, and in that sense it is clearly 'elitist'. Nonetheless its central tenets relate, not to the particular conditions and preoccupations of those working in higher education in 1915, but to the liberal scientific method and Enlightenment ideas about the nature of knowledge. Cary Nelson, writing in *No University Is an Island,* suggests the *Declaration* 'relies on the scientific method as a model for the ideal exercise of academic freedom. In a broad, multi-disciplinary context, that means rationality, willingness to test hypotheses against evidence, openness to counterclaims by peers, and so forth' (2010, p. 24).

The origins of academic freedom

One reason why the AAUP *Declaration* has stood the test of time is that it recalls a far older philosophical discussion of intellectual freedom as crucial to passing judgement on existing knowledge and the development of new ideas and original perspectives. Such a belief in the relationship between freedom, criticism and the pursuit of knowledge first emerged in Ancient Greece. Socrates, Aristotle and Plato are all credited with promoting ideals of free speech and free inquiry. Intellectuals in the ancient academy were 'dedicated to the art of critical debate, the posing of questions, and the search for solutions' (Poch, 1993, p. 3, in Papadimitriou, 2011). Socrates has been recorded as arguing for the freedom to keep challenging people in the agora, or marketplace, on the basis that only the gods are wise and humans can be wise only in recognizing their own ignorance (Annas, 2000, p. 59). Sentenced to death for corrupting the youth of Athens with his ideas, Socrates' defence in relation to the charges levelled against him is often cited as the first recorded statement of the need for freedom in teaching (Hofstadter, 1996, p. 3).

It is important to note that for Socrates, the freedom to inquire was less a special privilege of the learned than a duty upon everyone. A Socratic theory of academic freedom can be considered closer to general individual free speech rights, rather than one that depends upon the professional legitimacy of the speaker. In contrast, for Aristotle, intellectual freedom was a privilege earned through knowledge gained. He wrote that 'All men by nature desire to know' and that 'humans are most like gods in the act of knowing' (in O'Brien, 1998, p. 35). From this tradition emerges the belief that freedom of inquiry, specifically in the form of tenure, is based upon proven professional competence. One legacy of these ancient origins is that academic freedom has been enshrined within Article 16 of the Greek constitution since 1975 (Papadimitriou, 2011, p. 105). More broadly, we see the emergence of two conflicting views of academic freedom that persist to this day: a declaration of general free speech rights on the one hand, and a privilege based on professional competence on the other.

Centuries later, during the time of the Enlightenment, such ancient principles were revisited and the Socratic notion of intellectual liberty appeared at first to have won out. John Stuart Mill acknowledged a debt to Socrates, the 'acknowledged master of all the eminent thinkers who have since lived' (2005, p. 35). The Enlightenment philosophers first established the principle, which has continued into the modern era, that freedom was necessary to advance knowledge as it permitted the criticism and collective acts of judgement through which existing orthodoxies could be challenged and new ideas proposed.

Prior to the Enlightenment, knowledge within the medieval universities had been rooted in tradition and religion: the justification for its pursuit and transmission lay in bringing people closer to God. The first European universities were established by the Catholic Church and, although largely preoccupied with training men for the priesthood, were influenced by the work of Plato and St Augustine. They drew upon Plato's Academy in offering a model for 'essentially secluded non-utilitarian study of the higher spiritual purpose and destiny of human beings' (Carr, 2009, p. 5). From the time of their founding, the Catholic Church did much to establish the principle that universities should have freedom from outside interference, most particularly from the nascent state.

As Conrad Russell indicates in his book *Academic Freedom,* 'the claims of Universities to academic freedom have always been rooted in an intellectual tradition created to defend the autonomy of the medieval church' (1993, p. 1). This defence was needed to protect individuals when the religious affiliations of the ruling elite changed. Persecution, resulting even in death, occurred when scholars found their religious affiliations suddenly out of kilter with those of the monarch of the day. In 1533, during the English Reformation, Protestant scholars at New College Oxford were expelled and others fled the country or were killed for not renouncing their religious convictions. Peter Quinby, a Lutheran, was locked in the college tower and left to die of starvation (Prickard, 2010, p. 70).

For medieval universities, the principle of 'liberty' emerged to defend a realm of society into which the state could not enter. However, the relationship between universities and the state could at best be described as ambiguous. Despite demands for institutional autonomy, from their inception universities sought physical protection and some degree of resource, often in the form of financial endowments, from state or monarch. Russell describes the relationship as one of 'high assertion of intellectual independence, combined with a total physical dependence' (1993, p. 17). This allowed for only limited freedom: universities had a degree of institutional autonomy from the state as long as they did not challenge the authority of the ruling monarch. At the same time, universities were completely under the control of the church. In many ways, this meant the Catholic Church often served the role of censoring on behalf of the state. For example, it was the church that, in 1546, published the *Index Librorum Prohibitorum,* a list of prohibited books.

Significantly then, the freedom of universities from state interference did not imply a concomitant freedom for individual academics to criticize the church either as an institution or its teachings. As the personnel and authority of church and university were closely intertwined, little questioning of dominant religious ideologies emerged from within the cloisters of academe; rather, the institutionalized creation and transmission of knowledge was inherently linked to a divine concept of Truth. The intellectual leaps that began to occur with the dawning of the Enlightenment therefore posed a significant threat to the authority of the church. For example, the philosopher René Descartes' 1637 declaration, *cogito ergo sum,* with its focus upon the individual and its location of the source of human knowledge within man, challenged the church's view of God as the source of knowledge and authority.

Most significantly, Descartes developed a methodology for the pursuit of knowledge based upon principles of skepticism and doubt. From this we can trace the first underpinnings of the scientific method. Although later Enlightenment philosophers rejected many of Descartes' findings, they reasserted the importance of his methodological approach, which would come to characterize the enduring liberal academic project. Descartes was necessarily careful to avoid direct confrontation with the Catholic Church; he was all too aware of the imprisonment meted out to Galileo for espousing a Copernican view of the solar system. As a consequence, Descartes suppressed much of his work during his own lifetime while other writings, including much of his *Discourse on Method,* were published anonymously.

It was not until 150 years later that Kant, writing in *The Conflict of the Faculties* (1979 [1798]) was able to extol the need for a transition from the religious authority of knowledge, to a more secular, rational and empirical source of legitimation. Even then Kant, a teacher and scholar at the University of Konigsberg, came up against formal censorship throughout his working life. This became most pronounced in 1788 when state officials and monarch were united in a campaign to 'stamp out the Enlightenment' (Gregor, 1979, p. xi). A new Censorship Edict designed to limit 'the impetuosity of today's so-called enlighteners' (Gregor, 1979, p. x) was enacted that outlawed all writings on religious matters. In 1795, Prussian government ministers ordered the University of Konigsberg to forbid any professor from lecturing on Kant's philosophy of religion (Gregor, 1979, p. xi).

Kant's work brought him into direct conflict with the 'Biblical theologians' of his day and he had to write in such a way as to circumvent punitive censorship laws. In his personal correspondence, Kant complained that the Censorship Commission in Berlin met his arguments not with reason but with 'anathemas launched from the clouds over officialdom' (Gregor, 1979, p. viii). Through his battles with the censors, Kant formulated a defence of intellectual freedom by contrasting the obedience required from the civil servant paid to carry out public duties with the liberty of the scholar:

> ...the clergyman, as a representative of the state, is not free to argue with the tenets of the church when he addresses his

> congregation: here obedience, not argument, is called for. But the same man, as a scholar, has complete freedom to argue, to communicate to the learned public of the world the use of his own reason in religious matters. In his sermons he speaks in the name of the church and at its dictation: in his scholarly writings he speaks freely in his own name.
>
> (in Gregor, 1979, p. ix)

Kant's argument is that the professional role affords certain responsibilities which limit free speech; his concept of the scholar, however, was not a professional state functionary but an independent, critically autonomous individual.

The Enlightenment of the seventeenth and eighteenth centuries marked a paradigmatic break with the intellectual traditions of the medieval period and allowed a concept of knowledge based upon a secular view of truth to come to the fore. Empirical evidence and individual reasoning replaced religious faith. Kant argued that the capacity to reason, and therefore the basis for critical thought and the authority of knowledge, was to be found in the minds of individuals; indeed, this was what distinguished people from animals (Scruton, 2001, p. 92). He suggested that objective knowledge was only possible through the synthesis of experience and reason, which 'transcends the point of view of the person who possesses it, and makes legitimate claims about an independent world' (Scruton, 2001, p. 27). Kant's denial of the religious foundations of knowledge was not a rejection of truth; rather, he argued, individual reason and empirical evidence were a superior way of arriving at truth.

Knowledge was considered to encapsulate an inherent truth derived from the objectivity of independent reasoning. Kant declared, 'Reason is by its nature free and admits of no command to hold something as true' (1979, p. 29). He considered truth to be dependent upon individual freedom to reason; knowledge and understanding could advance only if people were free to allow their own inner reason to develop. As Kant argued, 'Truth gains more even by the errors of one who, with due study and preparation, thinks for himself, than by the true opinions of those who only hold them because they do not suffer themselves to think' (2009, p. 3). Kant's challenge to the church and state lay in his belief that the freedom for people to reach the wrong conclusions and make mistakes was ultimately better for the pursuit of knowledge than denying people opportunities to think for themselves through presenting them with a predetermined truth.

Kant suggested that the university – especially the philosophy faculty, with its relative freedom from the professional strictures charged to the other three faculties of law, medicine and theology – could play a role in protecting critical reason from political and clerical authority for the benefit of society more broadly. But for this to happen, Kant argued, the philosophy faculty needed the freedom to make 'its own judgment about what it teaches' (1979, p. 25). The 'medieval liberty' (Russell, 1993, p. 3) by which universities had freedom from the state was a necessary precondition for them to play this role.

Despite Kant's efforts, it took many decades before the influence of the church upon universities began to wane. The epistemological advances associated with the Enlightenment were made primarily by public intellectuals outside of the formal strictures of the academy; scholars within universities were expected to be obedient to church teachings. Walter Metzger, writing in *Academic Freedom in the Age of the University*, notes the extent to which, in the first half of the nineteenth century, a triad of assumptions ('traditionalism as an educational goal, "stamping in" as a pedagogical method, the contumacy of youth as a major expectation') prevented even the desire for academic freedom (1995, p. 5). Mostly universities sought to ally 'Christian piety and humanistic study against the skeptical rationalism of the Enlightenment' (Metzger, 1961, p. 3).

Academic freedom in the modern university

Individual intellectual freedom was not, then, a notable feature of universities in the early nineteenth century. Institutions sought primarily to conserve rather than critique or contribute to existing knowledge. Paternalistic and authoritarian, they aimed at disciplining and socializing young men. One effect of this was to prevent the development of a private sphere where students and scholars alike could be free to experiment and test out new ideas. Only from the middle of the nineteenth century did things gradually begin to change, largely as a result of the influence of German (then Prussian) universities that, at this time, were considered to be the best in the world.

In 1848, the Prussian constitution noted that 'science and its teachings shall be free'. This emerged from the concepts of *Lehrfreiheit*, the freedom to teach, and *Lernfreiheit*, the freedom to learn. The latter referred to the right of students to choose a course of study while the former hinted at a modern concept of academic freedom. That professors were free to pursue their area of expertise with no interference from the state was widely recognized and well protected by governmental institutions. The practice of hiring and retaining academic staff based upon their competence rather than political conformity or favouritism led to a more accomplished and expert faculty. A lack of political constraint led to faster and more innovative intellectual advances. Prussian universities had been influenced by Wilhelm von Humboldt's idea of the research university as 'an academically autonomous institution dedicated to the pursuit of knowledge and truth' (Carr, 2009, p. 6), although this privileging of pure research could be in quite a narrowly specialized way.

A significant number of American professors had received their degrees from German universities and witnessed the results of such freedoms in action. They brought ideas about academic freedom home with them and began to push for similar conditions in their own institutions, arguing for academic freedom on the basis that it led to more innovative research and scholarship. In the latter half of the nineteenth century, institutions resembling the modern research university began to emerge in the United States of America. It is no coincidence that this was also the period during which many of the modern professions started to organize themselves through establishing associations and formal entry requirements. American higher education began simultaneously to professionalize academic staff and the pursuit of knowledge as well as to carve out a role in preparing students for membership of a professional class. At this point, the founder of Harvard University, Charles William Eliot, introduced an elective system to allow students to acquire a specialized education shaped around the perceived needs of their chosen future careers (Menand, 1996, p. 7).

From the mid-nineteenth century, German universities began to differ from their British counterparts, which espoused a more liberal concept of scholarship as encapsulated in Cardinal John Henry Newman's *The Idea of a University* (1852). Newman urged that education needed no extrinsic justifications: 'Knowledge is capable of being its own end. Such is the constitution of the human mind that any kind of knowledge, if it be really such, is its own reward' (1852, p. 130). For Newman then, the relationship between the university and knowledge was embodied in scholars who were not just the custodians of society's collective intellectual capital, but fulfilled an important social role in inculcating a new generation of students into the world of ideas to which, through the development of their reason, they were able to contribute. Newman could claim with confidence, 'Education is a high word; it is the preparation for knowledge, and it is the imparting of knowledge in proportion to that preparation' (1852, p. 164). Newman's belief in knowledge for its own sake was driven by his religious calling. By the end of the nineteenth century, Britain's handful of universities still remained, outwardly at least, largely under the sway of traditions dating back to the medieval period.

Despite this, as the Enlightenment emphasis upon the empirical legitimation of knowledge played out within the academy, the influence of science and positivism came increasingly to the fore. In American universities, a marked shift in the academic goals of higher education occurred between the years between 1865 and 1890 alongside considerable growth in the number of institutions. As Metzger points out, 'To criticise and augment as well as to disseminate the tradition at hand became an established function of universities and this was a great departure for a system that had aimed primarily at cultural conservation' (1961, p. 3).

A significant impetus behind scholars challenging the influence of the church upon higher education was Charles Darwin's theory of evolution, published as *On the Origin of Species* in 1859. As Darwin's views gradually gained support among faculty, they increasingly became a focal point for conflict between academics and institutional benefactors. Professors risked dismissal for teaching or advocating the theory of evolution. Even by 1880, many college presidents still denounced the theory. Through privileging scientific knowledge over religious belief, academics were demanding the right to challenge existing understandings of the world and to propose an alternative, superior truth.

In many ways, the final decades of the nineteenth century and the first decades of the twentieth century represent the heyday of the liberal academic project. Scholars were becoming increasingly confident in espousing a notion of secular truth and had a strong concept of their own role in relation to its pursuit through knowledge. At no other point can the influence of Enlightenment values be seen so clearly within the academy. This sense of mission made the need for academic freedom both starkly apparent and practically meaningful. Scholars recognized that truth, although ultimately contestable, could not be pursued unless they had unrestricted liberty to follow the intellectual logic of their reasoning wherever it may take them.

Emile Durkheim, the founding father of sociology, claimed that the objective basis of knowledge was to be found neither solely in the minds of individuals nor in sensory experience of the material world. In his groundbreaking work, *The Elementary Forms of Religious Life* (2001 [1912]), he suggests knowledge is produced through people's collective action upon the world. For Durkheim, truth as something external to individuals emerged from the social (and therefore essentially human) nature of its origins and this gave knowledge an objective basis that allowed for the checking and critiquing of ideas as a collective act between scholars within the academy. It also lent weight to the importance of academic disciplines as communities of scholars who could legitimize knowledge and lend authority to truth claims. Durkheim drew extensively upon Kant's work on the problem of epistemology and developed a concept of truth dependent upon the universalization of individual reasoning.

However, as a critique of existing understandings and the pursuit of new ideas became possible, universities grew less concerned with the capacity for individual reason and more preoccupied with a faith in rational, scientific facts. Taking a lead from the authority afforded to science, academics began to seek the same empirical legitimacy for knowledge within other disciplines. Arguing for academic freedom became necessary to cement the break between universities and the church; as Metzger puts it, 'the assimilation of the values of science made academic freedom an ethic, an affirmative moral position, and not merely a negative condition, the absence of overt restraint' (1961, p. 89). The search for empirical legitimacy and objectivity demanded that knowledge be separated from individual reason and values. This began to bring about a shift in the concept of truth in relation to knowledge.

Despite Durkheim's foregrounding of a collective form of individual reason, the aspiration for and possibility of arriving at a notion of objective truth led to a privileging of fact and a rejection of value judgements. Truth, in turn, came to be defined more narrowly, as the specific outcomes of empirical investigation. This location of truth in quantifiable fact rather than individual reasoning was reflected in a wider millenarian crisis of authority. In Europe and America, the ruling political elite no longer considered tradition to be a justifiable basis for the social contract between state and citizens and instead sought scientific knowledge to lend credence to leaders and provide grounds for organizing society in new ways (see Furedi, 2013, p. 249). It is no coincidence that social science emerged as an academic discipline at this time.

An emphasis upon distancing the pursuit of facts from the work of individual scholars accelerated the professionalization of knowledge, and science in particular, within the university. One consequence of this was to delegitimize the work of talented amateurs and to promote the idea of the academic professional as expert. As Jonathan Rose points out in *The Intellectual Life of the British Working Classes,* in the early part of the nineteenth century it was not uncommon for 'proletarian naturalists' to contribute to scientific research:

> Thomas Edward, the shoemaker-naturalist (b. 1814), had an income of 9s. 6d. a week, little formal education, no books on natural history, and no community of autodidacts with whom he could discuss his research. Learning from the *Penny Magazine* and from observation, he eventually discovered twenty-six new species of crustacea in the Moray Firth; contributed to the *Naturalist,* the *Zoologist, Ibis,* and the *Linnaean Journal;* was elected as an associate of the *Linnaean Society* in 1866; and won a *Civil List* pension of £50 a year.
>
> (2001, p. 70)

With the formalization of science within the academy, it was far more difficult for the likes of Thomas Edward to make their mark. The replacement of autodidacts with experts reflects the erosion of knowledge as an end in itself; the more knowledge tended towards the empirical, the more it was expected to serve a social or economic purpose.

Into the twentieth century

The triumph of the scientific method brought the need for academic freedom into sharp relief. However, English universities did not gain freedom on the basis of having won intellectual arguments, but rather because the focus on science coincided with the concerns of the state. In the early decades of the twentieth century, the British government was increasingly preoccupied with matching the industrial advance taking place in America and Germany. Higher education was considered by the government to be a key means of securing the scientific developments that would result in national economic gains and the technological developments that would improve the nation's military prowess. 'Red-brick' universities were established in the heartlands of the industrial revolution. Granting universities freedom from the church and state was considered necessary for scientific progress to be made.

Freedom for institutions was not always matched by unrestricted liberty for individual scholars. Just as the run-up to the First World War made higher education more utilitarian in nature and scientific research more focused upon the militaristic demands of war, so it also led to more monitoring and restrictions upon academics. Karl Wichmann, Professor of German at the University of Birmingham, was one victim of such interference. A native German, employed because few British-born scholars could teach German to a sufficiently high standard, Wichmann took British citizenship shortly after the outbreak of the First World War. When war broke out, national sentiment turned against German residents in Britain, 'motivated by the more specific fear that they might be German spies' (Husbands, 2007, p. 494). Growing local controversy surrounded Wichmann, who 'was considered a security threat and obliged by the War Office to live and remain at least ten miles from Birmingham', thereby making it impossible for him to teach at the university. Wichmann was forced to resign his post of ten years in 1917 after Birmingham City Council threatened to withdraw its entire annual grant of £13,000 from the university if he remained a member of staff (Husbands, 2007, p. 500).

After the First World War, neither the church nor private business had as much influence over the direction of British higher education as the national government. The University Grants Committee (UGC), established in 1919, channelled what were, at the time, considerable sums of public funding into universities that had demonstrated an ability to meet the moral, intellectual and scientific needs of the state. At the same time as providing financial resources, the British government consciously sought to distance itself from the management of universities in a bid to protect institutional autonomy. The 'Haldane Principle', named after the founder of the UGC, 'reasserted the priorities of academic decision making over governmental prerogative' (Docherty, 04/12/14). British scholars therefore felt less impetus to make public declarations about academic freedom than their American colleagues who had, by this time, established the AAUP and published the *Declaration of the Principles of Academic Freedom*.

In the years immediately following the First World War, academic freedom was most under threat in Germany. German universities, once held in high regard around the world, had gained a reputation for nationalism and uncritical support of the country's war aims. Nonetheless, Hitler's National Socialist regime posited academics, and Jewish intellectuals in particular, as a threat to Nazism. After gaining power in January 1933, Hitler instigated punitive authoritarian censorship laws and oversaw a wholesale attack on all forms of critical thought and scholarly work. In May that year, German students began burning books considered a threat to the intellectual purity of the nation. In the years leading up to the Second World War, over ten per cent of the total university workforce, predominantly Jews, liberals and Social Democrats, were dismissed, including all members of the internationally acclaimed physics department at the University of Gottingen. Many more professors either resigned or emigrated to be replaced by those demonstrably sympathetic to Nazism.

Albert Einstein was one among many academics who fled to Britain in 1933 to escape an increasingly hostile environment for Jewish scientists. In London, Einstein spoke to an audience of 10,000 at an event organized by the newly formed Academic Assistance Council. In his speech, *Science and Civilisation*, Einstein praised the British people for having 'remained faithful to the traditions of tolerance and justice'. He expressed his hope that future historians, looking back upon this turbulent period of human history, would be able to report that 'Western Europe defended successfully the liberty of the individual'. Einstein was clear about why such individual liberty, 'without which life to a self-respecting man is not worth living', was important; he declared it is liberty that 'has brought us every advance of knowledge and invention'. Einstein concluded his speech with a warning:

> If we want to resist the powers which threaten to suppress intellectual and individual freedom we must keep clearly before us what is at stake, and what we owe to that freedom which our ancestors have won for us after hard struggles.
>
> (Einstein, 1933)

Perhaps understandably, within Germany itself relatively few academics publicly dissented from the Nazi regime. Self-censorship became habitual, and some professors went further, policing colleagues and exposing Jewish influence upon all aspects of intellectual thought. Einstein's Theory of Relativity was described by one Nazi writer as a plot against the non-Jewish world through 'bewitching it into spectral abstraction in which all individual differences of peoples and nations, and all inner limits of the races, are lost in unreality' (Victor, 2000, p. 162). Universities as a whole readily acquiesced to the Nazi project. The new government-approved rector at the University of Berlin, for example, had complete power within the institution and introduced twenty-five new courses to do with racial science (Grundmann and Stehr, 2012, p. 77). Few spoke out against such an approach as they were all too aware that the price for doing so could be not just their jobs but their lives. Some intellectuals who did speak out were sent to concentration camps.

In Britain, the Second World War had less obvious effects upon academia. Recruitment into the army led to a significant drop in the numbers of both staff and students although this did permit more women to take up available places. Universities in urban areas at risk of aerial attack were relocated to safer parts of the country. Some universities, such as Glasgow, became focal points for military training but elsewhere the presence of sandbags was often the only visible sign that academic life was not proceeding as normal. This veneer of calm concealed the fact that the British intelligence services carried out routine acts of surveillance on academics identified in the 1930s as having 'communist leanings'. Covert techniques employed to spy on private conversations as well as monitor academic work were maintained long after the war ended and throughout the subsequent Cold War (Russia Today, 24/10/14).

In public at least, the ready capitulation of German universities to Nazism led to a re-evaluation and reassertion of the importance of academic freedom in Britain and America after the Second World War. In his influential book, *The Crisis in the University*, Sir Walter Moberly wrote that 'a heavy responsibility rests on universities as the chief organs of the community for sifting and transmitting ideas' (1949, p. 294). The unspoken reference was to the collapse of German universities under the pressure of the Nazi regime. Universities were perceived by government ministers to be the 'intellectual conscience of the nation' (Shattock, 2012, p. 10) and the preservation of their intellectual freedom and autonomy were considered paramount. Such freedom demanded a special kind of organization; universities needed both liberating and protecting from external threats.

Moberly firmly linked universities' value to society with a minimalist role for the state: 'Direct state action, like surgery, should be occasional and rare; its function is negative rather than positive, it is to remove otherwise immovable obstacles' (1949, p. 241). This notion of academic freedom as arising from inaction on behalf of the state was supported by the American educational philosopher Robert Maynard Hutchins, who wrote in 1952 that 'Academic freedom is simply a way of saying that we get the most out of education and research if we leave their management to people who know something about them' (p. 21, in Shattock, 2012, p. 10). Although it is impossible to determine a 'golden age' in which higher education was securely funded and considered an end in itself, the more universities were freed from the strictures of church and state the more academics were able to follow liberal goals. The principles of academic freedom played an important role in allowing scholars to separate their work from all forms of external interference so as to better follow the pursuit of truth and the transmission of knowledge.

However, the experience of the Second World War ultimately posed a challenge to the ideas that had come to underpin academic freedom. Before 1945, the project of creating and transmitting knowledge as the goal of higher education could be asserted with confidence because knowledge was conceived as truth which was necessarily of universal relevance. From Aristotle, who claimed 'Philosophy is the science which considers truth', to Newman's argument that 'Truth of whatever kind is the proper object of the intellect; its cultivation then lies in fitting it to apprehend and contemplate truth' (1852, p. 170), knowledge simply was truth. Even Gramsci, who often stands accused of idealism, argued that Marxism was a superior theory of history as it was 'the historical methodology most fitting to reality and to truth' (in Martin, 2002, p. 218).

Truth had been conceived of in terms of the divine, individual reasoning or rational empiricism – but throughout, truth had remained the goal of the pursuit of knowledge. Irrespective of the views of individual academics, the role of the university was to pass critical judgement on existing knowledge and transmit that which was deemed closest to truth to a new generation of students, as well as, through research, arriving at new knowledge with its own truth claims. The experience of the Second World War called into question the confidence with which academics asserted the significance and interdependence of truth and knowledge.

The experience of the Second World War in both Britain and America prompted a national debate about the purpose of the university and, most specifically, the returns to the nation from public money spent on higher education. Politicians from both left and right agreed that the state funding of universities was important for the 'public good', which was defined variously in relation to scientific and technological advance or the preservation and promulgation of national culture. In America, the AAUP reconvened in 1940 and re-evaluated the 1915 *Declaration of Principles of Academic Freedom*. Those meeting at this time considered the 1915 *Declaration*, although offering an important first step towards establishing academic freedom, to be problematic. They were critical of the expectation that scholars should fulfil such a lengthy probationary period within the university before achieving tenured status, and at the same time wanted academic freedom to be more closely bound to the overall purpose of higher education which they saw as the realization of the 'common good'. In the *Statement of Principles on Academic Freedom and Tenure* published at this time, it was declared: 'The common good depends upon the free search for truth and its free expression'. Such sentiments are echoed some years later in the British discussion of higher education as a 'public good' prompted by the *Robbins Report* (Committee on Higher Education, 1963).

The 1940 AAUP *Statement* establishes an instrumental link between academic freedom and particular outcomes or aims of higher education. This was, in the long run, to undermine the foundations of the AAUP's earlier notion of academic freedom that hinged upon a liberal concept of scholarship with no aim other than the pursuit of knowledge. In 1940, the common good of higher education was defined in relation to knowledge; but a perceived need to explain why knowledge is important suggests its role as an 'end' rather than a 'means' has been called into question. When academic freedom is connected to the 'common' or 'public' good, its foundational value, to allow for scholars to pursue knowledge as contestable truth, is undermined by the imposition of instrumental objectives. Over subsequent decades this definition of the public good of higher education has come to be reassessed, by academics and politicians alike, far more explicitly in relation to a changing range of values (see the next chapter for a fuller discussion of this point).

The danger of linking academic freedom to a particular aim of higher education – even one as potentially far-reaching as the fulfilment of the public good – is that it risks transforming academic freedom into a *quid pro quo* arrangement between scholars and the state. Freedom is granted on condition that certain goals are fulfilled. Metzger makes the point that 'In the 1940 statement, each passage entitling faculty members to a different kind of academic freedom is followed by a clause or sentence introduced by "but" and laden with messages to faculty members admonishing them to do right things' (1990, p. 9). In this way, the 1940 *Statement* becomes more akin to a declaration of professional ethics rather than a straightforward demand for academic freedom. In shifting the meaning of academic freedom away from a negative concept of freedom from external interference to a positive freedom to meet the common good, academic freedom becomes a contingent right, dependent upon the individual academic remaining in good standing within their institution.

We do not know exactly how the 1940 Committee intended the balance between liberties and exhortations to be measured. However, the subsequent impact of this 1940 *Statement* has been to offer a far more limited concept of academic freedom than that presented in 1915, albeit one that is broadened out to more people working within universities through cutting the length of probation prior to tenure. One way in which the 1940 *Statement* limits academic freedom is in the instruction to faculty to avoid 'controversial discussion unrelated to their subject'. Far from freedom of extramural utterance, this restricts academics to speaking or writing only on topics relevant to their immediate professional specialization. This 1940 *Statement* would, in a very short time, become a supporting document for institutions seeking legal means of dismissing or denying tenure.

The 1915 AAUP *Declaration of Principles of Academic Freedom* was driven by the need to protect individuals from censure by institutional trustees. In contrast, the 1940 *Statement* was a response to perceived threats to the institution of higher education as a result of a more polarized and extreme political climate in the run-up to the Second World War. This perception was to prove prophetic in foreshadowing the impact of McCarthyism upon American universities in the decade following the war's end.

Academic freedom after the Second World War

One significant feature of the 1950s was the crusade against communism instigated by Senator McCarthy in response to perceived threats to the nation from the recently formed Soviet Union and Eastern Bloc, which aimed to remove people propagating 'un-American' ideas from positions of influence. Growing anti-communist sentiment spread throughout the nation as McCarthy-inspired inquisitions moved from Hollywood to business and into academia. Academics who were openly sympathetic to communism, or were otherwise considered controversial figures, were at risk of dismissal by university presidents motivated by political or marketing concerns. One argument frequently used against academics accused of membership of the communist party was that they had relinquished their intellectual independence and were therefore unqualified to teach.

The first recorded academic freedom case linked explicitly to the McCarthy trials occurred at the University of Washington in July 1948. Six academics had charges levelled against them, and three of them were dismissed: two who admitted to membership of the Communist Party and one who refused to answer any questions about his politics. The three were described as 'incompetent, intellectually dishonest, and derelict in their duty to find and teach the truth' (Schrecker, 1994). None was able to find a comparable academic post. This was just a precursor to the main round of dismissals from universities that occurred between 1952 and 1954. Many junior professors lost their jobs to little fanfare; others did not have contracts renewed or were never hired in the first place.

In the spring of 1953, immediately prior to the main congressional committee's investigation into academia, thirty-seven university presidents issued a statement urging professors to name colleagues they suspected of communist sympathies. Ellen Schrecker, author of *No Ivory Tower, McCarthyism and the Universities,* suggests it was the legacy of academic freedom that drove university leaders to clothe their response to McCarthyism 'in elaborate rationalizations about the academic profession's commitment to "complete candor and perfect integrity"' (1994). By the time formal investigations came to a close, almost one hundred academics had lost their jobs for refusing to cooperate with anti-communist investigators and several hundred more were probably 'eased out'.

The three decades following the end of the Second World War were, in many ways, far kinder to British academics, many of whom enjoyed privileged membership of a social elite and often informal access to members of the political establishment. During this period, universities continued to receive generous financial settlements from the state in recognition of their liberalizing influence upon society as a whole and their contribution towards the public good. The legacy of the Second World War led government ministers to safeguard academic freedom, partly as a defence against totalitarianism but also as a rhetorical means of self-consciously demarcating British higher education from the restrictions experienced by scholars from countries behind the Iron Curtain. This gave academics an unprecedented degree of academic freedom.

In 1957, the philosopher John Anderson declared that academic freedom

> does *not* mean that academics have the same standing "before the law" as any other citizen; it means that they have a special province, a field in which they can say: "*We* are the experts here;

> *we* can tell you (the Law, the State) what has force, what *runs*, in this department of social activity".
>
> (in Hayes, 2009, p. 107; emphasis in original)

The confidence with which Anderson declares 'we can tell you' is underpinned by a disciplinary framework: it is a confidence built upon the expertise of the professional subject expert. Parallels can be seen between this assertion and the AAUP *Statement* from 1940; both represent a strong defence of academic freedom albeit one that is restricted to a more narrowly focused terrain.

Although the McCarthy era was relatively short-lived, it left a marked legacy upon higher education in America. Cases against individuals that made it to the Supreme Court eventually resulted in academic freedom becoming enshrined as a First Amendment Right. In the 1957 trial of Sweezy versus New Hampshire, Justice Frankfurter argued that academic freedom was protected by the Constitution. He outlined the four essential freedoms of a university: 'to determine for itself on academic grounds who may teach, what may be taught, how it shall be taught, and who may be admitted to study' (in Levinson, 2007). It was a 1967 case that led to First Amendment Protection being extended to academic freedom. The Court declared:

> Our Nation is deeply committed to safeguarding academic freedom, which is of transcendent value to all of us and not merely to the teachers concerned. That freedom is therefore a special concern of the First Amendment, which does not tolerate laws that cast a pall of orthodoxy over the classroom.
>
> (in Levinson, 2007)

In *The Closing of the American Mind*, Allan Bloom points to another, less positive, legacy of the McCarthy period. He suggests it was the last time academics had any clear sense of belonging to a community defined by a common enemy and the last time academic freedom had more than just rhetorical relevance. Bloom argues that protecting unpopular ideas, which he claims were never, in reality, so unpopular within the universities, was a collective task and not an abstract proposition. Bloom suggests that what has been lost from higher education is a sense of the university as a preserve against public opinion. Instead, he notes, in the 1960s the ideas of the professoriate began to coincide with more generally popular ideas and academic freedom no longer needed defending to such an extent. As the 1950s gave way to a more liberal era, new threats to academic freedom came less from a repressive state and more from political radicals. As such they were either not recognized as attacks upon free speech, or were welcomed regardless. Reflecting upon the McCarthy era in 1987, Bloom wrote that, 'Today there are many more things unthinkable and unspeakable in universities than there were then, and little disposition to protect those who have earned the ire of radical movements' (p. 324).

One such example can be seen with the impact of the civil rights movement on campus towards the end of the 1960s. The free speech movement that began at Berkeley in 1964, before spreading to other universities across the country, was prompted by students wanting to engage, as adults, in political discussions and campaigns on campus. Students who had been active in the growing civil rights movement resented the imposition of infantilizing restrictions on debate. This powerful and liberating movement stands in stark contrast to today's supposedly radical calls to shut down debate in the name of protecting students from offence. Yet it is perhaps possible to trace the roots of today's censoriousness to later developments within the free speech movement itself. For some campaigners, the demand for free speech was only ever a pragmatic means to enable the promotion of particular issues, mostly connected to the civil rights movement. This made it possible for the demand for free speech to be superseded by what was perceived to be the greater importance of the cause being championed.

An example of this in practice occurred at the end of the 1960s with the growing influence of the militant Black Power group upon the Black Student Union (BSU). In September 1967, Larry Gossett, Head of the BSU at the University of Washington, reflected an emerging separatist and identity-focused response to the persistent racial discrimination experienced by black citizens. He wrote, in an article for the *Seattle Post-Intelligencer*, 'I believe that black people must be obsessed with thinking black. Then they will understand the need for determining their own destiny'. Growing increasingly angry at the slow pace of change, Gossett argued that Black Power meant, 'self-determination, self-respect and self defense, by any means necessary' (in Schaefer, 2015). The BSU argued for changes within educational institutions, including the establishment of a black curriculum and greater rights for students.

At Cornell University on 19 April 1969, students from the Afro-American Society responded to heightened racial tensions by taking over the students' union building on campus. The following day, students emerged from negotiations with faculty carrying guns. The university administration had agreed to meet all of the students' demands, including those that had been previously rejected concerning changes to admissions requirements and the academic curriculum. Shortly afterwards, Cornell launched its *Africana Studies and Research Center*. The hard-won freedom of lecturers to determine the content of their own teaching had been abandoned; professors capitulated to all attempts to influence the content of the curriculum.

The AAUP welcomed students trumping the rights of their lecturers and did little to defend academic freedom in such instances. The merit of the specific cause was judged to be more important than general principles of academic freedom. This marked a major turning point in defining and evaluating the perceived importance of academic freedom, the impact of which is felt to this day. Bloom describes the shift that took place, thus:

> ...in the fifties a goodly portion of the professors still held the views about freedom put forward by Bacon, Milton, Locke and Mill... [A]nother portion were of the Left, and they had a personal interest in the protection afforded them by those views. When the former lost their confidence, and the latter gained theirs, the strength of academic freedom declined dramatically. (p. 325)

The capitulation to political demands heralded the start of an enduring change in the academic project. A commitment to particular values began to supersede rational inquiry as the goal of both teaching and research.

Bloom hints at one reason why this shift from rational inquiry to a commitment to values came about so readily when he describes how the professors who had once believed in the concept of freedom 'lost confidence'. The experience of the Second World War, and of the Holocaust in particular, led to a broader questioning of Enlightenment values within society at large and within higher education in particular. As early as the 1940s, Theodor Adorno and his Frankfurt

School colleagues posed the Holocaust as a logical outcome of the dialectic of enlightenment, scientific thought, and reason (Markle, 1995). In a process explored more fully in Chapters 2 and 6, over the course of the following decades, this view gained traction in the universities. Values that had been associated with the liberal academic project and the scientific method such as rationality, the search for truth, the importance of empirical evidence, public acts of judgement and the potential for individual critical reason, all became discredited. More than anything else, the collapse of truth within humanities and social science disciplines that began at this time had a devastating and enduring impact upon the pursuit and transmission of knowledge and the meaning and purpose of academic freedom.

In the UK, the consensus surrounding the nature and purpose of higher education in the decades immediately following the Second World War meant that there had been little explicit public debate about the meaning or importance of academic freedom. In 1966, Lord Robbins, President of the British Academy, gave the first of a series of annual lectures sponsored by the Thank-Offering to Britain Fund. This was a financial trust, established by refugees, who sought sanctuary in Britain during the war. The trust's founders noted that academic freedom, 'is a matter of great importance to the welfare of our community [...] it was to escape a state of academic unfreedom and worse, that many of those who contributed to its endowment left the lands of their birth' (p. 45). In his speech, Robbins argued:

> [T]he demand for academic freedom in institutions of higher education is not the same as the demand for freedom of thought and speech in general: it goes considerably beyond that principle. It is not merely a demand that the academic, in his capacity as a citizen, shall be free to think and speak as he likes; it is a demand that, in his employment as an academic, he shall have certain freedoms not necessarily involved in ordinary contractual relations and that the institutions in which he works shall likewise enjoy certain rights of independent initiative not necessarily granted to other institutions which are part of the state system. (p. 48)

Robbins set out what he considered to be the contemporary threats to academic freedom, most notably, 'if the search for truth and values is subordinated to the exigencies of particular ideologies' (p. 46). He was clear that

> at the present day there are some to whom the concept of academic freedom, so far from being an ideal to be supported, is something which should definitely be opposed. The belief that academic life should conform to central regulations and disciplines is not something which is only to be found east of the Iron Curtain. (p. 58)

As the 1960s drew to a close, student protests spread from America to Britain and the rest of Western Europe. Often such protests were a response to contemporary political issues such as the war in Vietnam. Demands for free speech became part of a broader challenge to the authority of the university over students. British sociologist, Jennie Bristow, notes that 'concern about the apparent alienation, or detachment, of middle-class youth from the values and institutions of mainstream society becomes more pronounced in the 1950s and 1960s, and is seen to achieve a sharp expression in the student protests and the counterculture of the 1960s' (2015, p. 66). In 1967, the London School of Economics (LSE) became a particular focal point for dissent with students protesting against the appointment of Walter Adams, who had links with what was then Rhodesia, as Director of School. In response, Adams installed security gates at the entrance to the institution to prevent protesters occupying campus buildings. In January 1969, protests at LSE culminated in students smashing the gates.

As in America, academics once confident in their authority suddenly found themselves accountable to the student body. Students demanded places on academic committees and changes to certain courses. Again, this resulted in an undermining of once securely held academic principles. In a 2003 interview, one of the original cohort of protesters suggested with a note of triumph that their arguments were directed 'against the world our elders had bequeathed us – Vietnam, the prevalent class system in higher education, plus a smug and unmerited feeling of academic superiority ("objectivity") that permeated the LSE at that time. If nothing else, we punctured that' (Mair, 10/07/03).

In attacking the authority of the previous generation, protesting students challenged the basic assumptions that underpinned the liberal academic project. British students, like their American counterparts, often found themselves pushing at an open door as many academics were already beginning to question the aspiration towards truth and the possibility of objectivity as goals of the academic enterprise.

Academics at LSE and beyond often became involved in student protests, albeit sometimes unwittingly, as either supporters of the students or the focus of their anger. Two LSE lecturers, Nick Bateson and Robin Blackburn, were dismissed after they expressed support for the students who had dismantled the security gates. Although Blackburn drew upon academic freedom to defend his position, this was rejected by an employment tribunal, which decided that the university was entitled to dismiss Blackburn 'for misconduct in expressing support for the violent conduct of the students in removing the gates in a way that indicated a general support for and encouragement of violence in comparable circumstances' (Barendt, 2010, p. 86).

This judgement raised questions about the boundary between speech and action, and the extent to which academics may be considered to have more or less free speech than the population as a whole. The verdict appears to suggest that academics, in a position of responsibility over students, have to be more careful, and less free, in their speech. The events at LSE, and Blackburn's dismissal in particular, led to the formation of the Council for Academic Freedom and Democracy (CAFD) in July 1970. High-profile LSE academics such as John Griffith, Ralph Miliband and John Westergaard were among the founding members.

Throughout the 1970s, British government ministers, lecturers and university managers maintained an uneasy consensus about the importance of academic freedom. It was not until the late 1980s, when a vastly expanded higher education sector met severe financial cutbacks from the state, that this consensus began to be challenged. The government's proposed changes to the employment conditions of academics in the 1988 Education Act meant that for the first time in Britain, formally defining and defending academic freedom became a pressing issue for many in universities. In an *Academic Freedom Amendment to the Education Reform Bill*, Lord Jenkins of Hillhead proposed that academics needed:

> The freedom within the law to question and test received wisdom, and to put forward new ideas and controversial or unpopular

> opinions without placing themselves in jeopardy of losing their jobs or privileges they may have at their institutions.
>
> (in Russell, 1993, p. 2)

As always, there was a degree of pragmatism in arguing for academic freedom at this point. It could be seen as a means of defending the state-funded privileges of a selected few at a time when government money was no longer to be so forthcoming. The post-war British State has been described as a 'benevolent dictator' (Desai, 2003) and, perhaps unsurprisingly, academics were far happier to receive the benevolence than have their actions dictated. Even worse was the very real prospect of being dictated to while receiving little by way of benevolence. However, as with the AAUP's 1915 *Declaration*, although instrumentally motivated, such arguments for academic freedom were premised upon more universalist principles, and driven by a belief in the academic enterprise rather than simply a defence of private interests.

Academic freedom today

Since Lord Jenkins' confident assertion in 1988, academic freedom has become increasingly problematic as a concept and troublesome in practice. In 1955, Metzger usefully reminded his readers that 'the institutional setting, the educational objective, and the meaning and status of academic freedom are [. . .] intimately connected' (1961, p. 3). Today we see a decline in state funding for higher education in parallel with a period of dramatic growth in student numbers, alongside a managerialist demand that, as 'consumers', students must be 'satisfied' with their university experience. We also see a 'casualization' of the academic labour force so that tenured positions are no longer the norm, and an increasingly competitive market for research money that allows funding bodies and editorial boards to determine the topics, if not the direction, of investigations. Each of these factors shifts the purpose of higher education and the status of academic freedom.

Perhaps more than any of these, academic freedom has become problematized as scholars have rejected even the aspiration towards truth, and knowledge itself has come to be treated with suspicion. Battles fought in the name of academic freedom today, when separated from any greater project concerned with truth and knowledge, are quickly reduced to arbitrary and technical concerns with employment conditions or social media use. While employment rights and social media use are undoubtedly important, their significance lies in the security they provide scholars to rigorously pursue new knowledge into what may be controversial areas. This sense of mission has been lost from academia today.

Since its conception, the importance of academic freedom has been that it allows scholars to challenge existing orthodoxies and turn society's understanding of the world on its head with findings that may deeply offend the existing outlook of many. Academic freedom was fundamental to a scholarly enterprise based upon critiquing existing understandings and challenging established orthodoxies. However, this liberal academic project is only possible when knowledge takes on the status of a truth claim and its fundamental contestability becomes apparent. Academic freedom is therefore premised upon the notion of a 'marketplace of ideas' and the understanding that, within a multitude of competing truth claims, some will win out over others. The notion that not all knowledge is equally valid, that ideas should be set in competition with one another and can be assessed objectively rather than on the subjective identity of the knower, is unashamedly elitist.

Today's trend to add countless alternative, equally valid perspectives involves little fundamental challenge to existing ideas and rarely necessitates a staunch defence of academic freedom. When there is no longer a desire among scholars to partake in testing, challenging and disproving knowledge through setting it in competition with new findings, academic freedom becomes at best an individual and moral concern, and at worst an empty rhetorical slogan.

Some still maintain a connection between academic freedom, the pursuit of knowledge and the search for truth. Conrad Russell argued academics should have the 'freedom to teach the truth as we see it, with suitable acknowledgment of views which differ from our own' (1993, p. 18). Likewise, Cary Nelson suggests academic freedom 'embodies Enlightenment commitments to the pursuit of knowledge' (2010, p. 1). In *The Case Against Academic Boycotts of Israel*, the AAUP reminds academics that universities should be institutions committed to 'the search for truth and its free expression' (2015, p. 33).

However, there are three key ways in which academic freedom is being redefined today. Firstly, academic freedom is more strictly tied to the limited demands of the professional role. Gibbs, for example, argues the right to academic freedom is not a right to unencumbered free speech but instead a right to present, refer to and argue for (or against) claims or beliefs in an 'appropriately academic manner'. 'It is within the context of an institutional role and involves following as well as maintaining historic academic practices' (2013, p. 725). Proponents of the view that academic freedom should be limited to the demands of the professional role come from both the political left and right. Stanley Fish characterizes his own position on academic freedom as being from the 'It's just a job' school of thought (2014, p. 9). He argues academics have 'obligations and aspirations' which are defined by the distinctive task and therefore 'academics are not free in any special sense to do anything but their jobs' (2014, p. 10). David Horowitz argues, 'academic freedom does imply restraint – the restraint of disciplined and professional standards of inquiry and expression' (2007, p. 16).

Conrad Russell has warned that, 'If academic research is not devoted to finding the truth, it is a form of propaganda' (1993, p. 19) – and the second threat to academic freedom today results from the rejection of truth. Stanley Fish argues that faith in academic freedom implies a 'withdrawal from moral judgment and morality' (2001, p. 8). We could just as easily argue that as scholars have lost faith in academic freedom they have privileged passing moral judgement. The combination of abandoning goals of truth and objectivity at the same time as passing moral judgement can lead to the redefinition of academic freedom as a matter of justice. This results in the privileging of work based upon the identity of the scholar. As will be discussed more fully in Chapter 7, those committed to 'academic justice', who emerge predominantly from the political left, argue that inherent within concepts such as truth and objectivity is a privileging of the knowledge and assumptions of socially dominant groups – usually white, Western, male, middle class and heterosexual. The content of the curriculum, in the arts and humanities as in other disciplines, needs to represent the best that has been thought and said; and this requires that judgements be made that separate the value of a work from the identity of its author.

The third way in which academic freedom is restricted today is through a culture of conformity, which encourages academics to self-censor. Such self-censorship takes a number of forms, including suppression of research or teaching material that may be considered controversial. More often it is less about suppressing material than not raising particular issues in the first place, or bringing work into line with the expectations of funding councils, journal editorial boards, colleagues and students. In this way a particular political outlook can come to dominate higher education – academics are rewarded in terms of career success if they conform, and punished for idiosyncrasy if they do not. The creation of a culture of conformity within higher education is elaborated in the next chapter.

2
Conformity in the Academy

As the previous chapter has shown, there has never been a golden age of academic freedom within universities. In different historical periods, attacks upon academic freedom have come from the church, state, university managers and benefactors, or students and colleagues – or a combination of these forces. Confronting each new threat has posed its own particular set of challenges.

Today, academic freedom in the western world is rarely threatened by formal restrictions imposed upon scholars by interfering governments or overzealous university administrators. When such threats do arise, as with the global swathe of anti-terror legislation enacted since the 9/11 attacks, they are often easily identifiable, exposed and disputed. Likewise, many are quick to complain when there is any suspicion that big business or wealthy private donors may unduly influence the direction of scholarship. Groups such as the American *UnKoch My Campus* petition for greater transparency of higher education funding. Campaigners assume that some sources of income are more morally legitimate or politically neutral than others, and that private finance is incompatible with academic freedom.

But despite a lack of significant formal restrictions, there is little sense that universities are places committed to unbridled liberty and free expression. Rather than finding their words limited by external impositions, academics who want to say something that comes up against the norms of their departmental or disciplinary culture, or just goes against the grain of polite society, experience pressure to self-censor and conform. Many no longer have the employment security of tenure but instead serve lengthy periods working as temporary or hourly paid members of staff before gaining the prize of an 'open-ended' contract – which is often perceived as permanent only so long as employee, course and institution remain in good standing. This incentivizes obedience and dissuades people from saying or doing anything controversial for fear they will lose their job. Early career academics take their lead from more established colleagues, who compromise to satisfy the demands of student–customers, peer reviewers and funding councils. They guard their language so as not to breach speech codes, institutional safe spaces and equality and diversity policies.

Fee-paying students are increasingly treated like consumers of higher education who must be satisfied, flattered and appeased rather than challenged. Infantilized students consider themselves to be vulnerable and in need of protecting from anything offensive, or even just upsetting, while at the same time lecturers have their performance assessed on student evaluations of their teaching. Within this context, the urge to self-censor so as not to challenge students unduly, and to receive positive feedback which can support a promotion application, is strong.

In relation to research, the expectation that academics will secure peer-reviewed publications in a narrowing selection of disciplinary-specific journals similarly incentivizes self-censorship and conservatism. Instead of pushing into radically new intellectual terrain, the safer strategy is to determine which issues are currently of interest to a specified journal's readership, the opinions of potential reviewers and the body of relevant material that must be acknowledged. This leads to publications that often seem to specialize in saying very little and merely confirm that which has gone before.

When it comes to securing research funding, there can be even more pressures on academics to bring ideas in line with a particular, predetermined viewpoint. Funding bodies will often list research topics they are prepared to support that can be quite explicitly linked to the political agenda of the government of the day. This can go beyond identifying themes, and actually dictate the direction of the research. For example, over recent years funding into climate science has increasingly been made available for projects which consider ways to reduce carbon emissions and promote sustainability, rather than those that aim to use science to counteract anthropocentric global warming and promote industrial development (see National Association of Scholars (NAS), 2015).

In England, the Higher Education Funding Council argues, 'We want sustainable development to be central to higher education' (HEFCE, 2014). This means promoting a particular set of values and practices such as recycling, reduced energy use and the promotion of ethical consumption. As a result, there is apparently no room within the academy for the so-called 'climate-contrarian' Bjorn Lomborg's proposal to consider the role of technology in ameliorating the effects of climate change rather than trying to prevent them from occurring. Lomborg's failed attempt to establish a climate change research centre at the University of Western Australia showed that rather than challenging the imposition of a particular moral agenda, academics are often at the front line of enforcing the consensus.

In order to comply with an overtly moralistic and values-driven agenda in higher education, many academics choose not to venture into intellectual territory that may pose any sort of challenge to the status quo. Alternatively, they may self-censor their criticisms of the dominant ethos and take the easy option of saying nothing rather than questioning a consensus. This tendency for academics to censor their written and spoken words before they are ever publicly uttered offers one explanation for the limited need for institutional managers and national governments to resort to crude censorship. Self-censorship does not prompt public conflict; rather, it promotes a false sense of harmony and an absence of dissent.

Such lack of conflict is detrimental to the pursuit of knowledge. As Mill explained in *On Liberty*, 'Wrong opinions and practices gradually yield to fact and argument: but facts and arguments, to produce any effect on the mind, must be brought before it' (2005, p. 30). Self-censorship leads to some facts and arguments not being placed before students, colleagues or members of the public. In this way, entrenched self-censorship results from, and at the same time contributes to, a culture of conformity within universities. This chapter explores how and why higher education has become so conformist, as well as the potential impact of such a climate upon the pursuit of knowledge.

The end of knowledge

When John F. Kennedy spoke at Harvard University in 1956, he confidently described the university as a place whose 'whole purpose is dedicated to the advancement of knowledge and the dissemination of truth'. He could not have foreseen what a controversial statement this would later become. Although some politicians today may pay lip service to the importance of knowledge, they are most unlikely either to consider this as an end in itself or to link knowledge to a concept of truth. It is far more often argued that higher education serves comparatively mundane economic and social purposes for the nation in terms of innovation, scientific advance and the development of a skilled workforce; or creating a cohesive and democratically engaged society.

For over a century, successive governments throughout the western world have sought to link higher education to national economic and political priorities. In the UK, the start of the twentieth century marked the point at which the university, and its intellectual products, began to be considered instrumental to a range of essentially political goals (Delanty, 2001, p. 34). Whereas an earlier generation of scholars within the Ancient Universities maintained an almost monastic separation from the outside world better to pursue their studies, in the twentieth century higher education became part of the industrial landscape. This drive towards the instrumentalization of knowledge accelerated after the Second World War. Although by no means the first such document, the British government's 1963 *Report of the Committee on Higher Education* (the *Robbins Report*) represented a clear shift in the need for state expenditure on higher education, and on the pursuit and transmission of knowledge more broadly, to be justified in relation to tangible, preferably public benefits. This attempt to influence the direction and purpose of universities has increased markedly in recent years despite a global shift in the funding of higher education away from state financial subsidies and on to individual students in the form of tuition fees.

In *The Closing of the American Mind*, Allan Bloom describes the damaging impact of the removal of 'great books' from higher education. He reminds us that the concept of the canon – works of literature, art and music that have a publicly acknowledged quality superseding their historical and geographical context – has not always been written off as socially elitist. Rose similarly reminds us that in Britain at the beginning of the twentieth century, 'The mainstream of the labour movement agreed that great art and literature had eternal value, and ought to be disseminated among the workers out of a disinterested concern for truth, beauty and a higher morality' (2001, p. 50). Canonical works were not deemed to have any instrumental value outside of their intrinsic quality; as a result, Hannah Arendt argued that 'Higher education will either understand that the life of the mind is something to be cherished for its own sake, that learning can exist and flourish only if it is done for its own sake, or it will wither away and die' (1973, p. 12).

Arendt's very need to make such proclamations was a response to the markedly more instrumental attitude towards knowledge that had begun to materialize from the middle of the twentieth century. The post-war challenge to the idea of learning as an end in itself was met with relatively little opposition from within universities. It chimed with a growing lack of confidence about the pursuit of knowledge felt by many academics, and there was little questioning of the essentially political demand that knowledge should be a means of achieving social and economic goals. In 2003, the British Labour government's Secretary of State for Education and Skills, Charles Clarke, declared knowledge for its own sake to be 'a bit dodgy' – going on to explain that his department had no interest in supporting 'the medieval concept of a community of scholars seeking truth' (BBC News, 31/01/03). Back in 2003, such a statement was considered newsworthy. Today, though perhaps stated rather less boldly, it is often accepted as common sense.

Although an increasingly instrumental discourse about higher education has primarily emerged from beyond the university, it has met relatively little challenge within institutions. Many academics have become far more humble in their aspirations and do not consider themselves to be contributing what John F. Kennedy termed 'objective views' or a 'sense of liberty' to the affairs of the nation. No longer is there certainty about what constitutes knowledge, how it differs from practical experience and on what basis judgements should be made as to which knowledge is worthy of a place in the university. Today, there are few who confidently claim knowledge is its own reward. When, in October 2014, Professor Andrew Hamilton, the vice chancellor of the University of Oxford, spoke out in defence of 'apparently useless' study, the shocking nature of this declaration made it a national news story (Massie, 09/10/14).

It is not unusual for academics to question the aspiration towards truth or the possibility of objectivity in the pursuit of knowledge. Some express concern that 'knowledge, as we have known it in the academy, is coming to an end' (Griffin, 1997, p. 3). However, others welcome the fact that 'the legitimacy of any institution of higher education cannot be premised on prior assumptions regarding the provenance of truth' (Nixon, 2011, p. 42). They are upfront in rejecting the notion that knowledge serves a unifying purpose and argue that universities have outlived the role of 'producer, protector and inculcator of the national culture' (McLean, 2008, p. 38). This view is, perhaps unsurprisingly, most apparent within humanities and social science disciplines.

A great deal of confusion over the meaning and purpose of knowledge ensues when any connection to truth is rejected. Often, as discussions around the use of technology in education and the replacement of face-to-face teaching with online courses show, knowledge is reduced simply to data and easily internet-accessible facts. In an 'information age', the idea of reading books from beginning to end, or even attending lectures, can appear outdated when all that is known on a topic can be accessed at the push of a button. Gerald Raunig, writing in *Factories of Knowledge Industries of Creativity*, argues that knowledge is just information, a marketable commodity and the driving force of twenty-first century capitalism (2013). Others within the academy agree that knowledge has now become a valuable commodity, marketed through books, articles and conferences as well as patents and governmental contracts within a neo-liberal economy (see, for example, Oparah, 2014, p. 115).

Knowledge is further confused with skills, a term that has unhelpfully come to take on an increasingly wide range of meanings (see Winch, 2002, p. 137). Unlike knowledge, which can be entirely abstract and conceptual, skills tend to be practically oriented, often physically demonstrable and useful only within specific contexts. When skills are considered a component of 'human capital' to be invested in by individuals and governments in order to secure financial return, they also become seen as commodities with an appropriate exchange value (Williams, 2005, p. 186).

Most recently, skills have been posed as fundamental for participation in society and an essential component of social inclusion. This redefines education as more akin to general personal development. Although perhaps requiring committed intellectual and practical engagement, enhancing personal skill levels is not the same as increasing knowledge, which often takes individuals beyond themselves and places them in relation to a broader collective project of understanding the world.

The discussion about skills and information points to a more fundamental misunderstanding of the nature of knowledge today. An ability to cite, or even just access, facts on a particular topic is not the same as a deep understanding of a subject. Delanty argues that information is 'instrumental knowledge' (2001, p. 5) in that it serves a particular purpose and is useful only in that it provides answers to specific questions. When taken out of context, facts alone can rarely help in 'discovering new ways to interpret the world' – Rose's description of the goal of a liberal education (2001, p. 7). Knowledge suggests an awareness of facts in context, an understanding of how and why data has been generated and how various facts on a similar topic relate to each other. The purpose of the post-Enlightenment university has never been to teach information but rather, as Bill Readings puts it in *The University in Ruins*, 'to inculcate the exercise of critical judgement' (1996, p. 6).

When not confused with information, skills or personal development, knowledge is increasingly treated with suspicion. Michael Young reminds us that canonical knowledge was considered 'objective in ways that transcend the historical conditions of its production' (2008, p. 19). Yet Piya Chatterjee and Sunaina Maira, writing in *The Imperial University*, describe the production of knowledge as 'central to the imperial project' (2014, p. 8) and as such, Steven Salaita posits, 'no piece of scholarship has ever been nonaligned' (2014a, p. 229). Salaita scorns attempts at objectivity as methodological foolishness, 'if it claims to be objective then it's lying to you. And if it's not political, then it doesn't exist' (2014a, p. 234). Chatterjee and Maira argue that in disciplines such as anthropology, knowledge is used to 'other' 'indigenous and minoritized communities' providing 'both information and "intelligence" for the subjugation and administration' of such groups (2014, p. 15).

In scientific disciplines, knowledge is considered tainted by the development of the atomic bomb and other deadly weaponry, and presented as continuing to serve the interests of America as a global and military power. Instead of making the case for more objective, or better, knowledge, Oparah suggests: 'we ultimately fail to dismantle the academic–military–prison–industrial complex if we address it only through the production of more knowledge' (2014, p. 115). As she considers knowledge to be merely a commodity, Oparah argues 'better' or more progressive knowledge is no solution as it can still be co-opted for oppressive political purposes.

The use of the word 'production' in the context of such discussions suggests not just that knowledge is socially constructed but that it is made under almost factory-like production line conditions, applying rigid methods to formulaic theories. As a result, declining to teach subject content is considered by some academics to be a radical means of opposing the marketization of higher education and challenging the commodification of ideas considered inherent in the 'knowledge economy'.

When considered in historical perspective, such scorn for knowledge is a relatively recent phenomenon. In the first half of the twentieth century, a relationship between education, knowledge and the search for truth was taken for granted and drove the scholarly project. Delanty terms this era 'liberal modernity', when the pursuit and, importantly, the nature (or mode) of knowledge within the university was still compatible with the Enlightenment's ideal of truth and the ultimate unity of culture (2001, p. 33). As noted in the previous chapter, the experience of the Second World War, and the Holocaust in particular, prompted an intellectual process of questioning and discrediting Enlightenment values.

The Holocaust was considered by many to be a logical consequence of the endeavour to shape society through science and rationality. In *Modernity and the Holocaust* (1991), the sociologist Zygmunt Bauman argues against the idea that the Holocaust was an historical anomaly in which society temporarily regressed to a state of premodern barbarism. Rather, he presents this event as intrinsically connected to the project of modernity. Bauman highlights Enlightenment principles – in particular the drive for efficiency and rationality that lay behind the industrial division of labour, the attempt at the taxonomic categorization of different species and the tendency to view rule-following as morally good – as having been demonstrated in merely a more extreme form in the experience of the Holocaust. He suggests that after the Second World War, all 'grand narratives', including Enlightenment-inspired positivism, stood accused of oppressing minority views and promoting conflict and were therefore discredited.

The rush to abandon Enlightenment principles was led by academics on the political left who, in the post-war period, found it increasingly difficult to defend the ideals of reason, progress and universalism upon which their intellectual tradition had been built. As will be explored more fully in Chapter 5, theorists associated with the Frankfurt School, such as Theodor Adorno and Max Horkheimer, emphasized the temporality and context-dependence of truth in knowledge. Likewise, the German philosopher Herbert Marcuse, writing in *One Dimensional Man* (1964), argued that knowledge is ideology; in other words, simply a product of the dominant economic and political conditions that gave rise to it.

Berger and Luckmann, writing in *The Social Construction of Reality* published in 1966, lent further weight to claims that there was no inherent connection between knowledge and truth. They argued that the nature of reality itself was not objectively experienced but constructed through the interaction of people's knowledge and beliefs in society. Taken together, such views were interpreted as a denial of the possibility of objectivity or truth in knowledge beyond an exposure of the workings of power. In a 1977 interview published under the heading *Truth and Power*, Michel Foucault declared that there is 'no truly universal truth' and this dictum soon became widely accepted. Furedi notes that by the end of the 1970s, the views of these 'New Philosophers' had gained broader traction among a new breed of academic who 'promoted a stridently anti-universalist and anti-Enlightenment outlook' (2014, p. 176).

The new sociologists of education, who emerged out of this changing philosophical climate, posited curricular knowledge as socially constructed and merely reflective of the ideology of the dominant social elite. Contributors to books such as *Knowledge and Control*, edited by Michael Young and published in 1971, argued that the educational failure of many working class children was a result of *their* knowledge and experiences not being recognized in school and formally credentialized. The French philosopher Pierre Bourdieu, writing in *Reproduction in Education, Society and Culture* (1977), suggested that schooling was a form of 'symbolic violence' that reinforced class hierarchies through credentializing the children whose tastes corresponded to those of the social elite. Teachers and the school curriculum, Bourdieu argued, portrayed the tastes and opinions of the elite as universal and ideologically neutral. This created a false sense that it was the most academically able who were formally rewarded with success at school, and that society itself was a meritocracy based upon educational achievement rather than shared cultural capital.

Since at least the mid-1980s it has become commonplace for scholars to conceive of established bodies of knowledge as simply a reflection of the tastes, opinions and experiences of a social elite, while the concept of truth and the notion of objectivity are presented as myths propagated in an attempt to pass off a dominant hegemony as ideologically neutral. In America in particular, this has played out in a discussion around the concept of the canon. Without a sense of there being any intrinsic merit to canonical works, there is no means by which one poem, work of literature or musical score can be judged as better than any other: all are equally valid and all are reduced to the status of 'texts'. Paul Boghossian notes, in *Fear of Knowledge: Against Relativism and Constructivism,* the 'conviction of many scholars that the best philosophical thought of our time has swept aside the intuitive objectivist conceptions of truth and rationality [...] and replaced them with conceptions of knowledge that vindicate equal validity'. He argues this lends legitimacy to the notion that 'there is no such thing as superior knowledge only different knowledge appropriate to its setting' (2006, p. 6).

Whereas in the 1970s and into the 1980s, denying any relationship between truth and knowledge was considered to be a radical and subversive challenge to tradition, today it has become far more normal within the humanities and social science disciplines. Such academics have been diagnosed as suffering from acute 'veriphobia' (Bailey, 2001), and scholars who continue to defend the pursuit of knowledge as a search for truth are increasingly rare. In comparison to the perceived radicalism of abandoning truth, a persistence in upholding the values of rationality, truth and objectivity has come to be interpreted as, at best, an arrogant or foolish endeavour and at worst, an authoritarian, oppressive political act that serves only to reinforce existing power relations.

The paradigm shift that led to the recognition that knowledge was not always empirically discoverable but often socially constructed formed an important intellectual breakthrough within the social sciences and humanities. It paved the way for the development of a better understanding of the social world. However, Berger and Luckmann's work was often misinterpreted as denying the existence of reality altogether rather than suggesting an existing reality was conceived through people's interactions with each other and the world. Such a misinterpretation led to claims about the arbitrary nature of curricular knowledge that are not supported by a constructivist approach. Michael Young, in the 1970s at the forefront of arguing that curricular knowledge was selected simply to reinforce existing power relations, has reversed his position. He now mounts an intellectual challenge to the view that subject knowledge is arbitrary and, in the interests of social justice, best avoided. As Young points out in *Bringing Knowledge Back In*, 'education presupposes the possibility of both knowledge and truth' (2008, p. 83). The rejection of truth as the goal of knowledge leaves only 'voice discourses' and reduces higher education to an empty shell.

When scholarship was connected to goals of truth and objectivity, the separation of the identity of the individual academic from their work was a fundamental principle of scholarship. Today, rather than demanding that 'every subjective element be eliminated' (Metzger, 1961, p. 80) many academics argue that objectivity is a myth and call instead for recognition of the subjectivity of the researcher. Rather than celebrating the universal, people are limited to their own experiences and restricted to peering in at others. Instead of knowledge taking people beyond themselves, it reinforces a focus upon the self. This shift in emphasis undermines the justification for universities that were once premised upon the pursuit of knowledge through reason, critique and rationality.

The rejection of all truth claims has had a devastating impact upon the liberal academic project of the pursuit of knowledge. As Furedi indicates, 'without a relationship to Truth, knowledge has no intrinsic meaning' (2004, p. 7). Although a proponent of the rejection of truth, postmodern philosopher Richard Rorty illustrates the ensuing sense of futility: 'the whole project of distinguishing between what exists in itself and what exists in relation to human minds – the project shared by Aristotle, Locke, Kant and Searle – is no longer worth pursuing' (1996, p. 30). This nihilistic understanding of knowledge and education has much in common with Nietzsche's view that the quest for historical truth was impossible.

In abandoning a connection between knowledge and truth, anti-Enlightenment radicals reject the project of advancing knowledge through competing truth claims. The other side of this coin is the assumption that the truth of a particular issue is settled beyond question. The tendency to label critics, or skeptics, on issues as wide ranging as the Holocaust, climate change, patriarchy and rape culture, as 'deniers' suggests not a clash of opposing understandings but that the truth has already been determined and people who do not accept it are deluded. It suggests that any further discussion is not only futile but problematic as it detracts from dealing practically with the issues concerned. Both the rejection of truth and the notion that the truth is settled curtail academic debate by undermining the assumption that knowledge progresses through competing truth claims. The former position prevents any new knowledge superseding existing understandings; the latter suggests there is simply nothing to debate and no further intellectual progress to be made.

When universities are no longer committed to the advancement of knowledge they become hollowed-out institutions in search of a defining purpose. The philosopher John Searle argues, 'The biggest single consequence of the rejection of the Western Rationalistic tradition is that it makes possible the abandonment of traditional standards of objectivity, truth and rationality', and suggests that the rejection of the Enlightenment project 'opens the way for an educational agenda one of whose primary purposes is to achieve social and political transformation' (in Rorty, 1996, p. 25). This leaves a vacuum at the heart of higher education that becomes filled by a range of instrumental aims, from the promotion of individual employability skills to, as Rorty indicates, the inculcation of particular values.

End of criticism

The post-war rejection of grand narratives and the aspiration towards truth denies the possibility of passing authoritative judgement. This has consequences that reach beyond academia; as Furedi notes, 'Once truth is interpreted as a dubious claim in competition with many others, it ceases to play a key role in society's cultural life' (2004, p. 4). One impact of this upon broader society is to call into question the role of criticism. The freedom to be critical allows the best ideas and understanding to progress at the same time as less valuable or incorrect knowledge is critiqued, disproven and superseded. As Mill explained in *On Liberty*:

> Truth, in the great practical concerns of life, is so much a question of reconciling and combining of opposites, that very few have minds sufficiently capacious and impartial to make the adjustment with an approach to correctness, and it has to be made by the rough process of a struggle between combatants fighting under hostile banners.
>
> (Mill, 2005, p. 62)

The importance of truth in relation to both criticism and knowledge lies in its fundamental contestability. The liberal academic project was driven by a concept of truth that was permanently open to challenge. This was never a rejection of knowledge so much as an abandonment of certainty; indeed, it is precisely the tentative nature of truth that makes knowledge possible. Without truth to aspire towards, intellectual struggle played out as a battle of competing ideas is futile. There is simply nothing at stake. We end up with a consensus that all views are equally valid and a climate of criticality comes to be replaced by a culture of conformity. Judgement is reduced to a matter of personal experience or the expression of individual identity. As Angus Kennedy notes in *Being Cultured*, 'Even the *attempt* to argue that something might be better than something else is met with accusations of undeserved cultural authority, of an elitism that has somehow had its day: that smacks of an abuse of power and influence' (2014, p. ix, emphasis in original). As culture is a reflection of humanity, and high culture expresses the best of the human spirit, the rejection of criticism further represents the abandonment of a belief in the value of human freedom and the individual's capacity to reason.

Raymond Williams writes that the words 'critic' and 'critical' came into the English language in the early seventeenth century from the Greek word for 'judgement' (1983, p. 85). The philosophical approach of the Greek Skeptics led to the emergence of the radical social principle of public criticism (Rauch, 2014, p. 46). The core concepts of ancient skepticism were belief, suspension of judgement, criterion of truth, appearances and investigation. The importance placed upon the suspension of prior judgement implied a difference between criticism and opinion or response. Criticism came to be associated not just with a reasoned judgement based upon informed interpretation but also a judgement that was shared collectively. What was radical about a public act of passing judgement was the imperative to place faith in people, or the demos, rather than a social elite to determine the merit of any particular idea. The worth of criticism was dependent upon the public validity of the intellectual authority, rather than the social status of the critic.

The significance of ancient skepticism to more modern forms of criticism is the methodological precedent that this set. Passing judgement requires the critic to arrive at publicly acknowledged conclusions, yet at the very same time to consider none of their conclusions as being beyond challenge. As Rauch puts it, 'knowledge is always tentative and subject to correction' (2014, p. 45). Everyone in society, not just those in academia, can critically scrutinize the work of others and no knowledge is off limits. The pursuit of ideas depended upon people having the freedom to critique and challenge the knowledge they had inherited in order to counterpose new ideas.

The contemporary challenge to the authority of the critic can be seen as a rejection of faith in people's ability to understand and respond to intellectual judgements. Today, rather than focusing upon theoretical or abstract arguments, criticism is often wrapped up in discussions of identity. It is assumed that knowledge of the author or critic's biological, social and cultural background is necessary for a correct appreciation of the work. When criticism becomes simply a matter of proffering alternative but equally valid viewpoints, knowledge itself is reduced simply to perspectives.

Accepting alternative views makes no great calls upon individuals to exercise their capacity to reason. No beliefs are challenged: all is simply received, contemplated and dismissed. As this poses little threat to the status quo, the need for individual liberty to exercise reason becomes redundant. When criticism no longer poses a challenge to existing knowledge through offering a competing, superior truth, criticality collapses into cynicism and the passing of informed judgements is replaced by an equally nihilistic interpretation of all subject content.

One example of this can be seen in the popularity for labelling ideas as 'neo-liberal'. Neo-liberalism has been described as a 'catch-all term used with little discrimination' that has taken on the aura of a grand theoretical term (Barnett, 2010, p. 291). As such, 'neo-liberalism' is often used as rhetorical shorthand to indicate either the worst excesses of capitalism or simply anything perceived as distasteful. In effect, the charge of neo-liberalism is used to evoke all that is bad; only its ubiquity and lack of specificity makes it a vacuous insult that is designed to say more about the credentials of the critic than the material being critiqued (Furedi, 2014, p. 204). As such, its use has become *de rigueur* among academics seeking to demonstrate their presumed criticality. In this way, and somewhat ironically, the exercise of criticality in higher education actually serves to reinforce a culture of conformity.

When scholars no longer consider that the truth claims inherent in new knowledge must compete for veracity against alternative understandings of the world, the academic enterprise is fundamentally altered. No longer do we have a marketplace of ideas in which the best, or those closest to truth, win out. Instead we have a meeting ground where all ideas are afforded due respect according to the identity of the proposer. In *Higher Education and the Public Good,* Nixon argues, 'the legitimacy of any institution of higher education cannot be premised on prior assumptions regarding the provenance of truth' and that universities are instead places 'where arguments are held and divergence of viewpoint is valued' (2011, p. 42). Rather than the public good of higher education lying in knowledge as a search for truth, it comes instead to be concerned with the knowledge that there is no truth (Williams, 2014).

The consequence of Nixon's contention that there is no truth and the best we can achieve is to acknowledge difference would be that people can no longer access the powerful knowledge needed for some ideas to win out over others. As Young notes, 'The practical and political implications of such a rejection of all knowledge claims is that voice discourses are self-defeating. They deny to the subordinate groups, with whom they claim to identify, the possibility of any knowledge that could be a resource for overcoming their subordination' (2008, p. 5). In reality, despite the relativist rhetoric of simply acknowledging difference, it is clear that some knowledge, and some values, are to be rewarded more than others. For example, Monica McLean, writing in *Pedagogy and the University*, specifies a focus on addressing inequality, and tackling issues associated with poverty, the environment and conflict (2008, p. 17). Such radical academics risk denying people access to potentially transformative knowledge and, in the rejection of truth, preventing an intellectual challenge to the erroneous ideas used to justify oppression on the basis of race, gender or sexuality.

Promoting values

When transmitting knowledge, and particularly linking knowledge to truth, is considered problematic, many academics feel more comfortable concerning themselves with nurturing students' employability skills or personal values. Freed from the imperative to defend their own ideas from criticism and to pass judgement on the ideas of others, universities become places where intellectual conflict is replaced by coalescence around particular values. Academics and governments alike seek to redefine the public good of higher education away from 'universal knowledge and information' (Marginson, 2011, p. 416), and towards the inculcation of particular beliefs on one hand, or employment-related skills on the other. Academics wishing to move away from a perceived neo-liberal agenda that reduces knowledge to commodified skills or information prefer to consider higher education as essential for social inclusion. The skills students gain enable their participation in society and particular pedagogic approaches can be used to instil 'a common commitment to social justice and equity' (Nixon, 2011, p. 1). This results in a blurring of the boundaries between knowledge, beliefs and values, as well as a great deal of uncertainty as to the role of the academic and the purpose of teaching in higher education more broadly.

Although knowledge and values undoubtedly influence each other, losing the distinction between the two should be considered a major problem facing academics today. Values are a matter of personal conscience. Expecting people to demonstrate they hold values that have been determined for them, irrespective of whether they individually agree with those values or not, creates a climate of 'intellectual conformity' that is the exact opposite of what a university should be about. Rauch argues that the 'moral charter' of universities is 'to seek knowledge through criticism, not to instil correct opinions' (p. 68). Yet the promotion of values causes people to self-censor, to monitor their own speech and behaviour and to check that they say only what is considered acceptable. The role universities seek to play in determining the values of both staff and students suggests a deep suspicion of thinking critically and a belief that the 'wrong' conclusions may be reached if people are not told explicitly what to think.

One reason why a 'great books' approach to higher education went out of fashion is that such a body of material was often considered to be intrinsically connected to the promotion of national identity. As will be explored in more detail in the next chapter, the legitimization of literature as an academic subject within universities occurred alongside the development of the nation state. But as nationalism has waned in the post-war period, it is no longer looked to for an overarching ideological sense of purpose for higher education. Consequently, as Readings suggests, 'what exactly gets taught or produced as knowledge matters less and less' (1996, p. 13). Instead, a more politically radical approach to higher education sees a move away from teaching the supposedly nationalist content of 'great books' and onto promoting values more palatable to the current sensibility, such as those associated with 'global citizenship'.

The aim of global citizenship education is to bring about changes in students' attitude or outlook rather than teaching any particular knowledge about the world. As such, it involves a focus upon morality and pre-political virtues such as respect, care and responsibility. Students are asked to consider issues such as global poverty and globally unsustainable consumption, less through direct engagement with specific issues in the curriculum than through personal behaviour and consumption. In order to bring about a broader moral as well as spatial outlook, universities 'nudge' the behaviour of students through poster campaigns, removing trays from the dining room, replacing general rubbish bins with recycling bins, selling only Fairtrade or organic produce and stopping the use of disposable cups (see NAS, 2015). Similarly, universities from around the world have signed up to the United Nations Rio+20 Higher Education Sustainability Initiative. This requires institutions to commit to teaching sustainable development concepts as part of degree programmes; to encouraging research on sustainable development issues; to 'greening' campuses; and to supporting sustainability efforts.

The promotion of global citizenship through education requires students shift their perspective from identification with a nation state to recognizing themselves as members of a 'global community'. This is premised upon a sense that a national outlook is limited and parochial. Butcher and Smith, writing in *Volunteer Tourism: The lifestyle politics of international development*, suggest that global citizenship, in circumventing the nation state, downplays the significance of collective political action and instead emphasizes individual differences. Foremost among the assumptions underpinning this ethical stance is, Standish points out, a cultural relativism that is often expressed in terms of 'respect' for other cultures (2012). This respect for difference trumps recognition of common aspiration and values and restricts the individual's capacity to criticize or pass judgement as the relativist can neither judge nor question that which he or she considers fundamentally different from his or her own culture (Butcher and Smith, 2015, p. 97).

Global citizenship connects private feelings and qualities such as care, empathy and awareness, with the global issues of the day. While taking personal responsibility is a progressive impulse, in the advocacy of global citizenship an individual's decisions and emotions are cut adrift from broader political issues: the promotion of global citizenship places whole areas of knowledge beyond debate. In being asked to demonstrate particular behaviour, students are not expected to question the intellectual claims that underpin such requests, and issues such as climate change and global inequality become reinterpreted as a matter of personal ethics rather than political contestation. Strong cultural and political assumptions are often hidden behind a value-neutral veneer (see Standish, 2012), and a particular ethical stance is presented as a universal ethical imperative for all.

The extent to which values, or political attitudes and behaviours, have come to dominate higher education is reflected in the titles of new interdisciplinary degree courses and research centres. Students at Kingston University in London, Murdoch University in Australia and Roosevelt University in the United States can all study for degrees in 'Sustainable Development'. At the University of Central Lancashire in the UK, students can study for a Master's degree in 'Advancing Equality, Rights and Inclusion'. Goldsmith's University in London and York University in Canada both have 'Centres for Feminist Research'. The titles of such courses suggest the intellectual outcomes have been determined in advance and are bound up in an already agreed upon broader political goal. The imperative to conform becomes embedded in the curriculum when 'ideological claims are wrongly treated as objective truth, and observed deviation from that truth is treated as error' (Duarte et al., 2014, p. 9).

For some academics, proud of their credentials as campaigners, there is no apparent boundary between teaching and promoting a political cause. Contributors to *The Imperial University* argue the need for academics to 'embrace the idea of teacher–scholar activism' (2014, p. 261). At the University of Sussex's Centre for Gender Studies, prospective students are told, 'Sussex research has always had an activist slant, and Gender Studies is no exception'. This information, and the course titles, suggests that it will be difficult for students to question, let alone challenge, the political concepts of sustainability, inclusion or feminism and still successfully complete their studies. Hoff Sommers argues,

> Students are quick to learn that open criticism of the feminist classroom will not win them support from teachers who privately agree with them. The lesson they learn from the cravenness of their teachers is never lost on them: keep clear of controversy. Conformity is safest: practice it.
>
> (1994, p. 117)

The overt promotion of values creates an orthodoxy whereby some topics are placed beyond challenge. Students are denied access to the knowledge base that is necessary in order to construct an intellectual critique of a topic. They are not presented with contestable truth claims but with indisputable moral certainties, which lead to dogmatism and an insistence that 'truths are immune to criticism or change' (Scott, 1996, p. 171). This can result in entire areas of research being abandoned and scholars risking 'ostracism' if they do not fall in line with the explicit dominant value framework (Duarte et al., 2014, p. 14). Staff and students who disagree with the political agenda being propounded are under pressure to self-censor in order to ensure success, or to opt out and leave the academy.

However worthy the motivation, Rauch warns that attempts to eliminate prejudice through central authority mean 'eliminating all but one prejudice – that of whoever is most politically powerful' (p. 68). In this way, the promotion of values rather than a critical appraisal of knowledge creates a climate dominated by 'groupthink', where peer-group pressure serves to bring people into line with the correct way of thinking. As Russell describes it, 'the imitative quality now known as peer-group pressure, is the quality which makes groups of people so vulnerable to pressure to dress, talk or think alike, and it is one which, in academic life, tends to prop up established orthodoxies' (1993, p. 38).

The effectiveness of 'peer-group pressure' in promoting conformism and curtailing dissent was highlighted by Mill two centuries earlier: 'It is that stigma which is really effective, and so effective is it that the profession of opinions which are under the ban of society is much less common in England than in many other countries' (2005, p. 43). In late nineteenth-century England, much like in higher education today, the pressure to conform to particular socially acceptable ways of speech and behaviour was a far more effective means of control than any number of restrictive laws.

While, as adults, students are doubtless subject to other opinions and alternative values through contact with the world outside of academia, this is no substitute for knowledge, which is the unique claim of higher education and which provides the basis for informed judgement. As citizens, lecturers clearly have political opinions and personal values; academic freedom permits them the right to express such views in the public sphere as much as in the classroom. Indeed, to pretend not to have political opinions would be disingenuous and patronizing towards students. However, there is a difference between presenting students with opinions in conjunction with the knowledge base from which they are derived and denying the very existence of such a knowledge base.

Rather than this shift towards promoting values being considered problematic, it is welcomed by many within universities. New lecturers are often expected to gain 'professional recognition' with a certificate from the Higher Education Academy (HEA), a body that claims to 'champion excellent learning and teaching in higher education'. Part of the process of gaining recognition involves lecturers demonstrating that they have met the values specified in the HEA's professional standards framework. Lecturers are expected to: respect individual learners and diverse learning communities; promote participation in higher education and equality of opportunity for learners; use evidence-informed approaches and the outcomes from research and continuing professional development; and acknowledge the wider context in which higher education operates.

There is much to challenge in this seemingly arbitrary list of values, most especially what is not listed: a commitment to the pursuit of knowledge. The biggest problem, however, is with the principle of prescribing values for lecturers to hold at all. That the HEA expects lecturers to demonstrate collective values, and that universities have gone along with this, suggests criticality is no longer considered a fundamental part of the academic enterprise.

Rather than engaging in rigorous academic criticism, students are often expected to demonstrate having, through personal reflection, rejected erroneously held values and certainties in favour of a new set of officially sanctioned values. The questioning of such values in and of itself proves they have not been sufficiently taken on board. In this way, students are socialized into the university's culture of conformity, and they run with this outside of classes and reproduce its influence beyond the campus.

Students benefit from exposure to as much knowledge, and as many different values, political views and opinions as possible. When students are taught values in the absence of knowledge and when they are assessed on their ability to demonstrate having met values rather than their ability to critique a body of knowledge, universities and academics do students a disservice. Drawing upon academic freedom to defend the inculcation of values redefines its core principles; the focus on values closes down rather than opens up debates within higher education. When lecturers promote values, they deny students access to the knowledge that may be used to critique the intellectual basis of the agenda being propounded. Through the teaching and assessment of values rather than knowledge, staff and students buy into a particular, moralized framework, which then makes criticism of that agenda increasingly difficult. Russell points out that the basis of academic freedom is called into question by 'wilful error perpetrated deliberately for the sake of advancing a career or a cause' (1993, p. 42).

A culture of conformity

Promoting values appears to stand in radical opposition to a more 'neo-liberal' discourse of education as individual investment in future earnings. However, there is no right for scholars to use the lecture theatre as either pulpit or soapbox. Academic freedom demands that academics are free to teach their subject as they see best but it must also allow for criticism, if not in the immediate teaching context, then through the potential for developing critical thought.

A conformist academic culture can be characterized by the dominance of particular views and the suppression of opposing ideas, which only rarely takes place through formal mechanisms but rather is enacted through peer-group pressure. Within academia there is a general tendency for scholars to seek out like-minded individuals for collaborations and to reward those who share similar views to their own through processes of peer review and recruitment. Left unchecked, a climate that is intellectually hostile to opposing values and ideas can emerge. Such intellectual harmony is not a cause for celebration; it represents the dominance of a mentality which 'causes some questions not to be asked, and some answers not to be overly scrutinized' (Gobry, 17/12/14).

A team of American researchers (Duarte et al., 2014) explored the lack of political diversity within the discipline of Social Psychology; this provides a useful case study to illustrate what a culture of conformity within academia looks like and how it has come into existence. They show that whereas 50 years ago, academic psychologists held a diverse range of political affiliations, today this is no longer the case. In the 1920s, psychology professors were as likely to report voting Republican as Democrat and 'from the 1930s through 1960, they were more likely to report voting for Democrats, but substantial minorities voted for Wilkie, Eisenhower, and Nixon (in 1960)'. But, by 2006, 'the ratio of Democrats to Republicans had climbed to more than 11:1' (Duarte et al., 2014, p. 7). Such political homogenization can be seen across the social sciences where 'self-identified Democrats outnumber Republicans by ratios of at least 5:1'. This political polarization is most acute in psychology where '84 percent identify as liberal while only 8 percent identify as conservative' (Duarte et al., 2014, p. 6). Furthermore, the researchers suggest that this marginalization of Republicans from the discipline is a trend which looks set to continue: 'whereas 10% of faculty respondents self-identified as conservative, only 2% of graduate students and post-docs did so' (Duarte et al., 2014, p. 8). A survey of British academics, carried out before the 2015 general election, suggested 46 per cent of those questioned intended to vote for the Labour Party and 22 per cent for the Green Party. Only 11 per cent claimed allegiance to the Conservative Party.

A number of factors contribute towards the emerging homogeneity of political views. New entrants to the profession are, as students, enculturated into a dominant disciplinary perspective. As students progress through their academic career they either buy into this consensus or those with opposing beliefs opt out. Some disciplines, such as Cultural Studies or Women's Studies for example, may be quite explicitly political in nature (see Readings, 1996, p. 123 and David, 2004) and so sharing assumptions is a prerequisite for entering the disciplinary community. As will be explored more fully in Chapter 6, Women's Studies combines the political project of promoting women's rights with more traditional academic work, and scholars who do not share this desire to promote women's rights find themselves at odds with the rest of the disciplinary community. Such selection is reinforced through recruitment procedures and the practice of self-censorship by those already within the discipline.

This growing homogeneity of viewpoint is not especially concerning in terms of how individuals act in the privacy of the voting booth. Students and lecturers have lives away from the academy and are subject to all the same influences as everyone else in society. Political bias is a far greater problem to universities than mere factional infighting; it impacts upon the future direction of academic work and the range of legitimate ideas that can be pursued. The American social psychology researchers suggest that a lack of political diversity may result in 'the embedding of liberal values into research questions and methods, steering researchers away from important but politically unpalatable research topics, and producing conclusions that mischaracterize liberals and conservatives alike'. They point to the existence of high-profile replication failures and suggest 'one largely overlooked cause of failure is a lack of political diversity' (Duarte et al., 2014, p. 3). Indeed, the shock that greeted the outcome of the 2015 British general election, after months of opinion polls failing to predict a victory for the Conservative Party, suggests pollsters may have experienced a degree of confirmation-bias in the answers they received from members of the public. The creation of a culture of intellectual conformity within academia prevents the checks and balances upon research that emerge from discussion with colleagues who do not share the same political outlook or value framework.

The threat to free thought from the creation of a culture of conformity is far more insidious than formal acts of censorship. Instead of being collectively opposed, self-censorship and conformity are internalized by individuals. Academics are expected to demonstrate obedience and obsequiousness to students, funders, publishers and managers alike. Two key factors drive the reluctance of academics to challenge such pressures: a degree of moral cowardice and a loss of any sense of higher education as having an overarching sense of purpose. In the absence of a moral or intellectual mission in relation to the pursuit and transmission of knowledge, there is little to make it seem worthwhile to attract opprobrium.

From the students' perspective, university can seem to be less about confronting new and challenging, perhaps even dangerous, ideas and instead more concerned with a process of socialization into what can and cannot be said. Universities come to play a role in inducting the next generation into how to conform to the expected speech and behaviour codes of right-thinking, polite society. Demonstrating adherence to particular values is privileged above the intellectual challenge of articulating and confronting the unthinkable and unspeakable.

Academic freedom

Today there are few formal restrictions preventing academics saying or writing whatever they want. But it would be wrong to interpret this lack of censorship on the part of management as a licence for free expression within universities. It is not fear of libel which curtails debate; rather, it is the reluctance of many academics to say anything controversial at all. More problematic, particularly in the social sciences, is a growing sense that there are some views that just cannot be expressed.

On one hand, the pseudo-radical, broadly left-wing consensus that pervades universities means that castigating neo-liberalism, the influence of the popular media and the desire to consume, will automatically garner the support of the peers who will review your work for publication and you for promotion. On the other hand, not paying lip service to the importance of feminism, the welfare state and protecting the environment, is more likely to see your work rejected. New academics are often recruited because their research fits into the existing departmental culture, and new generations of students are taught the values of their lecturers. Today, the biggest threats to the freedom to exercise judgement come from within universities. Academics themselves, particularly those who conceive of their role as scholar–activists, are at the forefront of enforcing censorship.

Part II

Knowledge in the Disciplines

3
Criticality within the Disciplines

Dominated by consensus and conformity, the intellectual environment of today's university precludes all but the most determined attempts at truly groundbreaking free thought. Academic freedom thus comes to seem a largely abstract proposition disconnected from the pursuit of knowledge. This culture has emerged with the collapse of criticism, or the public act of passing judgement, which required both a concept of knowledge as contestable truth claims and an audience of people with the necessary expertise to validate the worth of a critique. Within the academy, such a public was formed of like-minded scholars who shared a common body of knowledge and similar theoretical and methodological assumptions.

For the past 150 years, this scholarly community has been formally embodied within the practice and structures of academic disciplines. It is the social collective of the academic discipline that provides the legitimate basis for claims of truth and objectivity within arts, humanities and some aspects of social science. While knowledge in these areas is socially constructed rather than empirically discoverable, its validity comes from being held by people in common. The disciplinary community can, at best, constitute a formalized and streamlined version of a marketplace of ideas when its members share knowledge, methods and understanding. New generations of scholars are inducted into disciplinary-specific ways of thinking primarily through undergraduate teaching.

The knowledge that comprises the content of the curriculum is, to a degree, arbitrary. However, its selection is determined by members of the disciplinary community on the basis of their understanding of the area: it is neither simply random nor just a politically driven reflection of elite tastes, as critics of the curriculum often contend. This chapter considers the emergence and institutionalization of the social science and humanities disciplines – specifically, Sociology and English Literature – and how these have played a significant role in regulating and legitimating knowledge, and creating the conditions necessary for intellectual critique.

Defining the disciplines

The unique complexion of academic work means individual scholars often relate less to the university as a distinct institution than they do to their particular faculty, discipline or subject area. The form the university takes in any one country or at any particular point in time can be considered as an embodiment of the collective assumptions of the nation's higher education sector at that historical juncture. In Britain, the late nineteenth and early twentieth century move from the university as a cloistered citadel to provincial red-brick buildings in the industrial heartlands represented a shift from a liberal to a more instrumental sense of purpose for higher education. However, this national shift was a step removed from the particular experiences of many individual academics.

More recently, universities have come to be re-conceptualized according to a business model, and there is a drive towards marketization to ensure customers and profitability. For lecturers, this often creates an additional bureaucratic burden to be managed; it rarely leads to a strong identification between an individual academic and their particular institution. Rather, academics are more likely to identify with disciplinary or subject affiliations that reach beyond the university campus and connect people with similar interests within and across national borders.

In *The Conflict of the Faculties*, Kant defines faculties as 'smaller societies, each comprising the university specialists in one main branch of learning' (1979, p. 23). He identified four faculties in the universities of his day: philosophy, theology, medicine and law. This organizational form reflected the purpose of the university at this time: to prepare young men for civic service. Since Kant's time, the formalized knowledge base of the university, as represented in the branches of learning, has proliferated. The most common university faculties have become established as science, social science and humanities. Each of these is further broken down into numerous more specific subject areas or disciplines: for example, the humanities faculty disciplines include philosophy, history, literature, languages, music and theology. Recently, as will be discussed more fully in the next chapter, there has been a growing trend towards interdisciplinarity, with more traditional disciplines combining or entirely new subjects emerging with content and methodologies selected from across a range of knowledge areas.

The phrase 'academic discipline' is today used mainly in its noun form, although its origins, and what is often still implied, stem from the verb 'to discipline'. In this respect, discipline means a mental training and obedience to particular rules and customs that arises out of the body of knowledge associated with the subject's content. Leavis suggests that the study of literature, for example, involves the practice of critical analysis and the training of sensibility (1979, p. 12). When disciplines are thought of as practice, the methodologies and ways of thinking which develop separately for each area are not rigidly fixed to a specific body of content. The particular topics that are taught and researched can vary in a relatively short period of time, while the underlying ways of approaching and critiquing content alter far more slowly. From their earliest days as an undergraduate, students are enculturated into the ways of thinking and behaving associated with their chosen disciplinary area through the mental training it provides. Students are encouraged to identify with the discipline, to read, write and even think according to its implicit rules and structures.

The significance of disciplines within today's universities can be understood in both a practical and epistemological sense. Dividing staff and students up according to subject, and grouping certain subjects together into schools or faculties, serve as an administrative convenience to institutions. Writing in *In Defense of Disciplines*, Jerry A. Jacobs describes academic disciplines as the 'key unit in the social organisation of the university' (2013, p. 3), functioning as intellectual, social, career and political systems. More fundamentally, such divisions represent differences in the members' understanding of the nature of knowledge, the terrain of content covered, the methodological approach to creating new knowledge and the theoretical framework for evaluating existing knowledge and critiquing new understandings. As such, disciplines can be seen as both a 'knowledge field' and 'a sociological object' (Fanghanel, 2009, p. 568), with interaction between field and object bringing about change in each.

Academic disciplines are constantly evolving in relation to both internal and external pressures. On the one hand, paradigmatic leaps in understanding can lead to a fundamental reappraisal of the existing disciplinary knowledge base. On the other hand, national policy directives or demands from professional bodies in areas such as law and medicine may also alter the direction of work within a disciplinary area. However, the intellectual traditions that bind members of the disciplinary community together have historically offered some immunity, or at least a time lag, to the need to respond to internal or external pressures. This can be considered both a strength and a weakness of disciplinary structures.

When viewed as objects, disciplines represent more than just an administratively convenient means of organizing university life. They reflect the dominant perception of the purpose of higher education. The idea of a liberal education, as propounded most explicitly by the British theologian Cardinal Newman in *The Idea of a University* (1854), required students to make meaningful connections between knowledge in a range of areas. The ideal student would have both a depth and breadth of knowledge. Since the earliest years of the twentieth century, this liberal ideal has been consistently challenged, due to pressures from within and without the university, for students to acquire ever-more specialist knowledge in increasingly narrow areas. By 1948, Leavis bemoaned the fact that 'the idea of liberal culture has been defeated and dissipated by advancing specialization; and the production of specialists tends to be regarded as the supreme end of the university' (1979, p. 25). At the same time as the knowledge base of each discipline has been narrowed, the range of skills students are expected to master has been broadened in response to pressures from outside the academy to make higher education more practically applicable and relevant to the world of work.

Criticisms of disciplines as 'academic silos' that constitute a barrier to intellectual progress and impede connections between universities and industry have gathered momentum since the late 1960s (Jacobs, 2013). Since this time, interdisciplinary subject areas such as Cultural Studies, Women's Studies and Business Studies have been formed. Students focused upon securing employment may select interdisciplinary courses that appear more immediately relevant to the labour market, and universities respond to this customer demand. As a result, the boundaries between even relatively 'pure' disciplines have blurred in recent years and conformity to rules and ways of thinking determined by subject content has given way to a celebration of the interdisciplinary. The 'cutting edge' of the university and the forefront in the development of new knowledge is today often considered to emerge from the meeting point between the frontiers of one discipline and another.

As the specific practices of an academic discipline emerge from an historical concept of knowledge, the collective norms provide a means of challenging existing understandings and developing new ideas. In this light, the questioning of the rules associated with academic disciplines, and the increasingly blurred boundaries between subjects, can leave scholars without a structured framework for criticality and unable to challenge existing understandings or make truth claims in relation to new knowledge. While the norms associated with disciplinary structures stand accused of enforcing consensus, ironically, abandoning such norms can also lead to the creation of a culture of conformity because the basis for criticism is rejected.

The origins of academic disciplines

As a practical means for administering university life, academic disciplines are historically young; sufficient numbers of people working in the same area must be employed in any one institution for disciplines to become organizationally meaningful. Such a concentration of scholars really only emerged with the post-Second World War expansion of higher education that occurred in the USA first and later in the UK. However, the demarcation of knowledge into different branches has a much longer history. The origins of many of the disciplines now located within the humanities can be traced back to the medieval university.

The first European universities were intrinsically connected to the Roman Catholic Church and their purpose, if it can be described as such, was intertwined with the idea of scholarship as an act of devotion. This view of the role of the university is reflected in the practice of separating knowledge of 'The Word' from knowledge of 'The World'. The Word was covered in the Trivium and involved lessons in logic, grammar and rhetoric. Study of the World was encompassed in the Quadrivium and included arithmetic, geometry, astronomy and music.

The roots of subjects such as music, languages, literature, philosophy, classics and linguistics reach back to the music, logic, grammar and rhetoric of the Trivium and Quadrivium. Students were expected to master the word of God as conveyed through scriptures and the world God had created. As the word of God was prior to the world He had created, students commenced their studies with the Trivium. This distinction between the word and the world represented an important 'ontological dislocation' (Fanghanel, 2009, p. 566) between knowledge of internal and external experiences; between the inner life of spirituality, ethics and logic on the one hand, and the outer world of mathematics and science on the other.

The Trivium, and to a lesser extent the Quadrivium, covered elements of knowledge that the French sociologist Emile Durkheim classified as unobservable, invented, arbitrary and external to the perceptions of individuals. Durkheim labelled such knowledge as 'sacred'. It had a collective structure and social basis, the origins of which could be traced back to shared religious beliefs which Durkheim considered the 'paradigm of all advanced forms of theoretical knowledge' (Young, 2008, p. 41). Sacred knowledge was held in common by communities and, Durkheim argued, it was this social basis which created the conditions for the objectivity of knowledge. Collective knowledge was not context-dependent and it was protected from pressure to change with the whims of individuals. Durkheim suggests the unique function of formal education is to enculturate individuals into the collective sacred knowledge of society that they could not be expected to master through their everyday experiences.

Although the knowledge base of the medieval university would have been studied by each student without early specialization, each component of the curriculum had a distinct identity and all elements were insulated from each other. For this reason, the subjects comprising both the Trivium and Quadrivium have been described as 'singulars' by the British sociologist of education, Basil Bernstein. It is the sacred nature of the knowledge with which singulars are concerned that makes them strongly autonomous, inward-looking and self-referential. Bernstein argues that their commitment to sacred knowledge 'legitimises their otherness and creates dedicated identities with no reference other than their calling' (1996, p. 68).

European universities were established primarily to prepare young men for a life in the church, and scholars went on to fill positions of various ranks within the clergy. In an age before the state as we recognize it today, the church was the dominant influence in shaping and governing society. Men who rose up through the ecclesiastical hierarchy were in powerful social positions and, alongside the monarchy, formed the ruling elite. The study of disciplines within what is now known as the humanities therefore became the dominant education of the social and political elite. The authority of such disciplines was considered to be both moral and intellectual; advanced training in the classics was thought to form both mind and spirit.

Up until the beginning of the twentieth century, long after the influence of the church upon broader society began to wane, a liberal education comprised primarily of disciplines from within the humanities, which was dominated by subjects that could trace their roots directly back to either the Trivium or the Quadrivium, remained 'unquestioned as the best way of preparing men of the appropriate lineage to rise to positions of power at home and abroad' (Muller and Young, 2014, p. 128).

The Enlightenment challenge to medieval tradition

The intellectual movement of the eighteenth and nineteenth centuries known as the Enlightenment largely occurred outside of the European universities. New ways of understanding the world that were driven by developments in science were not readily accepted into the still-religious institution of the university. Only very slowly did the cloistered world of academia begin to move beyond the medieval curriculum. From the eighteenth century onwards, vocations such as medicine and law began to develop more distinctive bodies of knowledge necessary for practitioners to master and such subjects began to be brought within the realm of the university. Other subjects at this time emerged from developments within branches of knowledge covered by the Trivium and Quadrivium: philosophy and classics, for example, began to develop as separate subjects.

Such new intellectual terrain still pointed to a sacred knowledge base, and it remained the case in many universities at this time that students were expected to complete studies of the Trivium and Quadrivium prior to undertaking work in more externally driven subjects. The mastery of a body of knowledge was considered to precede its practical application. In current parlance, law and medicine would be subjects studied only by 'postgraduate' students.

For Kant, the philosophy faculty's inherent challenge to law and medicine created more critical, and therefore superior, practitioners: just as for Newman a half-century later, only a rounded liberal education pursued for its own sake could provide a man with 'a clear conscious view of his own opinions and judgements, a truth in developing them, an eloquence in expressing them, and a force in urging them' (1959, p. 192). Universities remained predominantly organized around the pursuit of autonomous academic subjects throughout the nineteenth century, although this did not mean that knowledge in one area was pursued in isolation from other subjects. A liberal education would suggest the opposite: that learning is enhanced by 'bringing into relation a diversity of fields of knowledge and thought' (Leavis, 1979, p. 9). Newman's concept of liberal education (1854) hinged upon the notion of academic subjects having 'no reference other than their calling' and therefore being inherently worth pursuing solely for their own sake. It is in this sense that law and medicine can be considered as 'vocational' subjects: that is, pursuits which students were 'called' towards and which could be better practised when pursued within the context of other more inward-looking academic subjects.

As the rationalism of the Enlightenment slowly gained influence across more of society, the religious foundations for knowledge began to be called into question. New forms of legitimacy were sought for existing knowledge, and new ways of understanding and interpreting the world emerged. An overriding belief in the possibility of empirical truth and the spiritual mission of secular knowledge gained in popularity throughout the nineteenth century. When separated from its religious roots, philosophy came to be considered as a moral science. This shift in the source of authority of knowledge from God to man occurred primarily outside of the universities. Only very gradually did new areas of study, such as philology, become more formally organized as branches of learning within the university. This took place first in German universities which, influenced by the ideas of Prussian philosopher and founder of the University of Berlin,

Wilhelm Von Humboldt (1767–1835), began to embrace science as a serious concern.

The study of literature

In Britain, it was only in the nineteenth century that discussion as to the purpose of the university took off in earnest, with Newman's *The Idea of the University* making a key contribution to this debate that has continued ever since. As the rector of St Andrew's University in Scotland, John Stuart Mill argued for the importance of the arts as one element of a liberal education on the grounds that such subjects helped to preserve a cultural inheritance for subsequent generations in a way that went beyond the merely custodial but assisted ongoing human intellectual and cultural achievements (see Small, 2013, p. 13). This notion of the university playing a conservative and implicitly political role in preserving culture was returned to much later by F. R. Leavis, who argued:

> The universities are recognized symbols of cultural tradition - of cultural tradition still conceived as a directing force, representing a wisdom older than modern civilization and having an authority that should check and control the blind drive onward of material and mechanical development, with its human consequences.
>
> (1943, p. 16)

The relationship between higher education and culture as described by both Mill and Leavis suggests that the nineteenth century idea of a university was increasingly intertwined with the development of the nation state. There was a growing sense that universities could play an important role in advancing knowledge for the nation while also promoting national culture. This belief was most explicit in the German Humboldtian view of higher education, but also became increasingly influential in the relatively new United States of America. Interest in promoting national culture brought particular attention to the use of the national language most readily embodied in literature.

Terry Eagleton reminds us that 'literature itself is a recent historical invention' (2008, p. 177), and Alan Sinfield locates its emergence as occurring in the eighteenth century. He argues it was not until the nineteenth century that it became fully appropriated as meaning printed works of a certain quality. Literature was far more bound to the concept of the nation state than philosophy which transcended national borders; it inherently raised issues of national language, cultural tradition and identity, which were not evident in works of philosophy to the same degree (Readings, 1996, p. 70). However, while philosophy, having rejected overt connections to religion, developed as a moral science, literature struggled to make such epistemological claims; and despite being able to trace its disciplinary origins back to the study of linguistics and rhetoric in the medieval university, it was not readily accepted within higher education.

Franklin E. Court, writing in *Institutionalising English Literature*, notes that 'the history of English literary study in Britain has always been fraught with conflicts and uncertainties' (1992, p. 2). He suggests the first attempt at formalizing the study of English literature within higher education occurred in Scottish universities in the eighteenth century, and had a distinctly political profile as it supported the Union of Scotland into Britain and the promotion of 'cultivated English taste' (1992, p. 18). Court points out that it was in the 1820s that the modern history of the discipline of English really begins, with a Professorship and taught course in the subject at the newly formed University College London. He links this to the growth of utilitarianism and the idea that literature provided 'the ideal carrier for the propagation of the humanist cultural myth of a well-educated, culturally harmonious nation, in agreement on fundamental social goals and blessed with a sense of spiritual continuity' (1992, p. 14).

There was an assumption among early proponents of the subject that discussion of the philosophical and ethical issues covered in literature could be used to promote particular moral and ethical behaviour. From the middle of the nineteenth century, Matthew Arnold drove the study of English in schools as a means of encouraging literacy and providing an accessible form of cultural awareness and moral understanding. Decades later this came to be interpreted, especially by Marxist literary critics such as Terry Eagleton, as the promotion of the values of individualism that were needed to support free market capitalism. *Robinson Crusoe* is often cited as a novel used to inculcate such rugged individualism.

As Jonathan Rose makes clear in *The Intellectual Life of the British Working Classes*, literature was interpreted in all kinds of ways that were not always in keeping with the author's – or the literary establishment's – meaning. The desire of members of the working class for access to classic works of literature suggests a universal element that goes beyond the tastes of one particular social group. Indeed, it was this openness to interpretation and potential sympathy with a range of political viewpoints that left the academic study of literature without a theoretical centre. This lack of intellectual clarity meant that the study of English literature within British universities met considerable resistance, especially in 'the traditional centres of excellence' (Wright, 1993, p. 227). The Universities of Oxford and Cambridge refused to countenance offering the subject for serious study. Oxbridge dons wanted the discipline of English Literature to be put on a firmer intellectual footing that they assumed could only come from science and the logic of positivism. As Small notes, 'English literature was not widely studied at university level until the start of the twentieth century' (2013, p. 14). In large part, this reluctance stemmed from the challenge English literature posed to the study of the ancient Latin and Greek classical texts, which formed the mainstay of the university curriculum at this time.

Literature was more readily accepted as a subject for serious study in the new universities to emerge at the turn of the twentieth century that did not have Latin and Greek traditions to circumvent. The grounding of the subject in schools where it was deemed to provide children with relevant and useful moral lessons created a demand for suitable teachers. This slowly helped to legitimize the study of English within the new universities. For the most part, however, English literature was considered too readily accessible and therefore not worthy of serious study by university students.

In response, proponents of the study of literature attempted to align the subject with other more established disciplines. Linking the study of literature to the teaching of philology as a science would eventually lend the subject legitimacy and lead to its incorporation within the academy. Court notes that the turn towards philology, with its focus on 'positive fact and empirical analysis' created a distance from 'topical matters of social reform' (1992, p. 75) and politically neutralized the emerging discipline.

The drive to put the study of literature on a scientific basis can be seen in America too. The Modern Languages Association was founded in 1883 and, as Menand notes, its first members were philologists whose work on language conformed to a scientific model and could therefore be evaluated 'objectively' (1996, p. 12). Essentially, however, the literary was opposed to the scientific in ways that philosophy was not (Readings, 1996, p. 70). Once securely entrenched within the academy, the first task of literature scholars became to free the discipline from the tyranny of science. Leavis describes the English School at the University of Oxford as having, 'emancipated literary studies from the linguistic grinds' (1943, p. 7).

Literature took on particular significance as a university subject within German and American universities because of its explicit connection to national language and identity. Both Germany (newly founded from the state of Prussia) and America (newly freed from the British Empire) were keen to validate their statehood through the promotion of national culture. In America more than in Germany, students of literature could not rely upon tradition alone to lend legitimacy to the curriculum. Instead, the concept of the canon was employed to represent a list of books and other works regarded as being objectively of the highest quality. The quality of work was established through its enduring legacy over the passage of time; the authoritative opinion of the cultural elite; and significantly, the value afforded the work by members of the public.

In literature, as in other areas of knowledge, the canon was not a fixed entity: rather works moved in and out of the canon over time and as society's cultural values shifted. What was so significant about the canon for American universities was that it represented a body of literature which had been consciously and democratically determined, rather than simply inherited.

From science to social science

As well as opposing the study of literature, the Universities of Oxford and Cambridge also mounted considerable resistance to the teaching of science. As noted in the previous chapter, serious interest in science and the emergence of the scientific method began with the Enlightenment and took place largely outside of universities. A more formalized study of science within higher education – in contrast to an often decidedly unscientific study of medicine – started in German universities in the early years of the nineteenth century, and American universities followed suit. It was several decades later before a more formalized study of science began in Britain. However, this did not take place in universities but rather in colleges and institutes that were established and supported by local industrialists who sought scientific development to enhance technological progress, to build a more highly skilled workforce and to gain the social status conferred by a degree-level qualification for their sons.

Towards the end of the nineteenth and into the twentieth century, there was a more concerted bid by national governments to promote the teaching of science within universities. In part this was driven by a sense of competitiveness and the need for countries to maintain their global status. However, the formal move to institutionalize science also reflected an assumption that its study needed to be taken out of the hands of amateurs and professionalized within the academy. Furedi notes that 'by the mid-nineteenth century, the "man of science" gave way to the "scientist", representing a shift from gentlemanly vocation to a profession' (2013, p. 398). In Britain, the transformation of the nineteenth-century institutes and colleges into the twentieth century red-brick provincial universities marked the point at which science became formalized as an academic pursuit, although its antecedents in mathematics and geometry were already firmly established.

The turn towards empiricism and positivist methodologies led to the idea that people and society could also be legitimately studied according to the scientific method. Among the earliest proponents of this notion were John Stuart Mill and the French philosophers Saint Simon and Auguste Comte, who coined the term 'sociology' in 1838. Although these new areas of study sought to employ the methodological approaches utilized by the science disciplines, it took many decades before social science became incorporated as a field of study within academia.

The study of sociology

Enlightenment philosophers such as Kant, Voltaire and Spinoza aspired towards objectivity and universalism in their approach. By the end of the nineteenth century, Durkheim, considered by many to be the founding father of the academic discipline of sociology, could confidently assert that the capacity for individual reason was the unique quality that made people human. He claimed that it was both the exercise of individual reason and the sacred nature of collective knowledge that made objectivity and truth claims in relation to all types of knowledge possible. This focus on objectivity has been caricatured as assuming the possibility of a 'God's eye view'.

Durkheim recognized that the shift towards secularity that began in the late nineteenth century displaced not just God but tradition as the basis for the authority of knowledge. This meant society, and more specifically governing elites, could no longer rely on the authority of received wisdom but had instead to defer 'to the constantly re-evaluated and fluid knowledge of empirical science' (Furedi, 2013, p. 245).

At the end of the nineteenth century, the world seemed to many to be increasingly complex. Furedi notes that 'traditional notions of cause and effect could do little to illuminate the problems brought about by industrialisation, rapid social change and the rise of an interconnected world economy' (2013, p. 400). This crisis of authority fed into the universities and external pressures began to influence not just the formal structures of higher education but the content of knowledge. At this time, the status of the academic changed from being primarily that of a teacher transmitting subject knowledge, to that of a 'scholar-expert' who combined teaching with research. The growing influence in the USA and later in the UK of the ideas of Humboldt further precipitated this shift towards the scholar as expert in a research context.

In the *Theory of Human Education* (circa 1793), Humboldt locates education in relation to the 'demands which must be made of a nation, of an age and of the human race'. He linked education to truth and virtue to better the 'concept of mankind' (in Hohendorf, 1993, p. 668). The influence of Humboldt's ideas, particularly within American universities, represented a shift away from the more traditional concept of liberal education as practised in British universities.

The pursuit of knowledge endorsed by Humboldt could be quite narrow and specialized and led to the development of the research-led rather than liberal university. As academics took on the mantle of scholar-expert, they increasingly concerned themselves with social rather than abstract or theoretical problems. In 1880, T. H. Huxley gave a lecture at what would become the University of Birmingham in which he argued that sociology should be added to a basically scientific and technological curriculum (Halsey, 2004, p. 24). The extension of scientific principles to sentient human beings was thought to lend authority to leaders and provide grounds for organizing society in new ways.

For Durkheim, the constitution of moral authority represented the fundamental question facing scholars of his day. He believed that the task of moral regulation had fallen to the state, which did not have the same hold on citizens as non-state bodies such as the church. Durkheim considered the state to be too distant from people's lives to exercise moral authority over them, and that what was required were intermediary institutions such as schools to link the state more closely to the lives of individuals and to influence personal behaviour (see Delanty, 2001, p. 49 and Furedi, 2013, p. 310). Durkheim saw education as a process of socialization and a means of cultivating morality (1956, p. 28). He was interested in how the foundations of the knowledge that was taught through schools could be used as a means of developing an objective basis for moral values.

Durkheim argued it was society, 'through the moral regulation it institutes and applies' (in Furedi, 2013, p. 249), that created the resources necessary to subordinate the behaviour of individuals. He wanted to find an objective basis for moral values to counteract the dominant pragmatism of his time, which he derided as 'logical utilitarianism' (Young, 2008, p. 207). Durkheim considered that the unique feature of both knowledge and truth lay in the fact that they were compelling to people's innate sense of rationality (something he had in common with Kant), and that this compulsive drive towards truth was the major condition for new knowledge.

The source of this truth was, however, contested. Significantly, advocates for the study of literature argued it too could play a role in describing, analysing and explaining issues such as poverty and inequality. Victorian social problem novels such as those by Charles Dickens, Elizabeth Gaskell and Charlotte Bronte met more explicitly political works by Benjamin Disraeli, Friedrich Engels and, much later, George Orwell. From the outset, there was tension within sociology as to the legitimacy of such sources and the use of description, as well as statistics, for understanding society and better arriving at a concept of social truth.

In 1910, Ratcliffe, writing in a review of *Sociology and the English Novel,* claimed that modern fiction was descriptive sociology. Decades later, Berger (1960) notes that novels are the 'first and last resort of the sociologist in search of data' (p. 12, in Bristow, 2015). More recently, Krishnan Kumar (2001) locates the rise of sociology in the nineteenth century as located between literature and science. There was rivalry between the two fields for the intellectual territory of criticism and social reform. In Europe more than America, the arts formed a significant barrier to scientific sociology.

The era defined by Delanty as 'liberal modernity', which ended in the mood of crisis that set in towards the end of the nineteenth century and the culture of anxiety that surrounded the First World War, saw natural theology and the spiritual value of knowledge replaced by logical positivism and disinterested inquiry. Science became the dominant paradigm for the study of social problems with such new modes of knowledge demanding 'a far stricter separation of fact and value' (2001, p. 23). There was an assumption that value-neutral and rational scientific methods could be applied to the study of society and ultimately provide a basis for political action leading to social improvements.

A scientific approach to the study of social problems, and the legitimation of this practice within the academy through the disciplines of social science, took off in earnest in the period immediately prior to the First World War. Halsey notes that sociology as an academic subject began in the UK at LSE in 1907 (2004, p. 3). Again, Britain lagged behind other countries in this regard, primarily because of opposition from Oxford and Cambridge.

The 'golden age' of disciplines

In many ways, the first half of the twentieth century represents the heyday of the academic discipline. It was the era when national disciplinary bodies were founded and improved travel could bring together scholars from around the world. Disciplinary-specific academic journals flourished. For much of the twentieth century, universities received generous state subsidies allowing academics the professional freedom to align themselves with discipline rather than institution. The pursuit of knowledge flourished in such conditions, and new branches of learning emerged and took root.

However, this 'golden age' of the disciplines was both hard-won and short-lived. No sooner had subjects such as Sociology and English Literature secured their place within the academy than pressures from both inside and outside the university mounted a challenge to the autonomy of the disciplinary community and the authority of academic knowledge.

With the dawning of the twentieth century, pressure on higher education to serve the needs of the nation grew. This can be seen in the emergence of subjects such as engineering, metallurgy and mining, which were newly legitimized by universities at this time. Such subjects took direction from outside the academy and this privileging of extrinsic concerns began to call into question the intrinsic value of knowledge (Beck, 2010, p. 91). Between the First and Second World Wars there was a growing expectation among government ministers that universities would provide a return to the nation for finance received from the public purse.

This view was most explicit in statements linking teaching and research in science to the standing of the nation state on the world stage. The perceived purpose of higher education began to shift towards the training of a professional class who could meet society's need for a qualified workforce. Halsey notes that social workers, almoners and probation officers all had courses offered to them in the newly established provincial universities, as well as at Oxford, before the Second World War (2004, p. 13). Pressure to meet external imperatives challenged the autonomy of academic disciplines.

After the Second World War, the political role higher education had played in preserving and promoting national culture came increasingly to the fore and English Literature became firmly established as a discipline taught in British universities at this time. The British social and cultural elite saw potential for the values expressed through high culture, not just in relation to literature but also in other art forms, including music and drama, to play a role in the creation of a progressive modern society.

Exploring the positioning of art and literature within the post-war political settlement and the emergence of the welfare state, Alan Sinfield argues that high culture was envisaged as a 'good thing' that should be made generally available to all. The Labour Party manifesto from 1945 discussed the importance of making high culture accessible to everyone through public funding for the arts, and support for institutions such as the BBC and schools to promote high quality art. Once elected, the post-war government sought to exploit high culture in order to promote national unity by incorporating all of society into a shared cultural outlook. Sinfield notes that the definition of high culture was simply assumed – this had, he suggests, the effect of enshrining elite culture as universal culture (1997, p. 2).

Somewhat less cynically, there was a non-instrumental perception of access to art as being good in and of itself. Alongside this sat a belief in the educability of British citizens and that, once provided with high art and education, people would be able to understand, appreciate and share in the culture of the social elite. In recent times such sentiments have come to be viewed as both patronizing and elitist. At the time, however, the belief that high culture was universal and accessible was supported by the political left. By the end of the 1950s, there was money for the universities to pursue such aims more actively and this led to increases in the number of university students overall. With national attention increasingly focused upon who attended university, and what they did once there, arts subjects that had previously enjoyed a high degree of autonomy became open to greater scrutiny.

In 1963, Baron Lionel Robbins, in his influential government report on the future of UK higher education, argued that a key purpose for universities lay in 'transmitting a common culture and common standards of citizenship' (ch. 5.7). Despite stemming from a conservative desire to preserve what came to be perceived as essentially bourgeois culture as national culture, this argument reflected and encouraged a trend for previously self-referential, autonomous subjects to face outwards to the needs of society beyond the university. This brought about profound changes to the subjects affected, and has led to the frequently cited argument that the humanities have been in a permanent state of crisis since the mid-twentieth century. Indeed, the labelling of the humanities can itself be seen as symptomatic of this crisis of purpose and identity.

It was only in response to pressure to justify their relevance beyond the academy that the label of 'humanities' began to be used in relation to arts subjects. Helen Small, writing in *The Value of the Humanities*, suggests that 'humanities' arose from American efforts to define the special qualities of the study of literature, language, history and the arts in response to 'an aggressive form of positivism' (2013, p. 14). Unlike liberal arts, the label 'humanities' indicates a sense of purpose in relation to society and its collective culture. Significantly, it also suggests the final and formal replacement of God with man, and of religion with national identity. Leavis suggests that a study of literature should lie at the heart of the humanities because of its 'preoccupation with cultural values as human and separable from any particular religious frame or basis' (1979, p. 19).

For academics and students of literature, playing a role in relation to the promotion of national culture initially mounted little challenge to the traditional teaching of classic texts, whether selected according to tradition or for their status within a canon. It was yet to be assumed that 'political ideologies and ethnocentric traditionalism of one kind or another have never stopped shaping the discipline' (Court, 1992, p. 164). The formal teaching of English Literature in what has come to be recognized as a Leavisite tradition flourished within universities. Some scholars and writers were, however, opposed to the emerging form that the study of literature was taking in the early 1960s. Writing in *The Golden Notebook*, Doris Lessing bemoaned the fact that it was possible for students of literature to spend more time reading criticism, or criticism of criticism, than novels, poems or plays (1962, p. 19). Two years later, Susan Sontag similarly argued that such processes 'violated art': 'It makes art into an article for use, for arrangement into a mental scheme of categories' (2013, p. 10).

For social sciences, and sociology in particular, meeting external demands was also, by and large, considered to be unproblematic at this time. The need for empirical research that could offer insight into how to tackle persistent social problems confirmed the dominant belief among sociologists that rational scientific enquiry into the nature of people and society was both possible and could lead to social progress. A new enthusiasm for sociology saw the subject expand rapidly in the 1950s and 1960s. From the mid-1960s onwards, however, the scientific approach to researching social problems began to seem increasingly inadequate in the face of societies undergoing rapid social change. Scientific facts about the social world only told a partial story, and perhaps did not lead researchers closer to a concept of truth. Developments within sociology, and the sociology of knowledge in particular, began to mount a challenge to the orthodoxies of positivism.

The view that knowledge of the social world (though not the social world itself) did not just exist, waiting to be discovered, but was rather constructed by people in relationship to the world and one another became increasingly influential. The Hungarian sociologist Karl Mannheim had first argued in 1936 for a social scientific approach to knowledge which would consider knowledge in the context of its relationship to existence. This was not to deny an objectively existing world, but to suggest that the way people experienced reality was mediated by their subjective understandings at both individual and collective level.

As noted in the previous chapter, in 1966, Berger and Luckmann suggested in *The Social Construction of Reality: A Treatise in the Sociology of Knowledge*, that 'Society does indeed possess objective facticity. And society is indeed built up by activity that expresses subjective meaning'. However, they continued, 'It is precisely the dual character of society in terms of objective facticity and subjective meaning that makes its "reality *sui generis*" ' (1991, p. 30).

When knowledge comes to be considered as an interaction between the subjective and the objective, the limits of a scientific approach to the study of society are exposed. The social sciences needed to explore new, more qualitative, methodological approaches that would allow room for acknowledging and understanding the influence of the subjective. As Bristow suggests, when the subjective element is recognized in the construction of knowledge, understanding the development of history becomes predicated upon understanding 'the generational transmission of knowledge' (2015, p. 45). It is no coincidence that theories of the social construction of knowledge came to the fore in a period when students rebelled against 'the dead stuff' they were taught (Lessing, 1962, p. 18) and sought to challenge the 'elder generation's perceived stranglehold on knowledge' (Bristow, 2015, p. 60).

At the same time as a younger generation of scholars questioned the objectivity of knowledge, the establishment belief in the benefits of promoting high culture to the masses also began to wane. Political radicals, influenced by the notion that knowledge was socially constructed, questioned the extent to which high culture truly represented universal values. It was argued that declaring some forms of art as superior to others was an elitist attack upon the tastes of 'ordinary' people. Eagleton argues the very assumption that 'literature' is 'highly valued' means

> we can drop once and for all the illusion that the category "literature" is "objective", in the sense of being eternally given and immutable. Anything can be literature, and anything which is regarded as unalterably and unquestionably literature – Shakespeare, for example, can cease to be literature.
>
> (2008, p. 9)

Sinfield likewise derides the whole concept of 'literature' as an 'institutional arrangement' made 'to dignify some writing (at the expense of others)' (1997, p. 28). As such a view became increasingly dominant, the concept of a 'literary canon' also came to be seen as a social construct, 'fashioned by particular people for particular reasons at a certain time' (Eagleton, 2008, p. 10). The value of teaching the canon was called into question.

The challenge to the tyranny of positivism, and the recognition that understandings of the world were socially constructed, was a welcome and necessary move in the development of knowledge within social science and humanities disciplines. Likewise, questioning the 'given-ness' of traditional bodies of knowledge and canons of great work was an important intellectual leap. Both positions could have led to greater understanding and better knowledge of the social world, the meaning of literature and its relationship to society. However, the political climate of the 1960s and 1970s shaped the reception of such ideas. Bristow points to the student protests of the 1960s and 'the orientation of radical politics away from the material and towards the psychological and cultural' as leading 'to the realm of culture and ideas becoming a battleground'. She points out that 'In this context, the status and content of knowledge itself came explicitly under attack' (Bristow, 2015, p. 75). Academics began to question the possibility of truly knowing anything. Instead of gaining a greater understanding of the social and historical reception of literary texts, the concept of the canon was jettisoned.

It is undoubtedly true that a literary canon, just like a school or university curriculum, is constructed by people. Decisions are made (formally, in the case of curricula) based upon the subject knowledge, personal values and the sense of purpose of the people doing the constructing. Complex decisions as to what students should be expected to know at any stage in their educational careers are made by teachers, academics and government ministers. However, this does not mean that such decisions are arbitrary, or that all the knowledge included in the curriculum is also socially constructed. Such decisions are not made randomly but are based upon the knowledge and authority of the teacher which, in turn, is grounded within the individual's legitimacy through membership of a disciplinary community. The passing of collective value judgements when, for example, constructing a curriculum, is premised upon the idea that there is an objective basis for critiquing and evaluating works of arts, and that some are inherently more worthy of study than others. A reluctance to assert the superiority of some works of art over others and a shying away from established bodies of canonical knowledge has served to relativize curriculum content within the humanities.

From Literature and Sociology to Cultural Studies

In the latter third of the twentieth century, a number of initially positive developments came together to unravel the academy's drive towards the pursuit of truth and rationality and belief in the promotion of high art as representative of a unifying concept of national culture. A groundswell of opinion against positivism called into question the objectivity of the social sciences, first in sociology and later in strands of anthropology, economics and psychology. This challenge to positivism had a timely and welcome impact upon the nature of academic work. It opened up new topics for investigation and introduced new methodological approaches that had the potential to increase researchers' understandings of how the social world worked.

As the social sciences moved into a more qualitative terrain, sociologists began to reject structural functionalism, with its view that society's various institutions worked in relationship with one another to promote social stability. The scientific study of people and societies primarily through quantitative methods went out of fashion; the focus of research shifted from studying society and the behaviour of people *en masse*, to a growing concern with the more specific experiences of individuals. The political influence of the burgeoning civil rights movement of the 1960s and women's liberation movement of the 1970s led scholars to emphasize the importance of involving participants in the research process. 'Giving voice' to people from socially marginalized groups through narrative research and extended unstructured interviews became a priority for more radical academics.

Scholars attempted to grasp a more complete understanding of human experience than it was possible to gain from quantitative research alone, and this provided a badly needed challenge to what had become a limiting dependence upon positivism. This led to a further reconceptualization of knowledge within the social sciences. Knowledge was no longer considered to be solely determined by the empirically verifiable; nor did it necessarily have a theoretical and hierarchical basis grounded in the work of previous generations of thinkers. It could also be formed from the practical lived experiences of individual knowers. However, as will be explored more fully in subsequent chapters, the questioning of empiricism occurred in conjunction with a loss of faith in the capacity of individuals, as rational beings, to reason. It moved rapidly from a search for better means to pursue truth to an abandonment of truth as the end point of research. Delanty suggests this 'crisis of modernity' led to 'the rejection of objectivity, truth, autonomy and rationality' (2001, p. 21).

Literature students were meanwhile encouraged to question the elitism inherent within the concept of the canon and the liberal values classic texts were assumed to espouse. Eagleton argued that university literature departments 'are part of the ideological apparatus of the modern capitalist state' (2008, p. 174). To circumvent this perceived pro-establishment stance, more politically radical academics sought to displace the voice of the author with an array of possible interpretations. Scholars lost the vocabulary with which to defend teaching great books and as result, literature, as a category type, was often portrayed as of no greater significance than any other texts. Eagleton asks,

> whether it is possible to speak of 'literary theory' without perpetuating the illusion that literature exists as a distinct, bounded object of knowledge, or whether it is not preferable to draw the practical consequences of the fact that literary theory can handle Bob Dylan just as well as John Milton.
>
> (2008, p. 178)

He describes literary theory as a field of 'discursive practices' and argues for 'a different kind of discourse' – be it 'culture' or 'signifying practices' – that would include literature as an object of study but transform it by setting it, as text, in a wider context alongside other texts (2008, p. 178). In this way, both Sociology and Literature began to overlap once more in 'a blend of sociology and literary criticism' (Halsey, 2004, p. 17). In Britain, this took the form of Cultural Studies; across the Atlantic, American Studies emerged with similar goals.

The reasons for academics jettisoning the intellectual foundations of their disciplines in this way, and the consequences of such a move, will be explored more fully in the next two chapters. At this point it is worth noting that in moving to jettison disciplinary content, theories and methods, scholars risk rejecting the source of their authority, which lies in the collectively held intellectual heritage. Perhaps more fundamentally, in rejecting disciplines scholars reject the communities that provide the social basis for the objectivity of socially constructed knowledge and lend legitimacy to the passing of judgements. Without such a social basis there can be no objectivity to socially constructed knowledge, and therefore no aspiration for any knowledge to challenge and supersede that which has gone before.

When anything can count as an object of study, defining what constitutes the humanities becomes increasingly complex and the associated disciplines are left in search of a focus. Recent years have shown universities attempting to market the humanities in substantially instrumental terms, as producing broad social benefits and enhanced employability within the context of personal projects of transformation. While the drive towards instrumentalism within the humanities could be expected to bring about a renewed sense of purpose to their pursuit, attempts are vague and all-encompassing. Thus the UK government-sponsored funding body, the Arts and Humanities Research Council, suggests that research in the humanities: 'explores forms of identity, behaviour and expression, and seeks out new ways of knowing what it means to be human in different societies and across the centuries' (2013).

The humanities emerged with the final decentring of God from the university, and the replacement of a spiritual project of devotion with a moral mission to understand the universal human condition through the objective study of truth in art. The persistent trope of the humanities in crisis that has dominated recent decades is reflective of the decentring of universal man from the university, and with it any notion of truth that goes beyond individual experiences. Graham Good suggests:

> The carceral vision that now dominates the humanities could be seen as an attempt to cancel out the key values, not only of the Renaissance but of the whole western tradition – independent inquiry, realistic representation, and individual freedom – and to replace them with mere culture operating systems.
>
> (2001, p. 101)

He suggests this is 'a denial of human liberty, creativity and progress – and indeed of the very possibility of common humanity' (2001, p. 102).

As the social sciences have become more qualitative in nature, the boundaries between social science and humanities disciplines have become blurred. Dominant theoretical trends such as Critical Theory, feminism, post-colonialism and post-modernism have influenced both the humanities and social sciences, bringing about common methodological approaches and paradigm shifts within each. Cultural Studies has also come to occupy a dominant position within sociology at the beginning of the twenty-first century.

In presenting the humanities as separate from any particular body of knowledge content we end up with a mixture of the individual and the collective; the past and the present; the personal and the political. Any aspiration towards truth and objectivity has been replaced by the values of promoting cultural difference and diversity considered essential to a democratic community. This is echoed at Stanford University, where it is suggested that the humanities offer opportunities for: 'the study of the myriad ways in which people, from every period of history and from every corner of the globe, process and document the human experience'. We see here a mix of influences ranging from identity politics, a promotion of cultural diversity and the values necessary for democratic participation in society. Leavis' proposed mental training of the sensibilities and enculturation in a discipline of critical analysis have been replaced by a vague focus on practically applicable employability skills and the promotion of political values associated with equality, diversity and inclusion.

As with the humanities, social science disciplines have also become increasingly preoccupied with skills for employability and training students for entry to the world of work. Bernstein suggests that at the heart of the concept of 'trainability' lies 'an emptiness which makes the concept self-referential' (1996, p. 59). Beck argues that this is necessarily so as the whole point of trainability 'is the fostering of receptiveness to whatever set of objectives and contents comes along next' (2010, p. 90). The vacuum at the heart of trainability in the social sciences has most often been filled, as with the humanities, through projects of self-knowledge and personal transformation (see Abbas and McLean, 2010).

Since the end of the twentieth century, the search for legitimacy within the humanities has pushed some scholars out towards the boundaries of other disciplines, in particular science and social science. Most recently, and perhaps as a backlash to the intellectual hollowing out of the disciplines, there has emerged a trend towards scientism in social sciences and humanities alike. This has mainly occurred through applying methodological approaches from science to subject matter traditionally associated with the humanities, or social science.

Cognitive science is now applied to the study of human behaviour. Unlike an earlier empiricism, which was itself criticized for being too narrow, this is a science which seeks biological and environmental explanations for individual behaviour and in so doing downplays the significance of individual agency. Whereas Kant had suggested that the philosophy faculty played a unique role in critiquing the work of the other faculties, with the new scientism philosophers abdicate the moral responsibility to criticize, deferring instead to a weight of evidence.

Where now for criticism?

The academic disciplines that emerged in the twentieth century university reflected not just the status and organization of existing knowledge, but also the methodological parameters for constituting new knowledge. This is in line with Barnett's definition of 'fields of knowledge', which 'are identifiable in having their own key concepts, truth criteria and forms of life, for example, in their modes of reason and judgement' (2009, p. 436). Obedience to particular 'modes of reason and judgement' is required by all undertaking the mental training required for enculturation into a disciplinary community. Such discipline, to return to the verb form of the word, provides the basis for the exercise of critical judgement and the practice of academic freedom.

Meanwhile, the discipline as object provides the conditions for realizing such practice. Tracing the origins of humanities and social science disciplines and the interaction between their epistemological and sociological development makes it possible to explore the changing social status of knowledge and criticality. With the rejection of disciplines, scholars abandon the essential conditions for criticality and the historical basis of arguments for academic freedom. What remains is simply an array of alternative views, all of which are equally valid, none of which seeks to compete with any other. There is no longer a useful marketplace for ideas, nor any need for one.

In recent years a social realist approach to knowledge has emerged from the work of academics such as Michael Young, Karl Maton, Rob Moore and Johan Muller, who all build upon the ideas of Durkheim and Bernstein in relation to education and the sociology of knowledge. The social realists define themselves in opposition to both the 'neo-conservative' view that knowledge is neutral, objective and fixed for all time; and the postmodern, social-constructionist view that all knowledge is reducible to individual viewpoints and experiences. They take something positive from the social constructionists – that is, the idea that knowledge is not fixed for all time or naturally occurring. That knowledge is socially constructed in this way makes it open to being challenged and superseded by new truth claims. However, social realists reject the argument that knowledge is reducible to either individual experiences or a reflection of a dominant political ideology. Rather, they argue that it is the social composition of knowledge that makes it real.

It is this social composition of knowledge, within a disciplinary-specific context, that provides the authority for objectivity and truth claims in relation to knowledge, and that ultimately provides the epistemological basis for criticism and the foundations of academic freedom. This may point a way forward for an approach to the development of disciplinary knowledge that provides a basis for criticality.

4
Disciplines under Attack

From the late nineteenth century onwards, the pursuit of knowledge within universities became professionalized and formally channelled through the development of academic disciplines. The discipline, as both a structural mechanism for organizing academics in the workplace, and a community with knowledge, theories and methods in common, continues to play a significant role in regulating the behaviour and intellectual endeavours of academics. The emergence of the modern disciplines at the end of the nineteenth century created the conditions necessary for academic freedom to become a reality. However, disciplines also curb dissent and encourage conformity to particular norms. In relation to academic freedom, then, disciplines serve as a practical realization of a marketplace of ideas while at the same time imposing limits on what is considered acceptable academic work.

Current arguments against disciplinary structures tend to reject the positive feature of disciplines; that is, their ability to self-regulate and streamline the pursuit of knowledge. At the same time, arguments in favour of interdisciplinarity often replicate a tendency to impose conformity and the promotion of particular norms and values. This chapter explores how disciplinary structures both help and hinder the pursuit of knowledge and the realization of academic freedom. We then consider the attraction for academics of working beyond disciplinary boundaries, while acknowledging how interdisciplinary communities can also act as a mechanism for policing what counts as acceptable contributions to intellectual debate.

Freedom within disciplines

Academic disciplines have become so entwined with the nature of the modern university that evaluating their impact is difficult. Specific publications, forms of teaching, styles of writing, methodological approaches and canons of great works have all grown separately for each discipline. Key figures within each subject area and within each institution act as intellectual gatekeepers to regulate not only who enters the academy and in what capacity but, perhaps more significantly, what counts as a legitimate contribution to new knowledge within each subject area and the precise form such contributions should take. Despite Rauch's reminder that 'anyone is entitled to check (criticise) anyone, and no one is immune from being checked by anyone else [...] no one's experience or conclusion is supposed to get special weight by dint of who he happens to be' (2014, p. 50), the professionalization of academic work was too often concerned with limiting who *did* get to make such criticisms.

The push to establish disciplinary communities at the end of the nineteenth and the beginning of the twentieth centuries coincided with the heyday of positivism and a deeply held belief that empirical research could uncover truth and drive forward both academic knowledge and social progress. All academic disciplines sought the legitimacy of science. The demand for academic freedom which emerged at this time was firmly connected to the emerging organization of academic work into disciplinary communities.

In 1902, John Dewey argued that disciplinary communities 'were the guarantee both of the independence of the individual scholar in an increasingly centralized and oligarchic university, and of the integrity of his work. They were an immediate resource counteracting the dangers threatening academic freedom'. Dewey argued it was communal self-regulation based upon expertise that made academic freedom different from other notions of individual rights (in Scott, 1996, p. 168). For him, the importance of disciplinary communities lay in their ability to provide support for the individual academic, while at the same time checking, verifying and legitimizing the qualifications and credentials of members. Scholars in social and psychological fields, Dewey argued, needed 'the utmost freedom of investigation' because they dealt more closely than technical scientists with 'the problems of life' and were thus more likely to come up against 'deep-rooted prejudice and intense emotional reaction' (in Scott, 1996, p. 167). A disciplinary community could protect its members from such external pressures.

Arthur Lovejoy, a founding member of the AAUP, agreed with Dewey's view of the significance of disciplines. He argued that disciplinary communities, as 'qualified bodies', enabled individual scholars of the same profession to stand up against outside interference from 'political or ecclesiastical authority, or from the administrative officials of the institution in which he is employed'. Arguing for strongly bounded academic disciplines was necessary at this particular point in time, as they allowed scholars to break free from the regulations of institutions and trustees which had become so antithetical to the development of knowledge.

Writing in 1968, the Classics professor and AAUP activist Glenn Morrow made explicit the importance of disciplines to advancing knowledge. He argued that the advance of knowledge was premised upon certainty never being reached and truth claims being permanently contestable and subject to critique. He suggested such conditions were only achievable in practice with 'a community of scholars and scientists cooperating with one another through mutual criticism and selecting and recruiting new members through disciplined and systematic training' (in Scott, 1996, p. 169).

The creation of tightly focused communities of practice streamlined the act of criticism and lent impetus to the pursuit of knowledge. Many of the intellectual leaps that have occurred since the beginning of the twentieth century would not have happened, or at least not in so timely a manner, without academic disciplines creating a practical realization of a marketplace of ideas. Disciplines served to make the liberal academic project meaningful in reality. As we saw in Chapter 1, it was the drive to professionalize the role of the scholar and, in particular, for academics to claim the intellectual and professional autonomy of the subject-specialist, that led quite directly to the demand for academic freedom and the establishment of the AAUP at the beginning of the twentieth century. As Judith Butler suggests, the concept of academic freedom to emerge at this time was based upon a 'very specific historical set of presumptions about knowledge, social function and scientific progress that have, paradoxically, been revised and refuted on various grounds and in various directions over time, perhaps even as a consequence of the "advance" of knowledge itself' (2006a, p. 110). This notion of academic freedom granted scholars rights in proportion to their demonstrable level of disciplinary expertise and their status within an institutional hierarchy.

Despite the emergence of new subject areas and a continued interest in interdisciplinarity, the nature of the academic disciplines we have today would be readily familiar to scholars from a century ago. Jerry A. Jacobs suggests, 'There is much to be valued in the current arrangement of academic disciplines':

> This system is dynamic; competition occurs on many levels within fields as well as across fields. The very structure of the disciplinary system tends to push in the direction of competition and over time will generally arrest any tendency towards intellectual fossilization.
>
> (2013, p. 35)

Disciplines, through enculturating scholars into a shared epistemology, create the conditions for the rigorous checking of academic ideas and provide the rules for developing and evaluating new knowledge claims. The practices of an academic discipline are not arbitrary but emerge from an historical concept of knowledge. Rather than being restrictive, such shared norms provide a social foundation for the objectivity of knowledge and in so doing offer a means of challenging existing knowledge and developing new ideas. It is important to see disciplines themselves as a product of their historical circumstances. Butler notes, 'what is "too much" at one time may become a disciplinary paradigm at another' (2006, p. 119). She argues that all scholarly work is best understood 'as fundamentally conditioned by social and institutional structures and norms' (2006, p. 123).

Problematizing disciplines

Disciplines, as both sociological object and field of knowledge, have been under attack from within and outside of the academy from the point at which they were initially established, although this gathered momentum in the latter third of the twentieth century. In recent years, disciplines have been criticized for being relics from a bygone era, at best simply irrelevant to the pursuit of knowledge or, worse, a hindrance to the development of new ideas. Disciplines have been derided as academic 'silos' whose rigid boundaries constitute a barrier to intellectual progress and prevent communication between scholars who work on similar topics.

Disciplines stand accused of being inwardly focused on a narrow range of self-perpetuating topics and drawing academics into competitive game-playing, thereby wasting time and energy that could otherwise be spent on the search for solutions to practical problems. Jacobs outlines five main criticisms that are commonly levelled at disciplines: they inhibit communication; stifle innovation; thwart the search for integrated solutions to social problems; inhibit the economic contributions of universities; and provide a fragmented education for undergraduates (2013, p. 13). Menand also criticizes the structure of disciplinarity that has arisen with the modern research university for being expensive, philosophically weak, and encouraging intellectual predictability, professional insularity and social irrelevance (1996, p. 19).

While academic disciplines allowed for the emergence of powerful, truth-seeking communities of practice with a shared commitment to knowledge that led to demands for academic freedom, entry to these communities was tightly restricted, resulting in freedom for academics, rather than free speech for everyone. The late nineteenth century drive towards the professionalization of knowledge within academic disciplines slowly began to erode the intellectual contribution of talented amateurs and the general public to the pursuit of new knowledge, and, later, to the critique of existing ideas.

For those within the academy, disciplinary structures hindered a far more holistic approach to the development of knowledge in favour of the narrowly specific. In 1902, Dewey warned that specialization

> leads the individual, if he follows it unreservedly, into bypaths still further off from the highway where men, struggling together, develop strength. The insidious conviction that matters of fundamental import to humanity are none of my concern because outside of my *Fach*, is likely to work more harm to genuine freedom of academic work than any fancied dread of interference from a moneyed benefactor.
>
> (in Scott, 1996, p. 167)

Even today, disciplines provide both the shared knowledge foundation and membership of an intellectual community necessary to legitimize challenges to received orthodoxies; while that same community can also serve to prevent any challenge to entrenched and established views and enforce conformism. Butler argues, 'if the "profession" was charged with advancing knowledge, it also needed to safeguard dissent and debate to fulfil that charge' (2006, p. 113). In reality, this means any critic of established disciplinary norms must, ironically, 'find legitimation in the very discipline whose orthodoxy he or she challenges' (Scott, 1996, p. 166).

Disciplinary communities embody an inherent conflict between engaging in 'mutual criticism' and selecting new members through 'disciplined and systematic training'. Through regulating output and controlling membership, disciplines enforce conformity through threat of exclusion. Whereas disciplines were needed to organize knowledge and authorize its producers, they also served to constrain external input and curb internal dissent. Butler notes examples of significant developments in knowledge that have been hindered by disciplinary communities: 'Walter Benjamin's habilitations thesis was rejected by faculty at Frankfurt in the early 1920s. The Frankfurt faculty could grasp his study of baroque tragic drama neither as philosophy nor as literature', while 'James Watson, who was credited with co-discovering the structure of DNA, had his grant applications regularly rejected by his peers, who thought the routes he was following were worthless and without scientific promise' (2006, p. 118). She suggests that change in disciplinary norms, when it produces 'new configurations of knowledge and new lines of inquiry – is generally considered good, even if (or precisely because) it is controversial'.

When disciplinary rules are considered provisional and open to discussion they can serve an important role but when presented as dogma they can blindly enforce orthodoxies. As Scott notes, 'Freedom and subjection become two sides of the same coin' (1996, p. 175). Since their inception, then, the problematic nature of disciplines has been recognized. However, the particular problems identified have varied over time, and challenges to academic disciplines have often been quite selective in nature and have focused more upon some problems rather than others. There have, for example, been few demands to open up disciplinary communities to people from outside of the academy: the intelligent autodidact is all too often treated with suspicion. Indeed, as we saw in the introduction to this book, there are often attempts to restrict debate further to fully credentialized members of disciplinary communities. In addition, relatively few criticize disciplines for creating and cohering around intellectual orthodoxies that can then become very difficult to challenge from within a hierarchical community rigidly protected by gatekeepers.

Instead, academic disciplines are chiefly criticized for being too inward-looking and lacking relevance to students' future employment needs; for acting as isolated silos reluctant to embrace knowledge and methods from across subject boundaries; and for being unsuited to finding solutions to today's complex real world problems. Behind these seemingly practical concerns lie three distinct criticisms of the epistemological foundations of disciplines: the role they play in promoting obedience to a particular set of methodological rules; the credence they lend to the existence of a specific body of knowledge manifest in canonical works; and their tendency to promote a particular concept of truth. Such criticisms focus upon the role disciplines play in acting as a marketplace of ideas while making a case for interdisciplinarity, in the form of cross-disciplinary research centres or interdisciplinary subjects focused primarily upon ethnic, gender or area studies.

Why move towards interdisciplinarity?

The debate around disciplinarity serves as a useful reminder that the division of academic work into disciplines is neither natural nor inevitable. Disciplines impose rigid, often hierarchical divisions between different branches of knowledge and challenges to this formalism are to be welcomed. Menand notes that the discipline of English, for example, 'is neither natural nor inevitable, and it is very easy to see all the ways in which, by essentializing the object of its study and by marginalizing non-literary approaches, it limits and even distorts the understanding of literature' (1996, p. 18). The development of interdisciplinary research and taught programmes has increased markedly in recent years. Jacobs notes that 'interdisciplinarity is everywhere' (2013, p. 123), and he suggests today's universities can perhaps be best described as 'post-disciplinary' or even 'anti-disciplinary' (2013, p. 142).

To some degree, interdisciplinarity has been a feature of higher education since disciplines as we recognize them today first emerged. The idea of liberal education and the German concept of *Bildung* were never intended to be narrowly specific, but rather to allow for intellectual flourishing and the development of individual reason through enabling connections to be drawn between knowledge in different areas. In practice, an interest in interdisciplinarity emerged contemporaneously with the institutionalization of the disciplines: 'There was no long period of ossification; the one bred the other almost immediately' (Abbott, in Small, 2013, p. 33). As both Jacobs and Small conclude, the impulse towards specialization within disciplinary communities was immediately met by a desire to reach beyond subject boundaries and to 'correct for their narrowness' (Small, 2013, p. 33). Significantly, it was the existence of disciplines which created the conditions for their questioning and transcendence.

Readings makes the point that the university should not exchange rigid and outmoded disciplines for an amorphous interdisciplinary space: 'Rather, the loosening of disciplinary structures has to be made the opportunity for the installation of disciplinarity as a *permanent question*' (1996, p. 177). A connection can be traced between dominant assumptions about the nature of knowledge and the forms and structures used to organize academic work. Although there are many reasons to be critical of disciplines, it is important to consider the particular reasons why they have come under attack in recent decades and why this is a problem for academic freedom, the practice of criticism and the pursuit of knowledge.

A number of commentators have located the most recent vogue for interdisciplinarity as resulting from the marketization of higher education and the emergence of the student as consumer. The higher costs associated with attending university to be met by individuals may encourage students to pursue more applied fields of study rather than pure academic disciplines in order to secure post-graduation employment. University managers argue that the provision of multidisciplinary degree programmes such as Business with Psychology or interdisciplinary subjects more directly relevant to the world of work, such as Leisure Management, is demand-led. It is certainly true that currently fashionable courses such as Criminology or Journalism may attract more fee-paying customers than the less immediately employment-focused and more knowledge-driven rather than skills-based sociology or English literature.

Indeed, the impact of marketization and the need to attract fee-paying customers has begun to shape the focus of academic disciplines themselves. For example, over the past decade the UK has witnessed a decline in chemistry departments and the rise of forensic science as this is considered a more attractive option by student consumers. Often it can appear as if the decision to introduce interdisciplinary courses is driven by administrative or financial concerns rather than educational motives. This situation is compounded by the fact that funding bodies designed to allocate resources to scholars for the pursuit of academic research projects increasingly prioritize interdisciplinary work. Funding bodies see interdisciplinarity as a shortcut to meeting government targets in relation to 'knowledge transfer', 'economic relevance' and 'impact' (see Small, 2013, p. 16).

Basil Bernstein pointed to the pressures on disciplines to turn outwards and respond to external economic and social demands, thereby transforming the purely academic into more applied or multidisciplinary areas of study. The pressure experienced by chemists to reinvent themselves and their subject to meet the demands of both students and industry is an example of Bernstein's 'singulars', or 'pure' academic subjects, being increasingly displaced by 'regions', or subject areas that look out to other disciplines or the world beyond academia. Bernstein regarded this development as being 'a response to market conditions on the part of "autonomous" higher education institutions, rather than as being politically imposed' (Beck, 2010, p. 86).

Delanty likewise suggests that as the boundaries between education and the realm of production have become increasingly blurred, the role of the university in relation to knowledge production is challenged. Knowledge comes to be generated in its 'context of application' with 'commercial competition becoming the basis for the logic of discovery' (2001, pp. 108/109). The expectation that universities operate as businesses within a marketized environment has had an impact upon the nature of research conducted and the development of disciplinary knowledge.

Arguments that market pressures have weakened the insulation between the realms of education and production (Beck, 2010, p. 86) have a long history, and pre-date the most recent round of increases in the levels of tuition fees paid by individual students. While the marketization of higher education has exacerbated the relentless drive towards the hollowing out of knowledge in favour of the promotion of vocational skills training, the extent to which universities are creating or responding to demands from potential students is, however, debatable. If higher education was driven by a sense of purpose that went beyond simply the logic of the market, there may be room for factors other than customer demand to be taken into account in determining which subjects are worthy of a place on the curriculum.

The autonomy of fields of knowledge associated with specific disciplines was called into question from within universities before the more recent impact of marketization in both Britain and America was fully experienced. The challenge to academic disciplines dealing with a specific body of knowledge in a particular methodological way first arose within universities themselves. As the link between truth and knowledge was called into question by academics in the second half of the twentieth century, all disciplinary knowledge came to be seen as essentially arbitrary, representing little more than a reflection of the tastes and values of the social elite rather than any objective insight into the world. Halsey argues that from the 1960s the academy became characterized by 'vociferous anti-positivists, epistemological nihilism and moral relativism' (2004, p. 119). This manifested itself most visibly in the emergence of new hybrid subjects labelled 'studies'. Disciplines merged and developed to form new interdisciplinary subject areas such as Cultural Studies, Media Studies, Educational and Environmental Studies.

Academics themselves have been at the forefront of the hollowing out of knowledge as they seek to leave behind the rigid structures of the disciplines in favour of the presumed intellectual freedom and practical applicability of the interdisciplinary topic-focused research centre. As a result, interdisciplinarity has become something of a buzzword in academia, particularly in the humanities and social sciences. The British philosopher Roger Scruton notes that the trend for 'throwing together clusters of disciplines from the social sciences and the humanities in order to generate "studies"' first emerged in the 1960s and 1970s (2013). Cultural Studies began life at the University of Birmingham in 1964 led by Richard Hoggart, academic and author of *The Uses of Literacy*. Hoggart was associated with Britain's

New Left, a loose political grouping influenced by the Italian political theorist Antonio Gramsci, the Frankfurt School of Critical Theorists and post-structuralist thinkers like Louis Althusser and later, Michel Foucault. The Centre for Contemporary Cultural Studies at Birmingham became increasingly influential when Hoggart invited Stuart Hall, founder of the *New Left Review*, to join him in 1964. In 1972, Hall took over as the Centre's director. Cultural Studies became far more influential than a simple headcount of staff and student numbers may have indicated.

Women's Studies and African Studies also began to emerge as university subjects in the UK in the 1970s. In the US, various types of area studies, most notably American Studies, became increasingly influential. The trend for interdisciplinarity served a timely and useful function in promoting a discussion about the role of disciplines in asserting intellectual conformity and adherence to rules that were difficult to challenge. As the boundaries between even relatively 'pure' disciplines have become blurred, interdisciplinarity is celebrated along with a rejection of the need to conform to particular traditional ways of thinking. It can increasingly seem as if, particularly within the humanities, interdisciplinarity has become an end in itself.

Two distinct drivers – marketization on the one hand, and the rejection of knowledge on the other – have come together to ensure that the turn towards interdisciplinarity is considered favourably by both academics and administrators within the university. Radicals seeking to overcome rigid disciplinary structures and the imposition of particular bodies of knowledge find common cause with managers seeking to secure new sources of revenue. Readings suggests that one reason interdisciplinary subject areas can cohere disparate interests is that, lacking a shared historical legacy, such subjects are intellectually footloose and can bend to whatever expectations are projected on to them (1996, p. 39). There is a risk that as such new subject areas develop they jettison the key strengths of disciplines – namely, a group of scholars sharing a body of knowledge and distinct methodological approaches – yet keep the more problematic insularity and pressure to conform to the orthodoxies sustained by the community.

The recent vogue for interdisciplinarity speaks to the rejection of knowledge as the driving force of higher education. The idea of knowledge as intrinsically valuable carries little legitimacy today:

instead, disciplines increasingly seek to justify themselves in terms of 'relevance' which, as Muller and Young note, they 'can only do by weakening their boundaries with the world, which further weakens their traditional power and legitimacy' (2014, p. 133). Teaching an interdisciplinary subject that highlights the voices of marginalized groups, questions the concept of a subject-specific canon, encourages students to create their own knowledge or focuses on teaching skills as opposed to content, is often seen as preferable to passing on a particular body of disciplinary-specific knowledge.

Interdisciplinarity, in appearing to circumvent the limitations of academic disciplines, allows for a degree of intellectual freedom and liberation from the tight constraints of a disciplinary community. However, as Jacobs notes, one problem with interdisciplinarity is that it soon replicates new orthodoxies and creates new communities. Interdisciplinary fields themselves quickly become elaborately divided into specialities and develop their own forms of segregation, resulting in the proliferation of academic units, or 'schools' rather than the consolidation of knowledge into a more unified whole. Cultural Studies provides a useful illustration as to how interdisciplinarity plays out in practice.

In his 1990 article *The Emergence of Cultural Studies and the Crisis of the Humanities*, Stuart Hall argued that Cultural Studies 'emerged precisely from a crisis in the humanities', which had arisen because they 'were conducted in the light, or in the wake, of the Arnoldian project. What they were handling in literary work and history were the histories and touchstones of the national culture, transmitted to a select number of people' (p. 13). Hall was critical of the elitism inherent in the ideas of Matthew Arnold and F. R. Leavis – the conviction that it was possible to discern quality in the arts, and that educators had a moral and intellectual imperative to promote high culture. Readings notes that Cultural Studies arose at the point when culture ceased to mean anything vital for the university as a whole (1996, p. 91), and there was growing disillusion with the idea that elite culture could play a role in cohering society behind a unified national vision. Through Cultural Studies, Hall sought to develop 'an ideological critique of the way the humanities and the arts presented themselves as parts of disinterested knowledge' and did not allow contemporary cultural forms to 'constitute a serious object of contemplation in the academic world' (1990, p. 15).

Cultural Studies also arose out of political disillusionment with revolutionary politics, particularly in relation to the experience of Stalinism in the Soviet Union. Hall acknowledged this legacy of political disillusion in his suggestion that: 'The Centre for Cultural Studies was the locus to which we *retreated* when that conversation [about political transformation] in the open world could no longer be continued' (1990, p. 12, emphasis in original). The founding assumption of Cultural Studies was that mass or popular culture needed to be studied in order to understand 'what was wrong with Britain in particular and capitalism in general' (ibid).

From the outset, then, Cultural Studies relativized academic content through its rejection of high culture and focus on popular culture. Indeed, the word 'culture' itself came to be disassociated from the arts and was instead used to refer to everyday experiences. Cultural Studies began by applying the tools of literary criticism to mass culture to expose the interplay of culture, power and politics. Hall's aspiration was to develop an entirely new interdisciplinary approach to analysing popular culture that drew upon sociology, linguistics, critical theory and Lacanian psychotherapy. This approach, in relation to both content and method, has since had an impact across much of academia.

Cultural Studies was the first incarnation of a subject to be built on the explicit premise that all knowledge is political and ultimately reducible to an ideological expression of power relations. The Australian academic Toby Miller, a leading light in Cultural Studies, describes the subject's commitment to exposing power structures for 'progressive social change' as being 'animated by a desire to reveal and transform those who control the means of communication and culture' (2006, p. 7). This belies any pretence to truth or objectivity, values previously fundamental to the academic enterprise. Instead, as Young says of the sociology of education in the 1960s and 1970s, the outcome of scholarship had been predetermined; it lay in the link between power and knowledge, and the aim of academics was to show how this relationship manifested itself. Miller argues his subject has had a profound impact 'on a host of disciplines' and that it 'accretes various tendencies that are splintering the human sciences: Marxism, feminism, queer theory, and the postcolonial' (2006, p. 1). One problem with such interdisciplinary studies is that lacking a particular knowledge base, collectively held theoretical assumptions or methodological approaches, they can easily become intellectually vacuous and filled by their proponents' political ideologies.

The instrumental use of education to serve political ends resulted in some peculiar tensions within Cultural Studies concerning what 'counted' as mass culture and whether it was to be celebrated or critiqued. Miller describes Cultural Studies as offering a celebration of the counter-culture as opposed to the 'achievement-oriented, materialistic, educationally driven values and appearance of the middle class' (2006, p. 2). This caricature of middle-class values leads to a privileging of ignorance as somehow more authentic than submitting to the mores of elite culture. In *The Intellectuals and the Masses*, John Carey draws a parallel between the elitism and disdain for ordinary people shown by early twentieth century writers and thinkers and the later generation of critical theorists that influenced the subject of Cultural Studies. He points to Roland Barthes' decoding of popular culture in *Mythologies* which shows how its real meaning, 'discernible to the intellectual, escapes the gullible masses' (1992, p. 216). Carey suggests that to Barthes, the mass of the population 'reveals itself as unnatural, and not fully or wholesomely human' (1982, p. 216).

Hall described his aim with Cultural Studies as being 'to take the whole system of knowledge itself and [...] attempt to put it at the service of some other project' (1990, p. 18). In this, Hall was perhaps more successful than he initially imagined; the impact of Cultural Studies on academia has been substantial. As Miller notes, 'the "cultural" has become a master trope in the humanities' (2006, p. 1). An emphasis on personal identity and the more recent concept of intersectionality now hang over the social sciences. This has led to Cultural Studies becoming a victim of its own success. Readings suggests that Cultural Studies 'proceeds from a certain sense that no more knowledge can be produced since there is nothing to be said about culture that is not itself cultural and vice versa' (1996, p. 17). When every discipline treats all content as political, there is less need for Cultural Studies as a specific subject. The Birmingham Centre for Contemporary Cultural Studies has now closed, and students can no longer study the subject at undergraduate level.

In many ways, however, much as with Women's Studies (discussed in Chapter 6), all subjects are Cultural Studies now and higher education as a whole has become increasingly political as a result. The politicization of academic work means the subject community becomes less a marketplace for ideas and more a means of ensuring conformity to a particular political outlook.

The well-rehearsed assumption that like-minded individuals are attracted to one another plays out within the academy and academics with similar interests and perspectives gather within subject communities. As interdisciplinary fields become increasingly established, they develop distinct leanings which reflect the perspectives and interests of their members. The field then replicates such perspectives and viewpoints through regulating entry and controlling the outputs of its members. Duarte et al. suggest that over time, the group itself may become characterized by its group members: 'Professors and scientists may come to be seen as liberal just as nurses are typically thought of as being female'. They argue that such processes apply equally to political persuasions and that once that happens, 'conservatives may disproportionately self-select out of joining the dissimilar group, based on a realistic perception that they "do not fit well" ' (2014, p. 28).

The drive towards interdisciplinarity often reflects a positive impulse to go beyond the strict boundaries of disciplines and push the pursuit of knowledge into new areas. In recent years interdisciplinarity has often come to be about little more than either an instrumental means of meeting the requirements of funding bodies or attracting new student-customers. This is more about narrow specialization than broadening out academic debates. In such instances the creation of an interdisciplinary community of like-minded individuals can reproduce the drive to conformity inherent in disciplines, while losing the corresponding drive to advance knowledge.

In defence of disciplines

Disciplinary communities provide the foundations for a concept of knowledge that goes beyond individual identity and experience. Without this social basis, the means by which both new knowledge is determined and existing knowledge is challenged becomes increasingly baseless. Jacobs argues it is the specific training provided by disciplines that enables scholars to pass judgement: 'The community of scholars in a field establishes understandings and contentions about what constitutes important questions and what constitutes good research' (2013, p. 141). The questioning of the rules associated with academic disciplines, and the increasingly blurred boundaries between subjects leaves scholars without a structured framework for criticality and unable to challenge existing knowledge or make truth claims in relation to new knowledge. A disciplinary community of practice makes criticality both possible and meaningful. In the absence of a disciplinary community, criticism is reduced to individual experience, and the need for academic freedom dissipates.

Durkheim's contribution to the sociology of knowledge is important in determining the social origins of abstract knowledge. He describes social knowledge, or collective representations, as 'the product of an immense cooperation that extends not only through space but also through time; to make them, a multitude of different minds have associated, intermixed, and combined their ideas and feelings; long generations have accumulated their experience and knowledge' (1967, p. 15). In arguing that knowledge had a social foundation, Durkheim did not mean that knowledge was merely a product of the circumstances of its creation. He did not, as Delanty puts it, consider there to be a complete identity between knowledge and society to the point that all knowledge claims are relativistic (2001, p. 14). Instead Durkheim argued that once socially constituted, knowledge took on an objective status; indeed, it was the social constitution of knowledge that gave it its objectivity. Durkheim suggested such collective views that historically began with religious beliefs provided the 'paradigm of all advanced forms of theoretical knowledge' (in Young, 2008, p. 41).

Durkheim's argument that knowledge has a social basis points to the significance of academic disciplines as communities of practice. As Jacobs crucially reminds us, 'In organizing research, advancing knowledge is the goal, and reforms should be undertaken when they represent the best means of achieving that objective. Disciplines as currently constituted are central to the creativity and dynamism of the modern research university' because they provide 'the conditions for relatively unfettered critical inquiry' (2013, p. 9). As Durkheim indicates, knowledge takes its objectivity precisely from the social conditions of its production.

This point has been lost in debates around the social construction of knowledge, and many academics today assume that knowledge is reducible to personal perspectives. Instead of testing the truth of existing knowledge, it is argued that the notion of truth is itself an outdated concept and we have multiple, equally valid truths all dependent upon the status of the speaker's social group. As Graham Good puts it in *Humanism Betrayed*, 'Objectivity and disinterest are dismissed as pretences concealing the motives of power' (2001, p. 4).

Disciplines are at once necessary and problematic for the pursuit of knowledge. They provide the conditions for its production but also act as a curb on originality and dissent. They created the conditions for academic freedom to become a practical reality while simultaneously enforcing obedience. Haidt (2012) suggests that disciplines form a cohesive moral community and create a shared reality that 'subsequently blinds its members to morally or ideologically undesirable hypotheses and unanswered but important scientific questions' (in Duarte et al., 2014, p. 8). As broad and general self-regulating academic communities, disciplines served, and could continue to serve, a useful purpose. However, the more disciplines, or new interdisciplinary subject groupings, tend towards narrow specialization, the more they both curb the production of knowledge and promote conformity.

Cultural Studies both emerged from and contributed to an intellectually provocative and badly needed challenge to a conservative academy and caused scholars to question teaching and research practices which were often based on little more than historical legacy. Cultural Studies also acts as a useful case study to illustrate what is problematic about rejecting academic disciplines. The expectation that academics will become experts in a narrow specialism has not disappeared but this specialism can now lie outside of traditional academic disciplines. It can no longer be assumed that academic colleagues who share an interest in a particular topic will also share a collective knowledge base and theoretical or methodological assumptions. Interdisciplinarity encourages the emergence of narrow specialists, who can work with contextual knowledge but without the broader intellectual framework provided by the disciplines.

We need a guarded defence of disciplines, not based upon nostalgia, or in a protectionist sense of marking out academic territory. As Muller and Young argue, the search for truth through disciplinary enquiry has proved itself over two centuries to be the best way of advancing knowledge (2014). The rules associated with disciplines offer an epistemological framework for evaluating knowledge and a shared basis for criticality, which is essential for the exercise of academic freedom.

Part III

Beyond Criticism

5
Uncritical Theory

It took many decades for the intellectual movement of the Enlightenment to have an impact upon universities. In the UK and the US in particular, institutions remained steeped in their religious origins and medieval traditions until well into the nineteenth century. The eventual influence of values such as reason, rationality and individual autonomy played out within academia in two seemingly contradictory ways: the development of liberal education on one hand, and the drive towards disciplinary specialization on the other. Both trends brought to the surface assumptions about the purpose of a university, and the need for scholars to be able to question previously held knowledge, that resulted in demands for academic freedom.

Proponents of liberal education needed freedom from the strictures of church and state to pursue knowledge for its own sake. Subject specialists needed freedom from institutional interference to allow the professional academic community to self-regulate, to determine what counted as new knowledge and to pass judgement on competing truth claims. The organization of knowledge into disciplines and the alignment of academics with such professional communities provided the basis for making academic freedom a meaningful practice.

As discussed in previous chapters, the heyday of both the academic discipline and a belief in liberal education was relatively short-lived, corresponding to the latter half of the nineteenth and the first half of the twentieth centuries at most. Across society as a whole, there has never been a time when Enlightenment thought has gone unchallenged. The counter-Enlightenment, best characterized in the philosophy of Rousseau and the Romantic Movement in poetry and art, began in the eighteenth century as a conservative attempt to return political, social and scientific progress to the morality of church, monarch or nature. The academy, initially slow to co-opt Enlightenment values, took longer to develop a recognizably coherent counter-Enlightenment position of its own. The emergence of Critical Theory in the twentieth century marked such a transition.

This chapter explores the impact of Critical Theory on the enactment of Enlightenment values within the academy. Ideas associated with the Frankfurt School and, later, post-structuralist literary criticism, provided a welcome challenge to the newly established orthodoxy of positivism but in doing so, called into question other fundamental academic principles such as a belief in the possibility of arriving at (albeit contestable) truth claims through the pursuit of knowledge, individual reason and rationality. Michel Foucault's argument that there is 'no truly universal truth' and that all knowledge is ideology – in other words, simply a product of the dominant economic and political conditions that gave rise to it – has come to dominate academic thought, particularly within the humanities and social sciences.

Although many thinkers associated with Critical Theory champion the cause of individual liberty, their simultaneous rejection of the notion of autonomy, and the perhaps inevitable interpretation of their ideas as a celebration of relativism, erodes the fundamental tenets of academic freedom. With the abandonment of truth claims, Critical Theory loses its power to be truly critical, and the initial impetus behind scholars' demands for academic freedom is made redundant.

Critical Theory has presented a further, though perhaps less immediately obvious, challenge to academic freedom. Critical Theorists focused attention upon the role of the cultural realm in maintaining the conformity of citizens to an inherently exploitative capitalism. They argued that political and social change could be prompted by developments in the cultural sphere: this turned an older interpretation of Marxism on its head. Rather than material and economic circumstances shaping a dominant hegemony, Critical Theorists argued that cultural change alone could bring about a new consciousness among the working class and that this, in turn, would lead to more structural changes in society. The significance of culture, particularly popular culture in the form of film, music and advertising, was brought to the fore in academic and political discussions.

The seductive power of images and language in creating false needs and selling a consumer lifestyle came to be considered fundamental to understanding the continuation of capitalism. Later, French literary theorists went further in arguing that language helped shape people's perceptions of reality. This foregrounding of images and vocabulary paved the way for an understanding of words as all-powerful in shaping, not just a dominant ideology, but reality itself. The identity of individuals whose autonomy was considered to be constructed through discourse was consequently vulnerable to attack by offending words. Although far from the intention of Critical Theorists, this view would later contribute towards a justification for restrictions on free speech and academic freedom.

The Frankfurt School

The Institute for Social Research at the University of Frankfurt was founded in the aftermath of the First World War and the Russian Revolution. Max Horkheimer brought together like-minded academics to study the foremost social and political problems of a world left shattered by conflict. From the start, the interdisciplinary centre posed a challenge to more traditional academic ways of working. Scholars such as Theodor Adorno, Herbert Marcuse and Walter Benjamin sought to marry philosophy, sociology and psychology – in particular, the works of Marx and Freud – to explain why the working class in Western Europe had not engaged in revolution as had their Russian contemporaries.

Later, focus shifted to explaining why the majority of German citizens went along with the descent into barbarism marked by the rise of fascism, while Russia's communist revolution had given way to Stalin's totalitarianism. The rise of anti-Jewish sentiment within the German academy, discussed in Chapter 1, led key members of the Frankfurt School to flee Germany for America and it was there, in 1937, that the term 'Critical Theory' was coined. The experience of the Second World War brought about a change in emphasis in the work of the Frankfurt School and created an academic and political climate that was significantly more receptive to their ideas.

From the start, members of the Frankfurt School wanted to explore and build upon the works of Marx in order to understand how totalitarian regimes kept society under control. In this, they drew relatively little distinction between Stalinism and fascism, and considered fascism itself to be on a continuum with capitalism rather than something unique. In *Dialectic of Enlightenment*, a key text of the Frankfurt School written during the interwar period and published in 1944, Horkheimer and Adorno claimed, 'One day the Diktat of production, the specific advertisement, veiled by the semblance of choice, can finally become the Führer's overt command' (2002, p. 129). They argued that although the external means for keeping society in control may have varied, the internal logic of capital, and what they assumed to be an illusion of individual autonomy, remained the same. In their bid to critique totalitarianism they focused on some elements of Marx's work, in particular his writing on ideas and consciousness, above others. They were especially interested in Marx's views on the formation of human subjectivity and the role of ideas in encouraging the proletariat's acquiescence to the ruling elite.

Marx argued the material conditions people experienced helped to shape their consciousness: 'By thus acting on the external world and changing it, [man] at the same time changes his own nature' (1977, p. 173). Labour not only produces man's physical means of existence; it simultaneously produces man as a subjective being. However, Marx also recognized that people did not interact with the external world in isolation but experienced it mediated through ideas which had gained dominance within society more broadly; subjectivity was not just created through man's interaction with nature, but through his interaction with others in society. In *The German Ideology* Marx and Engels explained, 'The ideas of the ruling class are in every epoch the ruling ideas, i.e. the class which is the ruling material force of society, is at the same time its ruling intellectual force' (2011, p. 67). Marx argued what is particular about the ideas of the ruling class is that they take the form of universality, the ruling class has to represent its ideas as the 'only rational, universally valid ones' (2011, p. 68).

The Frankfurt School theorists were influenced by Antonio Gramsci's interpretation of Marxism. Gramsci argued that changes in the material circumstances of people's lives, or structural economic changes within society more broadly, do not automatically bring about political change. Rather, Gramsci noted, such economic shifts simply created the conditions in which social change became possible, and it was political factors which determined whether or not change actually happened. He pointed to the political 'relations of force', in particular, 'the degree of political organization and combativity of the opposing forces, the strength of the political alliances which they manage to bind together and their level of political consciousness, of preparation of the struggle on the ideological terrain' (Forgacs, 1999, p. 190), as being crucial in determining the likelihood of social change.

In order to instigate such change, the proletariat needed an understanding of hegemony, or of how the ruling class had made their ideas appear natural, universal and incontrovertible. Gramsci argued that, 'The realization of a hegemonic apparatus, in so far as it creates a new ideological terrain, determines a reform of consciousness and of methods of knowledge: it is a fact of knowledge, a philosophical fact' (in Forgacs, 1999, p. 192). Through foregrounding the importance of knowledge in this way, Gramsci affirmed the educability of the working class, and of some 'organic intellectuals' in particular. The connection Gramsci made between exposing the dominant hegemony and instigating social change was based on his belief in the importance of knowledge and the capacity of people to comprehend and act upon knowledge. Gramsci did not reject elite knowledge; nor did he lose faith in the educability of the working class.

Horkheimer, Adorno and, later, Marcuse further developed Gramsci's concept of hegemony. They explored the processes by which social class divisions were made to appear natural and the ideas of the ruling class seem universal. They sought to explain how a dominant hegemony manifested itself within society. In trying to answer these questions, members of the Frankfurt School were influenced by the work of Sigmund Freud, in particular his argument that people's unconscious being shapes their consciousness. They drew a parallel between Freud's notion of the individual psyche being formed through an interaction between id, superego and ego; and Marx's dialectic of historical struggle and resolution. While society engaged in a struggle between social classes, individuals engaged in a struggle between their experiences of reality and their understanding of the world.

Exploring how the contradictions between an individual's experience and their understanding are resolved so as to sustain existing social relations became a key goal of Critical Theory. Horkheimer and Adorno suggest that capitalism both creates an illusion of personal freedom – 'The blessing that the market does not ask about birth' – while at the very same time constantly restricting liberty: 'the possibilities conferred by birth are molded to fit the production of goods that can be brought on the market' (2002, p. 9).

In highlighting the limitations of 'the possibilities conferred by birth', Horkheimer and Adorno expressed their commitment to bringing about individual freedom and emancipation from both capitalist and communist 'systems'. They recognized that in both instances, the state was able to lessen the impact of the exploitation inherent within the mode of production, but that it did so by using culture to reinforce and conceal the dominant power relations. Critical Theory developed as an approach to exposing these contradictions and took on a renewed urgency with the turn towards fascism in Germany in the 1930s.

By focusing on the concept of hegemony, Critical Theorists highlighted psychological and philosophical rather than just material or economic concerns with capitalism. An interpretation of the Marxist concepts of reification and alienation became central to the Frankfurt School's analysis of how exploitative regimes sustained themselves. The concept of alienation was employed in relation to both individuals and society as a whole to highlight the psychologically damaging consequences of people being subsumed within the totality of a system of production. In their critique of the Enlightenment, Horkheimer and Adorno argued: 'Technical rationality today is the rationality of domination. It is the compulsive character of a society alienated from itself. Automobiles, bombs, and films, hold the totality together until their levelling element demonstrates its power against the very system of injustice it served' (2002, p. 95). Here we see how the intellectual gains of the Enlightenment come to be equated with capitalist exploitation, in the same way that bombs are equated with films.

In the *Dialectic of Enlightenment*, Horkheimer and Adorno explicitly link reification, or the externalization of repressed desires through making abstract and incoherent thoughts and emotions take a concrete form, to the legacy of the Enlightenment. They suggest, 'The expulsion of thought from logic ratifies in the lecture hall the reification of human beings in factory and office' (2002, p. 23). The positivist emphasis on the quantitative over the qualitative is reproduced in the workers' preference for the material over the emotional. Peter Thompson notes that reification 'forms the base of Herbert Marcuse's concept of the one-dimensional man, that dimension representing merely the reified desires of consumer culture' (06/05/13). Marcuse was also critical of the way in which capitalism appeared benign yet subsumed people within an all-encompassing system. He argued that while people's material needs were met and culture convinced people to be happy with what they had, they remained willing victims of their own repression. Constitutional equality simply hid structural inequalities.

The culture industry

In *Dialectic of Enlightenment,* Horkheimer and Adorno turn their attention to the role played by all forms of culture in legitimizing and naturalizing exploitative social relations. They suggest culture plays a specific role within a totalizing system such as capitalism, 'Each single manifestation of the culture industry inescapably reproduces human beings as what the whole has made them' (2002, p. 100). Horkheimer and Adorno were critical of 'high' culture, which they suggest universalized the ideology of the ruling class as a dominant hegemony. However, their primary focus was 'mass' culture, especially film and popular media, which they perceived as crucial in making the working class willing accomplices in their own exploitation.

Mass culture in particular, they argued, was responsible for propagating a false consciousness among the working class whereby capitalism, and social class differences, appeared natural. Mass culture further supported capitalism through artificially creating needs and desires that people could only fulfil through consumption. Horkheimer and Adorno argued that the power of false consciousness lay in the fact that people were enthusiastic consumers of popular culture and no element of coercion was needed to maintain the status quo: 'Entertainment is the prolongation of work under late capitalism. It is sought by those who want to escape the mechanized labour process so that they can cope with it again' (2002, p. 109).

The dishonesty of the culture industry, to Horkheimer and Adorno, lay in its propagation of the view that satisfaction was achievable: 'The culture industry endlessly cheats its consumers out of what it endlessly promises' (2002, p. 111). They held it chiefly responsible for reification: 'The most intimate reactions of human beings have become so entirely reified, even to themselves, that the idea of anything peculiar to them survives only in extreme abstraction: personality means hardly more than dazzling white teeth and freedom from body odour and emotions' (2002, p. 136).

The 1960s student protests led to renewed interest in concepts such as false consciousness, reification and alienation: Herbert Marcuse's *One Dimensional Man*, published in 1964, rapidly became a defining text of the era. Radical students and academics associated with the New Left defined themselves in opposition to Stalinism in Russia and Eastern Europe while also rejecting the resurgent capitalism in the West. Here, the absence of widespread political revolt in conjunction with the triumph of consumer capitalism led followers of the New Left to consider the collusion of the working class with capitalism. Again, the culture industry was implicated in legitimizing this collusion. Writing in an earlier political era, Horkheimer and Adorno had suggested that 'individuals experience themselves through their needs only as eternal consumers, as the culture industry's object'. This sentiment found resonance with the student-led protesters of the 1960s who, unlike the more materially aspirant working class, sought to 'drop out' and reject capitalist consumption.

Politically, the New Left became increasingly focused upon the role of mass culture in sustaining capitalism and, as discussed in the previous chapter, this played out in the academy with the development of new interdisciplinary areas such as Cultural Studies. One key topic of interest was the role culture was perceived to play in propagating a myth of people as autonomous individuals who were able to exercise free choice. Marcuse summed up the mood of the era in his declaration that 'Free choice among a wide variety of goods and services does not signify freedom if these goods and services sustain social controls over a life of toil and fear – that is, if they sustain alienation' (1991, p. 10).

The perception that people laboured under a myth of personal freedom, and had been hoodwinked into believing that it was possible to be in control of their own destinies, created a political divide between those who saw through the workings of the culture industry and those who suffered false consciousness. As Horkheimer and Adorno note, 'As customers *they* are regaled, whether on the screen or in the press, with human interest stories demonstrating freedom of choice and the charm of not belonging to the system. In both cases *they* remain objects' (2002, p. 118, my emphasis). We can see how a distinction begins to emerge between 'us' and 'them'; between those with insight into the system and those who have been duped; between subjects and objects; and between intellectuals and the masses.

Unlike in earlier decades, the ire of political radicals did not stop at the culture industry, but increasingly extended to members of the working class themselves. Workers were seen less as potential comrades and instead as complicit in their own exploitation through willingly sustaining consumption, the culture industry and ultimately capitalism itself. Thompson notes, 'it was during this period that the working class began to be seen as part of the problem rather than the solution' (13/05/15). Political opposition to the role of mass culture in propagating false consciousness and false needs turned, if not directly to opposition towards the consumers of mass culture, then at the very least to either pity or contempt. In a very few decades, the political left's perception of the working class shifted from Gramsci's view of an educable class ('all men are intellectuals') capable of acting upon knowledge to instigate change in their material circumstances, to that of a body of largely uneducable victims of a mass-market culture industry.

While Gramsci had argued that high culture played a role in universalizing the ideas of the ruling class, his faith in the working class led him to conclude that they could appropriate such knowledge without being further conditioned into accepting their subservience. In fact, critical engagement was essential for people to better understand the nature of the dominant hegemony and to capture the culture for themselves. The New Left's questioning of the educability of the working class and belief in the role of all forms of culture in normalizing and reproducing a dominant ideology, led to a reappraisal of Enlightenment thought and, in particular, a problematizing of the notion of individual autonomy and freedom.

Individual freedom

In *One Dimensional Man*, Marcuse argued that any notion of individual freedom under capitalism was illusory. Rather, 'A comfortable, smooth, reasonable, democratic unfreedom prevails in advanced industrial civilization, a token of technical progress' (1991, p. 3). This notion of 'democratic unfreedom' chimed with the broader political climate of the late 1960s, where formal systems of democracy and parliamentary politics came to be seen as increasingly problematic. As Marcuse went on to explain, '"the free society" can no longer be adequately defined in the traditional terms of economic, political and intellectual liberties' – instead, 'Political freedom would mean liberation of the individuals from politics' (1991, p. 6).

Having pointed to a disjuncture between the rhetoric and reality of democratic freedom within capitalism, Marcuse went on to question the possibility for free expression. He argued:

> Freedom of thought, speech and conscience were – just as free enterprise, which they served to promote and protect – essentially critical ideas, designed to replace an obsolescent material and intellectual culture by a more productive and rational one. Once institutionalized, these rights and liberties shared the fate of the society of which they had become an integral part. The achievement cancels the premises.
>
> (1991, p. 4)

Marcuse is correct to identify the significance of free speech in allowing societies to move from a 'know-your-place' feudalism to capitalism premised upon a notion of 'economic individualism'. However, Marcuse assumes that once free market capitalism has been established, free speech becomes incorporated within a totalizing system and rendered meaningless. As freedom within the system is illusory and real freedom is only to be found outside of the system, so too is free speech an elaborate myth.

Marcuse suggests that the concept of free speech is little more than a useful tool to propagate the status quo and replicate existing power relations. This idea was to gain ground within the academy several decades later but there was a further argument that needed to be made before it could fully put down roots.

As we have noted, Critical Theorists questioned the extent to which people could be considered as autonomous and rational beings, capable of exercising agency and determining their own destiny. Instead, it was argued, people simply play out an allotted role within a totalizing system which propagates an illusion of individual freedom. With the 'abolition of the individual', Horkheimer and Adorno argue, 'pseudoindividuality reigns' (2002, pp. 124/125). This view of individuals as playing out a preordained destiny would later be echoed in the French sociologist Pierre Bourdieu's concept of 'habitus'. Bourdieu defined the concept of habitus in relation to the tastes and dispositions people acquire through socialization into family and social class communities. Such dispositions both shape and are further consolidated by future life choices. Rather than rational beings exercising agency, individuals are reduced to 'acting out' a path which is at every stage influenced by their habitus. Robbins notes that, 'Bourdieu's overall position stands Rousseau's contention on its head. It's not that we are born free but are everywhere in chains. On the contrary, we are born in chains and constantly strive to construct the functional fiction that we are free' (1993, p. 159).

Bourdieu's work has gained traction in education research as a means of exploring why some people go to university and others do not, as well as more specifically how individuals select institutions and courses. There are undoubtedly useful insights to be gained from this work and recognizing that people do not make choices in isolation from the rest of their lives, or in circumstances of their own choosing, is important. However, Bourdieu's work builds upon the ideas propounded by members of the Frankfurt School and, when taken to its logical conclusion, contributes towards a downplaying of the concept of individual agency.

When social and political elites assume both a degraded notion of personhood and a greater significance for popular culture, the potential impact of speech – be it in the form of an argument, song or article – is overstated, at the same time as the ability of people to engage critically with challenging or offensive speech is downplayed. When this is combined with a view that all attempts at freedom within capitalism are illusory, arguments for restricting both free speech and academic freedom are able to gain ground.

Challenge to Enlightenment

The Frankfurt School of the 1920s and 1930s emerged as an interdisciplinary exercise at a time when tightly demarcated divisions between academic fields and strict adherence to rules within disciplinary areas determined the shape of academic life. It focused upon ideology at a time when the legitimacy of academic work was based upon a scientific, positivist method. The academy at the beginning of the twentieth century carried the imprint of Enlightenment principles, though it often lacked its spirit of intellectual curiosity and a belief in the capacity for people to reason rather than be reliant upon empirical evidence. The early ideas of the Frankfurt School provided a welcome challenge to an academic environment which risked becoming inflexible in its approach to both content and method.

However, Critical Theory was to develop in such a way that went beyond merely tempering the excesses of the academy's interpretation and enactment of Enlightenment values. It was to call into question the very principles of Enlightenment thought. Rather than stopping at a rejection of the excesses of positivism, later Critical Theorists questioned even the aspiration of truth as the endpoint of the pursuit of knowledge.

The experience of the Second World War, and of the Holocaust in particular, lent weight to counter-Enlightenment thought. The notion that scientific principles could lead to a greater understanding of social problems came to be discredited by association with Nazi ideology. This assumption, however, was underpinned by a false correlation between positivism and the Enlightenment and an erroneous sense that fascists were driven by an obsession with scientific rationality or universal categorization, which, as Bronner (2011) notes, was never the case in reality. Bronner suggests, 'They instead made ideological use of notions like "Jewish physics" or "Italian mathematics."' He argues that the clearest exponents of positivism were politically liberal, such as the philosopher Karl Popper, and that 'contempt for positivism (not its embrace) was a hallmark of fascism' (2011, p. 59). Despite the existence of little evidence to support the frequently propagated notion that Enlightenment values led directly to the logic of the Holocaust, this view became entrenched within society more broadly, and areas of academia more specifically, at this time.

In the decades following the Second World War, work associated with the Frankfurt School that presented a fundamental challenge to the intellectual gains of the Enlightenment received a receptive audience. Critical Theorists went beyond questioning the dominance of positivism and developed a broader critique of rationality, logic and the possibility of arriving at truth. Horkheimer and Adorno challenged the notion that post-Enlightenment society was progressive; anything potentially liberating, they argued, was lost in the submission of individuals to the totality of the system and 'enlightenment is totalitarian as only a system can be' (2002, p. 18). They argued, 'For enlightenment, anything which does not conform to the standard of calculability and utility must be viewed with suspicion' (2002, p. 3), and on this basis rejected the scientific methodologies that had come to dominate all areas of the academy.

Marcuse blamed positivism, 'in its denial of the transcending elements of Reason', for comprising 'the academic counterpart of the socially required behaviour' (1991, p. 16). There is an important point to be made here. With its focus on the empirical and quantifiable, a commitment to positivism often denied the role of individual reason. Independent thought and critical judgement lost out to the authority of the data.

However, having already called into question the notion of individual autonomy, Marcuse could not now employ this as a much-needed temper to the excesses of positivism. As a result, a useful critique of positivism developed into a rejection of its underlying methodological approaches and a broader abandonment of truth claims in relation to knowledge. The concept of truth, it was argued, contributed to reinforcing existing hegemonic assumptions by masking the vested interests of an economic and social elite and presenting their partial understandings as universal facts.

This questioning of both scientific method and the notion of truth was continued and developed most notably by the French intellectual, Michel Foucault. Foucault argued, 'The price Marxists paid for their fidelity to the old positivism was a radical deafness to a whole series of questions posed by science' (1980, p. 110). The main question posed by science that Foucault sought to challenge was the possibility of arriving at truth, however provisionally held. For Foucault, the entire concept of truth was tarnished through association with positivism and scientific method. 'Truth' he argued, 'is centred on the form of scientific discourse and the institutions which produce it; it is subject to constant economic and political incitement'. He continued, 'it is produced and transmitted under the control, dominant if not exclusive, of a few great political and economic apparatuses [...] it is the issue of a whole political debate and social confrontation' (1980, pp. 131/132).

For Foucault, it was not so much that truth did not exist, but rather that truth was a social construction and not a statement about reality:

> 'Truth' is to be understood as a system of ordered procedures for the production, regulation, distribution, circulation and operation of statements. 'Truth' is linked in a circular relation with systems of power which produce and sustain it, and to effects of power which it induces and which extend it.
>
> (1980, p. 133)

Foucault argued truth was nothing other than an expression of the dominant power relations constructed through discourse, 'produced only by virtue of multiple forms of constraint' and inducing 'regular effects of power' (1980, p. 131). Foucault explored the concept of ideology as that which 'stands in a secondary position relative to something which functions as its infrastructure, as its material, economic determinant' and at the same time 'always stands in virtual opposition to something else which is supposed to count as truth'.

'Truth', for Foucault, is not a reflection of reality but a concept or an 'effect' which is 'produced within discourses which in themselves are neither true nor false' (1972, p. 118). As Graham Good suggests,

> Truth is seen either as an outdated concept or as a function of who is speaking: a person's credibility depends on the status of his or her group. All propositions are seen as ideological, as advancing the interests of a group. Knowledge is equated with power. Objectivity and disinterest are dismissed as pretences concealing the motives of power.
>
> (2001, p. 4)

Uncovering layers of multiple discourses would not lead researchers to the truth, according to Foucault, but to a greater understanding of power relations that both produced and were produced through discourse. He proposed a 'genealogy' of knowledge or, in other words, 'a form of history which can account for the constitution of knowledges, discourses, domains of objects etc.' (1980, p. 117).

This unpacking and questioning of knowledge establishes a significant academic principle and raises important questions around the taken-for-granted assumptions surrounding canonical and curricular knowledge in particular. However, the claim that the social and historical context of knowledge can be traced is not the same as arguing that knowledge is reducible simply to a product of the power relations shaped by the historical context in which it was produced. When culture is considered reducible to ideology, and truth constructed through discourse, then the argument that more, or better, knowledge is needed for people to make sense of the world and engage critically with its contents loses out to a view that impartiality, objectivity and rationality need to be treated with suspicion.

This takes us beyond Foucault's useful intellectual insights and has a devastating impact upon the project of knowing the world. As Halsey notes of social science in the 1970s, 'positivism and its patient counting of heads became for some a term of abuse, relieving students of the obligation to read the books so labelled'. He suggests that epistemological nihilism and moral relativism 'removed respectability from all but the totally committed opponents of capitalist society' (2004, p. 119). In rejecting not just what was presented as truth, but the very possibility of making truth claims, Critical Theorists abandoned the intellectual foundations that made criticism possible. Their 'assault on system, logic and narrative' undermined 'the ability to generate criteria for making ethical and political judgements' (Bronner, 2011, p. 33).

Impact on academia

As disillusionment with alternatives to Western capitalist society grew alongside a loss of faith in the ability of the working class to act as a progressive force, increasing numbers of intellectuals looked inward to the university as a potential site for political change. Cultural Studies began life in 1964 but really gained momentum as an academic subject in the 1970s. At the same time, the ideas associated with Critical Theory began to have a broader impact within the humanities and, to a lesser extent, the social sciences. Its impact today can be seen in a number of key areas.

Walter Benjamin's argument that 'There is no cultural document that is not at the same time a record of barbarism' played out in the academy as Horkheimer and Adorno's more moderate assertion that 'the claims of art are always ideology' (2002, p. 103). Such sentiments were taken to the heart of universities primarily through humanities disciplines from the early 1970s onwards. As discussed in Chapter 3, within university English departments, there was a retreat from an Arnoldian or Leavisite liberal humanist appreciation of literature towards literary theory and the study of literature as texts rather than art. The goal of criticism shifted from interpreting to dominating literature. The aim was not to offer an appreciation of art but to deconstruct it and expose it as an instrumental account of power relations.

This posed a fundamental challenge to the nature of disciplinary knowledge. The literary critic Terry Eagleton argued in his now classic work, *Literary Theory: An Introduction*, 'The claim that knowledge should be "value-free" is itself a value-judgement' (2008, p. 12). He went on to explain:

> I do not mean by 'ideology' simply the deeply entrenched, often unconscious beliefs which people hold; I mean more particularly those modes of feeling, valuing, perceiving and believing which have some kind of relation to the maintenance and reproduction of social power.
>
> (2008, p. 13)

Eagleton argues the move towards theory in the 1960s represented a rejection of the idea that great literature could only be appreciated 'by those with a particular sort of cultural breeding'. He suggests, 'Theory was a way of emancipating literary works from the stranglehold of a "civilised sensibility" and throwing them open to a kind of analysis in which, in principle at least, anyone could participate' (2008, p. xii). One impact of this approach to the study of English was that the coherence to the subject, which stemmed from its content, was replaced by an arbitrariness as to what counted as text. As the old rules of judgement were jettisoned, discernment and the exercise of discrimination were also abandoned.

The challenge to both curriculum and canon gathered speed throughout the 1970s and into the 1980s. It moved from universities to schools and back into higher education once more, prompting significant debates about what should be taught and why. Basil Bernstein formally linked the social control function of schooling to the content of the curriculum and the nature of the knowledge taught to children. He noted that, 'Both Durkheim and Marx have shown us that the structure of society's classifications and frames reveals both the distribution of power and the principles of social control' (1971, p. 48). Michael Young took this a step further and drew a connection between the disciplinary function of schooling and the social construction of knowledge, asking: 'Are we then reluctant to accept that academic curricula and the forms of assessment associated with them are sociological inventions to be explained like men's other inventions, mechanical and sociological?' (1971, p. 41).

It came to be accepted that selection of cultural content, be it in the form of a canon or a curriculum, was a site of vested interests. The assumption was that education should move away from a straightforward transmission of knowledge, or the promotion of an appreciation of arts in an Arnoldian sense, towards the exposure of ideology.

When all knowledge and culture are considered reducible to ideology, the argument that more knowledge, better knowledge or a greater degree of criticality is needed loses out to a view that impartiality, objectivity and rationality need to be treated with suspicion or dismissed as ideological cover-ups for patriarchy and the vested interests of a dominant social class (see Good, 2001, p. 17). This shifts the focus of education away from a concern with knowledge for its own sake, or for the better appreciation of high culture, towards the idea of the curriculum as a construction which serves the politicized interests of the ruling elite. Louis Althusser (1971) classified schooling as part of the ideological state apparatuses which he described as functioning 'massively and predominantly *by ideology*', although, he noted, 'they also function secondarily by repression, even if ultimately, but only ultimately, this is very attenuated and concealed, even symbolic' (1971, p. 141). This led educators to ask important questions about the role that schooling played in disciplining, preparing and sorting children for an 'allotted' role in life.

The equation of culture, and more recently knowledge, with ideology was used to draw attention to the role of education in transmitting a dominant cultural hegemony from one generation to the next. When knowledge was reducible to ideology, teaching could be seen as the imposition of a particular hegemonic perspective in order to further the interests of a social elite. This involved acts of 'symbolic violence' as working class children were enculturated into what was considered to be an alien ideological outlook. Bourdieu and Passeron argued, 'All pedagogic action (PA) is, objectively, symbolic violence in so far as it is the imposition of a cultural arbitrary by an arbitrary power' (1977, p. 5). They continued:

> In any given social formation the cultural arbitrary which the power relations between the groups or classes making up that social formation put into the dominant position within the system of cultural arbitraries is the one which most fully, though always indirectly, expresses the objective interests (material and symbolic) of the dominant groups or classes.
>
> (1977, p. 9)

The notion that curricular content spoke to particular class interests rather than any universal human interests was reinforced by Bourdieu and Passeron's argument that:

> The selection of meanings which objectively defines a group's or a class's culture as a symbolic system is arbitrary insofar as the structure and functions of that culture cannot be deduced from any universal principle, whether physical, biological or spiritual, not being linked by any sort of internal relation to 'the nature of things' or any 'human nature'.
>
> (1977, p. 8)

While schooling could enforce obedience upon children through rules and punishments designed to modify behaviour, it was the teaching of culture which was considered to serve as 'a vital instrument' for the 'deeper entrenchment and wider dissemination' of certain social values (Eagleton, 2008, p. 16). For radical educators, teaching high culture has little merit beyond an opportunity to expose the ways in which hegemonic values are given the appearance of universality. Curriculum content has come to be determined less on the intrinsic merit of the knowledge to be covered than on the perspectives it represents. By this argument, classic texts, especially those written by 'Dead White European Men', have less to offer students than works by people previously under-represented within the academy. Students are encouraged, not to take ownership of an intellectual birth right and to make it anew for their own generation, but to reject the past in favour of an ever-present focus on identity.

The questioning of the role played by knowledge in enforcing a dominant hegemony led to knowledge being perceived in a very instrumental sense as a means to an end and a way of promoting particular political objectives, usually those of the dominant elite. The Frankfurt School-inspired project of exposing how high culture was not universal but a codification of elite values resulted in attempts to subvert the role of education through encouraging the teaching of counter-hegemonic knowledge. Marcuse wanted to employ art and technology to reveal to people the possibilities for their own liberation. Later, Habermas (1985) argued that knowledge and interest are one, and that communicative action could become a vehicle for resistance.

This view, while appearing radical, does little to challenge the instrumentalization of knowledge. It is simply an alternative ideology that is being promoted. Furthermore, it has the consequence of relativizing what counts as knowledge: high culture is rejected in favour of the study of the everyday. This suggests that there is no intrinsic sense of beauty or value in art. Yet artists, writers and composers were rarely working as agents of the state; their primary intention was not to promote a hegemonic position but a work of art. Similarly, readers and other consumers of culture are not so shallow as to imbibe uncritically. People can read, appreciate and, importantly, criticize high culture – but they do this all the better from a position of knowledge.

In opposition to the relativist view of knowledge and the curriculum stands a liberal humanist perspective. Graham Good argues that the core value of a liberal humanist approach to education is 'freedom of inquiry, discussion and research. Teaching is viewed as an open exploration of texts and ideas without a predetermined outcome. The aim is to teach students how to think rather than what to think' (2001, p. 16). This assumes people are more than mere siphons of the dominant ideology and that culture is about more than just a crude attempt at masking and repackaging power relations. In so doing it makes criticism possible.

Language shapes reality

Since the 1970s, what was once perceived as a radical counterpoint to dominant academic thought has itself become increasingly mainstream within higher education. The post-structuralist idea that truth is relative, context-dependent and constructed through discourse, found a particularly warm welcome within the humanities, particularly in literature departments. Although those most closely associated with post-structuralism were philosophers rather than literary theorists, it was English that was most open to their influence. English easily took on board the ideas of Critical Theory, as both its content – literature, and its medium – language, were open to question. The selection of works for study could no longer be justified on the basis of tradition, and the whole concept of the canon, as well as approaches to its critique, were to be treated with suspicion. As Eagleton puts it, '"pure" literary theory is an academic myth', as it is another means of serving and reinforcing 'the particular interests of particular groups of people at particular times' (1983, p. 170). After having established itself within English, Critical Theory began to reach out to influence other disciplines within the humanities.

With the view that notions of truth were constructed through discourse and dependent upon the identity of the individual doing the proclaiming, language itself became implicated in shaping ideology. Years after Horkheimer and Adorno had argued that language was an 'an instrument of power' (2002, p. 29), structuralists, influenced by the work of the Swiss linguist Ferdinand Saussure, highlighted the arbitrary relationship between language (signifiers) and reality (signified). This led to an interest in the role of language in shaping people's perceptions of reality. It produced the politically driven notion that changing language could become a means of altering power relationships.

Foucault takes arguments about social constructionism to their logical conclusion and argues not that language represents reality, but rather that it constructs reality. He suggests that discourse could no longer be treated as 'groups of signs (signifying elements referring to contents or representations) but as practices that systematically form the objects of which they speak' (1989, p. 54). Eagleton, in arguing, 'What is thinkable will of course be constrained by the language itself [...] certain meanings and positions will not be articulable within it' (1983, p. 175), does not go so far; he is suggesting that language shapes our perceptions of reality but he is not denying that reality exists: there is life beyond discourse. For Foucault, however, discourse *is* reality, 'One remains within the dimension of discourse' (1989, p. 85). Similarly, for later post-structuralists, signifiers referred only to other signifiers without ever reaching a final signified. As Good suggests, 'the new Theorists developed a strange kind of reversed Marxism, where representation produces reality and not the other way round' (2001, p. 43).

Literary theorists in the 1970s and 1980s, unable to assert the authority of text or language, looked instead for new ways to highlight the socially constructed nature of both. They were influenced by trends in post-structuralism, feminism and psychoanalysis. The French psychoanalyst Jacques Lacan's statement that 'It is the world of words that creates the world of things' (2004, p. 229) echoed Foucault's emphasis on discourse. The French philosopher Jacques Derrida further emphasized this point with his claim that, 'There is nothing outside of the text' (1967). Derrida denies that meaning is first embodied outside of language and then captured, or reflected, in it; instead he asserts that meaning is an effect of, or produced through, language.

Without a relationship to reality, the meaning of texts becomes elusive and entirely contestable. Derrida suggests that as texts are all form and no content, then arriving at meaning is impossible and we only see the world through an endless interplay of differences; meaning *becomes* difference. As the philosopher Raymond Tallis suggests, this implies signs refer only to other signs, and that 'the chain of signs is endless; or, rather, it terminates only where it breaks down, where interpretation generates something that resists interpretation – that is, in other words, unintelligible' (1988, p. 91). However, people can only live their lives by making sense of the world they inhabit; people form meanings, both individually and collectively within society. They can do so precisely because words stand in relationship to an existing reality; this is what makes communication possible. As Good argues, it is the 'system of differences' that 'makes language so successful at distinguishing various aspects of reality' (2001, p. 51).

The separation of language and meaning further called into question the significance and nature of literature as a category type. It was no longer considered to be the case that literature universalized an ideological perspective that favoured a ruling elite, but rather that as simply 'books' or 'texts' it referred to nothing beyond other books or texts. Foucault argued:

> The frontiers of a book are never clear-cut: beyond the title, the first lines, and the last full-stop, beyond its internal configuration

> and its autonomous form, it is caught up in a system of references to other books, other texts, other sentences: it is a node within a network.
>
> (1989, p. 26)

In this way, literature came to be seen as entirely self-referential: there was neither an escape from previous texts nor a possibility of referring to a world beyond text. The theory of intertextuality reinforced what Tallis refers to as 'the closed system view of language', that is, 'the view that reality is not independent of language and the view that language cannot reach outside of itself to a genuine extra linguistic reality' (1988, p. 16).

Myth of the autonomous self

If literature has no relationship to a world beyond text but refers only to other works of literature, then the unique role of the author, as the authoritative creator of the text, is called into question. The individual was seen as responsible not for creating a text, still less a work of literature, so much as constructing a discourse from pre-existing language and concepts. The idea of intertextuality gained ground as a means of challenging the nature of authorship, the concept of authorial intent and the existence of meaning, or reality, beyond the text. Julia Kristeva speaks of 'the notion of intertextuality' coming 'to have the place of the notion of intersubjectivity' (in Tallis, 1988, p. 46).

Just as reality dissolves into discourse, so too the concept of the self, the autonomous individual, the agent capable of exercising personal freedom, is also reducible to a web of discourse. Roland Barthes decreed, 'the birth of the reader must be ransomed by the death of the Author' (1977, p. 148). This further reinforced the idea that texts had no fixed meaning, not even a meaning intended by the author, but were open to a multitude of different interpretations with every new reader.

When everything, even individuals, can be considered as discourse, or text, the aim of theory becomes the deconstruction of text and with it the deconstruction of the individual who is also constructed through discourse. As Catherine Belsey notes, 'it is language which offers the possibility of constructing a world of individuals and things, and differentiating between them' (2002, pp. 2–3).

Individuals are seen as intersubjective entities, identifiable only at the boundaries between their relationships with other individuals. Eagleton, for example, is scornful of the assumption that 'at the centre of the world is the contemplative individual self, bowed over its book, striving to gain touch with experience, truth, reality, history or tradition' (1983, p. 171). He criticizes liberal humanism for constructing a view of individual freedom while 'the freedom of any particular individual is crippled and parasitic as long as it depends on the futile labour and active oppression of others' (1983, p. 181).

Exposing the 'myth' of individual autonomy is presented as a radical anti-capitalist critique that challenges the notion that people are willing workers and enthusiastic consumers. However it also leads to an attack not just on the possibility of individual freedom within capitalism, but on the very notion of individual autonomy and the possibility of liberty.

Individuals who perceive themselves as lacking autonomy and constructed through relationships and discourse are uniquely vulnerable to attacks on their sense of self. As Good puts it, 'The unity of the self is dissolved by the assertion that the apparent autonomy and liberty of the subject is actually a construct of bourgeois ideology which we have now outlived or seen through' (2001, p. 49). This challenges the very tenets of what it means to be human. Without control over our own destiny, aspirations for emancipation are pointless; we are reduced to the level of automatons in some unknowable and uncontrollable system. The gains of the Enlightenment, the assertion of humanity as in control of its own destiny, are surrendered.

The end of criticism

As literary criticism rejected any relationship between text and a reality beyond the text, there could be no objectively correct readings, merely subjective interpretations that were themselves bound within discourse. The subjective identities of both author and reader, as constructed through discourse and in relation to other subjects, became pre-eminent. This focus on a fragile and constructed subjectivity, rather than an autonomous and rational individual, marked the final end of any appreciation of literature in the Leavisite sense. Instead, readers were asked to appreciate, or respect, the subjective responses of author and other readers.

The shift from appreciation of literature to respect for identity was encapsulated in the move towards postmodernism, the influence of post-colonialism and, as will be explored more fully in the next chapter, the impact of feminism. Eagleton welcomes the focus upon post-colonialism and feminism as a 'return to everyday cultural and political life' (2008, p. ix). The logical consequence of demanding respect for competing identity claims is a relativism where there is no basis for judging some ideas better than others, and a breakdown in not just the possibility of communication, but the aspiration for communication.

When criticism comes to be about respect for identity rather than passing judgement, it becomes increasingly conformist in nature. There are no new truth claims being made to challenge existing understandings: 'Concepts of truth, fact, and certainty have been eclipsed by theories of social constructionism and contingency' (Koppelman, 2015, p. 204). Rather, alternative perspectives based on standpoints are projected with no basis for critique.

As far back as 1964, Susan Sontag argued that 'the project of interpretation is largely reactionary, stifling' and that 'Interpretation makes art manageable, conformable' (2013, p. 8). If criticism is not concerned with counterposing one idea to another, then academic freedom becomes unnecessary. Menand points out that this state of intellectual affairs has

> made it seem so difficult to argue that professors need the protections associated with the concept of academic freedom, since so many professors in the humanities are now willing to assert that their work is not about reaching the truth about a field, but about intervening in a conversation – a 'discourse' – that is already partial and political.
>
> (1996, p. 12)

The impact of Critical Theory goes further; it tames criticism by denying any connection with a reality beyond the text and any connection between authorial intent and text. The plethora of readers' interpretations, each equally demanding of respect, renders criticism meaningless. Worse, it enforces conformity because when people's identities are fragile constructions and words are a source of oppression and a threat to identity then people are encouraged to think carefully before passing any comment whatsoever. Theory, it seems, 'creates an undeclared politics of representation that determines what may or may not be said' (Good, 2001, p. 52). The veneer of criticality attached to Critical Theory allows it to assume an illusion of subversion while at the same time posing no challenge to any particular viewpoint, least of all the status quo.

6
The Impact of Feminism

Feminist scholars are often at the forefront of arguing that academic freedom is an outdated, elitist concept that needs to be redefined to allow greater opportunity for the voices of under-represented groups to be heard. This chapter focuses upon how such attempts to redefine academic freedom and curb free speech on campus often emerge from the notion that there are gendered ways of knowing and a particularly feminist concept of knowledge.

Feminist thought has moved a long way from demanding that the intellectual gains of higher education be made equally available to men and women. From the early nineteenth century until after the Second World War, individual women fought for, and often won, the chance to pursue and develop knowledge for themselves. In challenging the idea that learning mathematics or science was unfeminine, such 'bluestockings' had to overcome obstacles and continually prove themselves to be both academically capable and morally virtuous in a way that was not expected of men (Robinson, 2010). These pioneers were clear about the reward for doing so: access to the same knowledge that men were being taught. Women were not expected to take up graduate-level jobs after leaving university and so they were granted admission to institutions without any possibility of receiving a final degree qualification. It was not until 1948 that women were permitted to graduate from the University of Cambridge.

Since this time, women, and feminism in particular, have had an impact upon all areas of higher education from who attends university to what is considered legitimate knowledge. However, it is important that the changes brought about in the name of feminism are placed within a broader context. Feminism, as a political movement, began outside of the academy and made significant social gains long before it was legitimized within universities. Its eventual incorporation within the academy from the mid-1960s onwards needs to be seen in conjunction with other social and intellectual developments also occurring at this time.

In the US, and later in the UK, the post-war baby boom and an improving national economy led to overall growth in numbers attending university. This gradually led to greater diversity within the student body, with middle-class white women being the first group to benefit to any great extent. However, these women joined a higher education sector already undergoing considerable change, not just in terms of the student body but in overall sense of purpose. In 1963, British Prime Minister-elect Harold Wilson hailed the era of 'the white heat of technology'. In the same year, the Robbins Report argued for educational expansion as a means of capitalizing upon scientific and technological advance that would in turn have a direct impact upon the national economy (see Williams, 2013, p. 32). The universities women began to enter in large numbers were a far cry from the bastions of liberal education that had only ever really existed in a very few institutions for a short period of time.

By the 1970s, the years of steady growth in the proportion of female students slowly began to have an impact on the number of women academics, researchers and senior administrators. Women had entered the academy in significant numbers at the same time that second wave feminism, with its assertion that 'the personal is political', gained momentum within society more broadly. People influenced by this burgeoning women's liberation movement met an academic environment that, through the discrediting of positivism, the post-war challenge to Enlightenment thought and the influence of Critical Theory, was slowly becoming receptive to new ideas about the nature of knowledge. The notion that traditional bodies of knowledge were ideologically neutral, or that an objective truth could be a conceivable end point of research, was already being called into question. Feminism's further challenge to the content of the curriculum and ways of knowing ultimately fell on fertile ground.

Academic feminism has been most influential in shifting the direction of scholarship towards a focus on identity and a preoccupation with the self. Identity politics takes its clearest expression within feminism and, in turn, feminists have been quick to exploit broader trends in identity politics. This turn towards identity rejects any sense that knowledge is of universal relevance and abandons an aspiration towards truth claims as the goal of research. Whereas the rationality of the Enlightenment demanded a separation of ideas and self, today this has given way to a privileging of the subjective, and one consequence of this is a heightened sensitivity to perceived offence. This chapter explores the challenge that feminism poses to the pursuit of knowledge and the impact this has upon academic freedom.

Challenging knowledge

When feminist thought first began to make an impact upon the academy in the late 1960s and early 1970s, it chimed with other intellectual trends such as post-structuralism and the new sociology of education that were also beginning to question the composition of the canon and the taken-for-granted nature of knowledge. An initial priority for feminist scholars was to address the under-representation of women writers and thinkers within the higher education curriculum. It was argued that in many academic disciplines the intellectual contribution made by women was not recognized (Solomon, 1985, p. 79).

This early challenge was not to knowledge itself, but to the assumption that knowledge was ideologically neutral. Feminist academics argued that all 'scholarship reflected the perspectives and ideals of its creators' and that established canons reproduced patriarchal and elitist assumptions (Nicholson, 1990, p. 3). The dominance of work by men did not always mean their work was intellectually superior; rather, such work confirmed the political outlook of those constructing the curriculum. An alternative feminist canon, it was argued, would be neither more nor less political than traditional bodies of knowledge; it would simply represent previously marginalized voices.

This interrogation of contemporary practice provided a useful challenge to tradition and prevented the university curriculum ossifying through being passed without criticism from one generation to the next. Today it is unusual for academics to construct a course or reading list that does not include women writers. In addition, it can no longer be assumed that teaching a traditional, male-dominated curriculum, such as Shakespeare or Milton, to literature students, is of value unless it is taught in such a way as to expose the reproduction of power relations, including those forged by patriarchy.

Questioning the way universities reproduced existing power relations and played a conservative role in presenting new generations of students with incontestable knowledge was an important development. However, it would be wrong to infer from this that feminism and other intellectual challenges to the status quo were readily welcomed into the disciplinary structures of the day. Feminist thought was initially perceived as a threat to existing practice and, much like Cultural Studies, had to forge a way in to the academy – first as a separate interdisciplinary entity in the form of Women's Studies.

The first Women's Studies course was developed at Cornell University in 1969, with degree programmes established at many American universities throughout the 1970s. The scholarly journal *Feminist Studies* launched in America in 1972. In the UK, the first academic conference on feminism took place at Ruskin College Oxford in 1970, and was primarily attended by female academics and postgraduate students from across a range of disciplines, but most notably from sociology. Ideas and theories were influenced by key feminist texts to have emerged from outside the academy by writers such as Simone de Beauvoir and Betty Friedan. Women's Studies formally entered UK higher education as interdisciplinary research centres offering postgraduate degrees. The University of Kent's MA in Women's Studies, the first formally accredited taught programme, was established in 1980 (Downing, 20/06/13).

In developing away from the strictures of traditional academic subjects, scholars involved with Women's Studies were free both to investigate new areas of research and to adopt new methodological approaches. As a new academic field, Women's Studies was liberated from the need to locate its emergent theories within the context of an existing body of knowledge. Instead, texts, theories and methods were selected from across disciplinary boundaries, often in previously overlooked pockets of academic work, and from outside of the university altogether.

The idea that 'the personal is political' drove Women's Studies lecturers' interest in teaching and researching topics connected to the private sphere of relationships and the family, 'from the state and the economy to such domains as sexuality and mental health' (Nicholson, 1990, p. 4). It paved the way for the emergence of more qualitative research methods that explored women's daily lives and subjective identities. Carolyn Steedman's *Landscape for a Good Woman* (1986) explored the lives of working-class women through autobiography and the life history of her mother; she argued that interpretation 'can only be made with what people know of a social world and their place within it' (1986, p. 5). This push by Women's Studies to open up new areas of research and emphasize the qualitative over the quantitative was a further important, and potentially progressive, development within the post-war academy. The knowledge base of Women's Studies brought together interdisciplinary sources with work produced from outside of the academy, and introduced new topics and approaches to research.

More problematic, however, was the explicit endeavour to combine an approach to knowledge with a political imperative to instigate change. Feminist sociologist Miriam David describes Women's Studies at this time as being 'based upon essentially intellectual ideas' but notes that 'its aim was to challenge political ideas to transform women's positions in social and public life, questioning their traditional confinement to the private family' (2004, p. 106). Others point to the imperative towards action as providing an important counterbalance to postmodernism: 'Women whose theorising was to serve the struggle against sexism were not about to abandon powerful political tools merely as a result of intramural debates in professional philosophy' (Fraser and Nicholson, 1990, p. 26).

The aims of teaching and research in Women's Studies were quite explicitly political in their concern with, as David identifies, the 'deep power relations between men and women' (2004, p. 103). By legitimizing the politicization of academic work, Women's Studies and feminist academics more broadly, consciously abandoned the aspiration towards objectivity. The role of researcher and teacher no longer assumed a position of neutrality; an instrumental approach to teaching and research in order to promote particular political rather than intellectual goals was assumed. Gradually this new approach to academic work began to have an impact beyond the confines of Women's Studies and across the academy more broadly.

Throughout the 1980s and into the 1990s, more women entered the academy than ever before. In the UK, female students first outnumbered male students in 1992 and this has remained the case every year since. It was also the case that by the 1990s, greater numbers of women influenced by feminism had embarked upon postgraduate study and taken up academic positions across all disciplinary areas. As this happened, feminist thought moved from the sidelines to the mainstream of the university, although its influence varied considerably by discipline. As with Critical Theory, the impact of feminism has been most acute within the social sciences and humanities.

Feminism became embedded within academic disciplines that had already become accustomed to questioning assumptions about curriculum content, pedagogy and the nature of knowledge. This challenged not just the content of the canon but the very concept of passing judgement and arguing for some works to be more worthy of study than others. As American scholar Christina Hoff Sommers notes, 'Talk of "greatness" and "masterpieces" implies a ranking of artists and works, a "hierarchical" approach considered to be unacceptable because it implicitly denigrates those who are given lesser status. The very idea of "genius" is regarded with suspicion as elitist and "masculinist" ' (1994, p. 65). Feminist literary theorists began to argue for the inclusion of texts within the curriculum not on the basis of their inherent worth but as an instrumental means of exploring the construction of patriarchy as 'perhaps the most pervasive ideology of our culture' and one that 'provides its most fundamental concept of power' (Millet in Moi, 1989, p. 118).

Academic feminism combined with other contemporary intellectual trends, most notably postmodernism, to interrogate contemporary approaches to scholarship. This lent further weight to schools of thought influenced by Critical Theory and the work of Continental philosophers such as Foucault, Derrida and Barthes, who were calling into question the possibility and the desirability of truth and objectivity as goals of academic work. Nicholson, writing in *Feminism/Postmodernism*, notes, 'there are many points of overlap between a postmodern stance and positions long held by feminists. Feminists, too, have uncovered the political power of the academy and of knowledge claims. In general, they have argued against the supposed neutrality and objectivity of the academy' (1990, p. 5).

Collectively, these schools of thought challenged the assumption that the role of scholarship was to critique existing knowledge and to counterpose new truth claims. Instead, the postmodernist claim was 'that the pursuit of totalising theory is mistaken, for such theory is inevitably "essentialist" in that it makes invalid generalisations, universalising what should be seen as local and historically specific' (Crowley and Himmelweit, 1992, p. 3). This led to a rejection of traditional epistemological beliefs and methodological approaches. It initiated what David refers to as 'a major shift from "outsider" and objective approaches and accounts to more subjective and "insider" approaches' to research and teaching (2004, p. 103). Feminist philosopher Judith Butler is typical in questioning the assumption that knowledge progresses in an augmented, linear fashion that she argues 'is hardly represented by any of the prevailing paradigms of knowledge in the humanities or, indeed, the social sciences'. She proposes instead that 'how we conceive of knowledge has everything to do with what we consider our professional activity to be, and to be for' (2006a, p. 111).

Butler's arguments build upon the assumption, entrenched within the humanities and social sciences since the 1960s, that knowledge was not empirically discoverable but socially constructed. The primary motivation of feminist scholars became to expose and critique knowledge that had been constructed according to, or in defence of, patriarchal power relations while enabling the construction of new knowledge that put women, and feminism, to the fore. Feminist scholars, like many other academics influenced by postmodernism, argue that there is no one particular body of academic knowledge worth learning. David labels this moment the 'social and cultural turn' and argues it has 'led to a diversity of biographical, autobiographical and personal subjective theories and practices within sociology and the wider forms of policy sociology and sociology of education' (2004, p. 106).

When separated from a particular body of knowledge, yet explicitly political in its aims, higher education comes to be concerned with personal projects of transformation that enable people to recognize their own privileges and limitations. One example of how this has played out in practice can be seen in the way the feminist mantra that the personal is political has been incorporated into academic work. There is now a widely held assumption that the voice of the researcher should be recognized, and that the subjective or even emotional response to the research topic be acknowledged. Most recently this has led to researchers themselves being considered a legitimate source of enquiry in autoethnography, auto/biographical research or the more colloquially labelled 'mesearch' (Rees, 19/03/15). Feminism is not solely responsible for the appropriation of the self into scholarship, but it has been influential in the widespread adoption of such trends into the humanities and social science disciplines. Such ideas, chiming as they did with other branches of postmodernist thought, have become mainstream within the academy to such an extent that the fundamental challenge they pose to education is often overlooked.

The social construction of gender

The view that all knowledge was socially constructed led to the major intellectual assertion of academic feminism that gender itself was not a result of biology but a product of society: people were not born as men or women, but were socialized into acting in gender-specific ways from the moment of their birth. This idea that gender was separate from sex, socially constructed and enacted in performance came to dominate feminist thought in the late 1980s and early 1990s. Butler argued, 'gender is in no way a stable identity or locus of agency from which various acts proceed; rather, it is an identity tenuously constituted in time – an identity instituted through a stylized repetition of acts' (1988, p. 519).

This view promoted a paradigm shift in the way issues concerning women were discussed within the academy. As Hoff Sommers notes, ' "the sex/gender system" became 'the "controlling insight" of academic feminism', and, once made visible, 'we can see it everywhere' (1994, p. 26). As well as texts and ideas being interrogated for their reproduction of patriarchal relationships, they could also be used to explore the means by which both men and women were conditioned into performing gender roles.

The argument that all knowledge, including understandings of gender differences, was socially constructed challenged the view that men and women made sense of the world, or constructed knowledge, in the same way. It was argued that ways of knowing were gender-specific and that women's particular experiences of the world led them to a different understanding than men. In *Knowing Women,* Helen Crowley and Susan Himmelweit argue that women have a 'specifically gendered consciousness' (1992, p. 5). Such claims resulted in a rejection of the assumption that knowledge had the potential to be universal or of a relevance that superseded gender divisions; instead it was assumed that 'the norm itself comes from a model which is completely inappropriate to understanding a gendered, self-reproducing society' (Crowley and Himmelweit, 1992, p. 2). The Victorian argument that women and men were more suited to learning different types of knowledge was being replayed, only this time it was feminists who claimed women were different only as a result of society rather than biology.

The belief in ways of knowing that were specific to women celebrated the qualitative, emotional and subjective over the quantitative, rational and objective. As Daphne Patai and Noretta Koertge explain, 'Logic, the analysis of arguments, quantitative reasoning, objective evaluation of evidence, fair minded consideration of opposing views – modes of thinking central to intellectual life – were dismissed as masculinist contrivances that served only to demean and oppress women' (2003, pp. xiii/xiv). Feminist academics argued that a shift towards the subjective revealed understandings previously denied a place within the academy. Feminist epistemology is less concerned with bringing all people closer to truth than it is upon uncovering particular experiences and interpretations of the world. In this goal, feminism is not unique; it provides the most coherent example of the influence of postmodernism and identity politics within the academy.

It was a short leap from arguing that men and women had different but equally valid ways of knowing, to the assumption that women's understandings were superior. Some feminist academics assumed that patriarchal social relations negatively affected both men and women and prevented men from having an unbiased view of reality. The experience of growing up female and always 'exiled' on the other hand, offered women the possibility of becoming organic feminist 'dissident intellectuals' who would employ thought 'as an "analytic position" that affirms dissolution and works through differences [...] in the face of conceptual, subjective and linguistic identity' (Kristeva 1986, p. 299 in Brooker, 1999). It was women's experiences within the private sphere, and as subordinate members of society, that were thought to give them, not just a different perspective, but an understanding that was grounded in a greater sensitivity to the emotional realm and therefore intellectually superior. Sandra Harding argues a feminist vantage point is 'more illuminating than any existing vantage point' (in Nicholson, 1990, p. 7). Women, having experienced 'reproductive as well as productive labour' were considered 'able to develop a more objective viewpoint than men who have more restricted experience and have more to gain from hiding the truth' (Crowley and Himmelweit, 1992, p. 4).

The argument that female perspectives are somehow more objective masks the essential 'veriphobia' at the heart of academic feminism. Hoff Sommers notes, 'It is now common practice to use scare quotes to indicate the feminist suspicion of a "reality" peculiar to male ways of knowing'. She highlights the work of the feminist philosopher Joyce Treblicot who 'speaks of "the apparatuses of 'truth,' 'knowledge' 'science' that men use to "project their personalities as reality"' (1994, pp. 65/66). The privileging of women's knowledge represented the triumph of the subjective or 'that combination of conscious and unconscious thoughts and emotions that make up our sense of ourselves, our relation to the world and our ability to act in that world' (Crowley and Himmelweit, 1992, p. 7).

This feminist challenge to Enlightenment thought is presented by Judith Butler as a battle between radical new ideas and the prevailing consensus. She reminds us of the importance of being able to challenge the professional norms 'that dictated how and in what form thinking was permitted to occur' (2006a, p. 141). Her argument is that the rules of the academy, the very norms that regulated and drove the pursuit of knowledge, were themselves underpinned by elitist and patriarchal values and needed to be challenged. Instead of arguing that women had an equal right to contribute to the pursuit of knowledge as men under existing rules, Butler suggests a better course of action is to change the rules altogether. Such a radical course suggests that because the Enlightenment values that determined the pursuit of knowledge were devised primarily by men, they have nothing positive to offer society as a whole or women in particular.

Butler rejects the traditional academic goal of objectivity, along with the importance of skepticism and truth claims, and argues that alternative methods for the pursuit of knowledge are more progressive. However, when the idea that knowledge progresses through competing truth claims is rejected, it becomes difficult to argue that some knowledge or understandings are better than any others. Without an agreed basis for passing judgement, feminism loses out because its ideas are not counterposed to existing understandings but rely offering an alternative viewpoint. New knowledge can no longer challenge that which has gone before.

This shift in academic feminism, from arguing for equality under existing structures to demanding the abolition of the principles that underpinned scholarship for centuries, fundamentally alters the nature of academic work. Traditional disciplinary structures meant that the academy as a whole could withstand poor scholarship, as processes of peer review and new intellectual challenges would eventually establish some work as having longevity and leave other work forgotten. By arguing for different norms, feminism poses no challenge to mainstream views. The radical rejection of the entire academic edifice makes it impossible to argue that teaching, or knowing, any particular content is more worthwhile than any other content. As such, the very basis of critical thinking – knowledge – is also rejected. Ironically, as Patai and Koertge suggest, academic feminism did not have to lead in this direction: the 'justified critique of much traditional knowledge as biased and limited (if not overtly misogynist), and therefore ultimately erroneous, could have led it to claim the high ground by insisting on broader, more balanced, less biased curricula and research' (2003, p. 10).

Feminist pedagogy

The feminist and postmodernist rejection of all truth claims was presented as 'a subversive response to oppression' and 'an act of liberation and empowerment' (Bailey, 2001, p. 166). In locating claims for intellectual insight within women's experiences of subordination, feminist scholars were drawing a direct link between oppression and access to knowledge. Sandra Lee Bartky describes the notion of a specifically feminist consciousness as 'a consciousness of victimization' (1975). It is women's status as victims of patriarchy that is assumed to give them a greater understanding than men: oppression is considered to lead women to develop a superior value system and more finely tuned sense of morality. By this logic, the most victimized sections of society are deemed to have the best understandings of the way the world works.

In the space of just three decades, academic feminism moved from controversially arguing that women writers and thinkers were equally as deserving of a place in the curriculum as their male contemporaries, to the widely accepted belief that there were distinctly female ways of knowing that offered a superior insight into subjective experiences of the world. This intellectual shift is highly problematic for the pursuit of knowledge, as it claims special insight for people based upon their biology or their lived experiences (Rauch, 2014, p. 56). The liberal academic project brokers no such special status, and demands that ideas be judged unencumbered from the identity of their originator. When they are not, assumptions about judging the quality or veracity of new knowledge are also called into question. Thus, Crowley and Himmelweit suggest that new parameters for testing feminist knowledge focus upon 'political effectiveness' (1992, p. 4).

The link between intellectual insight and oppression paves the way for more oppressed groups to trump the claims of feminist scholars in a process of identity-driven one-upmanship. As a result, feminist scholars become committed to maintaining women's status as victims, and with every social and political advance made they are obliged to seek out new sites of inequality. Patai and Koertge argue such logic indicates 'women who do not feel crippled by sexism must "learn" that in fact they were – and are – victims of this cultural offense' (2003, p. 77). They go on to suggest that, 'One effect of these practices is to stretch the meaning of words such as harassment and racism, so that everyone in the group is able to qualify as a victim' (2003, p. 78).

When women's superior insight is dependent upon the assumption that they are oppressed, academic feminism has little incentive to question the existence of either oppression or oppressors. Rather, its explicitly political aims demand women are aware of their status as victims yet at the same time celebrate this 'difference' as offering them a special intellectual and emotional understanding. It achieves this by arguing that logic and rationality are specifically masculine, and therefore negative, while subjectivity, instinct and emotion are distinctly feminine traits and therefore positive attributes for academic work. The risk with such assumptions, as Hoff Sommers notes, is that it 'allows insecure men once again to patronize and denigrate women as the naive sex that thinks with its heart and not with its head' (1994, p. 77).

Higher education as a whole is criticized by feminist academics for valuing competition, individual achievement and objectivity over cooperation, empathy and subjectivity. In order for students to engage in academic enquiry, it was traditionally assumed that they first needed to prove themselves capable of following rational debate and presenting logical arguments. Yet it is precisely this notion of the student as an autonomous, independent learner that has come under attack from some of today's feminist academics. Crowley and Himmelweit, for example, suggest that the concept of the rational individual is a masculine construct (1992, p. 2). Nicholson notes, 'Feminists have criticized other Enlightenment ideals, such as the autonomous and self-legislating self, as reflective of masculinity in the modern West' (1990, p. 5). Others similarly argue that the idea of the rational individual is a myth rooted in white, Western constructions of the self (Leathwood and O'Connell, 2003).

Higher education's assumption of a rational independent learner has been criticized for excluding non-traditional students. Perhaps more damagingly exclusive is the notion that non-traditional students, or indeed all students, are incapable of realizing intellectual autonomy and exercising rationality in relation to academic debate. More recently, it has been claimed that the concept of the individual is a construction of free-market neo-liberalism and 'brings off various changes in subjectivity by normalizing individualistic self-interest, entrepreneurial values, and consumerism' (Barnett, 2010, p. 3). This argument has very serious consequences: when universities can no longer defend the notion of the autonomous student, an individual academically free to pursue independent intellectual thought and logical arguments, the traditional goals of higher education are revealed to be transformed.

The challenge to the notion of the autonomous self is apparent in feminist teaching methods. Lecturing is considered representative of a male tendency to preach and profess – and, in so doing, to silence the audience. Seminars are also perceived as a forum for masculine competitive one-upmanship, where confrontational arguments win out over seemingly more constructive attempts at intellectual compromise. The assumption of these feminists is that female, working-class, and black and minority-ethnic students will feel out of place in such an educational environment (Burke and Crozier, 2012).

A distinctive form of pedagogy emerged from within Women's Studies and built upon many of the political activities adopted by feminist campaigners outside of the academy, such as consciousness raising and the validation of personal experience. As feminist teachers assume the existence of ways of knowing that are distinctive to women, their pedagogical approaches privilege the subjective and the experiential above the objective and the empirical. The feminist classroom focuses upon the centrality of women's personal experience to understandings and the development of 'knowledge' (Morley, 2001; Kamler, 2001). This often 'involves an exploration of personal experiences, reflections and narrative or biographical accounts of both professional and personal developments' (David, 2004, p. 104). Students are asked to recount and reflect upon their personal experiences as a legitimate academic resource.

Teaching sessions that focus upon personal experience as the primary source material become an arena for sharing feelings and issues. Such an approach encourages the emergence of explicitly political aims through expressions of empathy and the consequent emotive rather than objective treatment of particular issues. Individual identity is located as the driver of subjective response; statements that begin, 'Speaking as a . . . ' are privileged as offering special insight and being an expression of incontestable truth. The underlying assumption is that group identity, be it linked to gender, sexuality or ethnicity, will 'determine all arguments a person makes or any actions she takes' (Patai and Koertge, 2003, p. 75). The role of the academic is to mediate such discussions while simultaneously encouraging the sense of gender-based grievance and promoting empowerment through feminism as the solution to such problems.

Such overt politicization is often considered unproblematic, as traditional teaching methods employed by universities are thought to be representative of a white, middle-class, patriarchal hegemony that alienates non-traditional students. Feminists recall Pierre Bourdieu's description of pedagogy as acts of symbolic violence designed to reproduce the established social order. When traditional forms of pedagogy are blamed for propagating gendered power relations, feminist teaching is seen as neither more nor less political than alternative approaches.

An emphasis on the subjective justifies the idea of the non-hierarchical classroom where everyone's individual experiences are equally valid and the teacher, despite possessing academic knowledge built up over many years of study, holds no special status.

In fact, the emotional and personal response of the newest student may be privileged if she represents a particular subjective experience that illustrates the oppression felt by a marginalized group. This 'learner-centred' focus favours cooperation through group work and emphasizes peer review rather than intellectual conflict and judgement. There is little opportunity, or expectation, that students' misunderstandings will be corrected by the lecturer. Indeed, misunderstanding cannot occur if everyone is expressing their own truth as it is experienced by them.

The explicitly political focus of feminist pedagogy actively encourages a critique of texts and ideas that exposes the construction of gender identity and reveals the workings of patriarchy. This is a useful and often valid form of criticism, but it is intellectually limited and leaves little scope for internal dissent, as refusal to acknowledge the status of women as oppressed, and white, heterosexual men as oppressors, leads to accusations of internalized misogyny. This need to adhere to one particular outlook has been termed 'ideological policing' (Patai and Koertge, 2003, p. 2), which discourages criticality and promotes conformity. Although students are encouraged to interrogate everything that may have sexist connotations, they are not encouraged to question feminism itself.

The ideological policing of the feminist classroom is brought into sharp relief through the emphasis on sharing personal experiences and emotional responses to ideas and situations. Students who, for whatever reason, refuse to share and reflect upon personal experiences, come under pressure from lecturers and peers to do so, and continued refusal can result in the failure of a particular module. The focus on the personal rather than the objective permits no distance between the self and the concept under discussion. Any challenge to ideas raised in the classroom becomes a direct attack upon the person espousing the particular view. Students soon learn that sharing feelings and experiences alone is not enough to gain affirmation in the feminist classroom and that the correct emotional responses must also be expressed. Patai and Koertge report that 30 per cent of the Women's Studies students interviewed said they 'felt silenced or at risk expressing unpopular opinions' (2003, p. 171).

Central tenets of feminist thought have migrated from Women's Studies to other subject areas within humanities and social science disciplines. This has opened up new areas of research and could potentially lead to exciting new intellectual developments. All too often however, it simply results in a narrow preoccupation with the self. English Literature courses now encourage students to interpret texts for what they might reveal about gendered power relations. Sociology classes allow students to research the family as a site of oppression. Both are important areas of research that become narrowly focused when taught through teaching methods such as reflective practice, where students are asked to keep logs of their emotional responses to experiences or reading material. The dissemination of Women's Studies across disciplinary boundaries allowed the 'autobiographical turn' and the focus on individual identity to gather pace. This has become increasingly prevalent as feminism and postmodernism within the academy have intersected with a perception of students as increasingly vulnerable and the adoption of a more therapeutic approach to teaching (Ecclestone and Hayes, 2008).

The mainstreaming of feminism within the academy in the mid-1990s had the perhaps unexpected side effect of challenging the existence of specific programmes in Women's Studies. Students interested in exploring the issues covered by Women's Studies found they could do so just as well through more traditional, and more marketable, social science subjects. At the same time, the content of many Women's Studies programmes was being questioned for excluding other issues that intersect with sexism such as disability, ethnicity and social class. As a result, some Women's Studies departments morphed into the broader category of Gender Studies and instigated research and teaching into other topics around gender and sexuality, including issues to do with masculinity, homosexuality and transgenderism. At other universities, Women's Studies was subsumed into sociology or social policy departments.

Words can wound

In the 1980s, a politicized and feminist approach to academic work, grounded in a social constructionist assumption of gender as performative rather than biological, met an emerging postmodernism that assumed discourse constructed not just perceptions of reality but often reality itself. This led feminist literary theorists such as Julia Kristeva to argue that language itself creates power relations and the conditions for oppression: 'language, like culture, sets up a separation and, starting with discrete elements, concatenates an order' (1982, p. 72). The American legal academic Catharine MacKinnon and the author Andrea Dworkin focused upon the role of language and images in propagating the oppression of women. They were particularly concerned with the harm caused by the production, distribution and consumption of pornography upon all women. The basis of their argument was that pornography was inherently discriminatory and damaging as it shaped people's thoughts about women. The US city of Indianapolis passed an ordinance (although later struck down) that defined pornography as discrimination. The Federal Court found the ordinance unconstitutional and described it as 'thought control' (Kaminer, 20/02/15).

Other feminist scholars taught about and campaigned against sexist language, pornography and the depiction of women in the media. Mackinnon argued, 'What you need is people who see through literature like Andrea Dworkin, who see through law like me, to see through art and create the uncompromised women's visual vocabulary' (in Hoff Sommers, 1994, p. 272). The creation of such a 'visual vocabulary' led to the view that academics and students had a moral responsibility to use their feminist insight to ban images and words they perceived as oppressive. The concept of free speech was considered problematic if it allowed for the continued subjugation of oppressed groups. Political judgements about the content of what was being said were used to determine who had the right to speak.

Unlike the McCarthyism of just three decades earlier, this attack on academic freedom came not from outside the university but from within, and not from the political right but from the radical left. From the students' perspective, censorship went from being something to rail against, to a morally righteous and politically radical act. Free speech became perceived as a barrier to equality, rather than necessary for political liberation to take place.

Although the feminist crusade against pornography ground to a halt in the face of both new technology and the American First Amendment, the notion that words and images were pre-eminently important in shaping perceptions of reality and could inflict mental harm upon people remained. This view led to an increase in 'ideological policing' both inside and outside of academia. There was a particular focus upon the words people used. Patai and Koertge point out that this crusade against words, images and jokes brings modern day feminists into line with their bourgeois Victorian foresisters, who saw it as their job 'to monitor language and enforce norms' of what was socially acceptable (2003, p. 120).

The perception of linguistic threats and the accompanying ideological policing becomes internalized in women's increasingly vulnerable sense of self which is reinforced, rather than challenged, by the feminist and postmodern deconstruction of the autonomous individual as a capitalist myth. Most recently, students have demanded 'trigger warnings' or advance notification if their course is to include content that might be considered racist, sexist, classist, homophobic or in any other way offensive or potentially capable of triggering post-traumatic stress disorder. Such demands are inherently censorious: at Oberlin College in America in 2014, faculty were asked to remove 'triggering' material when it did not directly contribute to course goals. Worse, trigger warnings promote self-censorship as lecturers remove material from the syllabus in order to pre-empt complaints.

Academic freedom

Feminism is not solely responsible for the erosion of the principles that have traditionally underpinned academic freedom. Feminism found a ready home within higher education when it combined with intellectual trends such as postmodernism and the broader turn towards the therapeutic in the regulation of social life. Together, such approaches to academic work called into question assumptions about truth and objectivity and directly challenged the Enlightenment traditions of scholarship. While such a process could have contributed to a useful reappraisal of the methods and topics legitimized within the academy, the explicitly political aims of feminism led instead to a focus on the subjective experiences of women.

The perception that women are primarily victims, oppressed by patriarchal norms constructed through discourse, has had two dominant repercussions that continue to influence many areas within higher education. The first is a focus upon identity politics, with its unquestionable privileging of personal feelings. The assumption that no one can speak outside of their own biological or social experience or on behalf of anyone else prevents criticism of any particular perspective. The second, related, repercussion is the notion that debate is not to be welcomed as a means of advancing knowledge, but curtailed as an indulgent academic exercise that fails to respect people's lived experiences. Both these trends are fundamentally antithetical to academic freedom. Patai and Koertge suggest, 'The only remedy for such abuses is to stop using identity as a passkey to all questions of truth or responsibility' (2003, p. 80).

7
From Academic Freedom to Academic Justice

The legacy of history continues to compel many scholars to hold an emotional attachment to the rhetoric of academic freedom. It is drawn upon, often in a seemingly arbitrary manner, to defend particular individuals, to challenge political legislation or to question the influence of private donors. However, as the previous chapters in this book have shown, recent years have witnessed a reappraisal of academic freedom and its significance to the pursuit of knowledge. Today, the concept of academic freedom is, on occasion, openly criticized. It stands accused of propagating a 'neo-liberal' view of the scholar as an autonomous individual, travelling free from experiences of prejudice, unencumbered by practical and emotional commitments, through a politically neutral intellectual terrain. Academic freedom stands accused of reinforcing the right to a platform for those who are already in dominant positions while doing nothing to challenge the structural inequalities that make it more difficult for less powerful groups to have their voices heard.

Alongside such criticisms sit attempts to redefine academic freedom. The rhetoric of academic freedom is increasingly attached to principles that run counter to free speech and free expression. It is reimagined as a matter of academic justice and called upon to silence supposedly powerful groups while allowing the voices of previously under-represented groups to be heard. This chapter explores what academic justice means, how it differs from academic freedom and how it is used to silence dissent and enforce conformity.

Academic justice

In 2014, the term 'academic justice' was employed by Harvard University student Sandra Y. L. Korn in a column in her campus newspaper. In an article carrying the subheading 'Let's give up on academic freedom in favor of justice', she explained, 'When an academic community observes research promoting or justifying oppression, it should ensure that this research does not continue' (18/02/14). The column provoked outrage, although arguably Korn's only crime was to put in writing what many far senior people within the academy had been suggesting for several years. Korn had imbibed a view that dominates higher education today: that academic freedom is not always compatible with other political principles such as fairness, equality, respect or sensitivity and has no superior claim on scholarship. Judith Butler expresses this view when she suggests, 'academic freedom is sometimes in conflict with basic human rights' and concludes, 'when such conflicts occur it must be that basic human rights are the more important good to defend' (2006b). Stanley Fish has caricatured this argument as meaning, 'while academic freedom is usually a good thing, when basic questions of justice are in play, it must give way' (2013).

Attempts to redefine academic freedom as a matter of justice have arisen most clearly in American and British campaigns to boycott Israeli universities. Proponents of Boycott, Divestment and Sanctions (BDS) argue that Israeli universities receive government funding in return for playing a cultural role propagandizing on behalf of a state that engages in systematic acts of oppression against Palestinians. They claim that interaction with the rest of the world legitimizes and politically neutralizes Israeli universities and, by default, the nation state. In addition, those in favour of sanctions argue that global Israeli influence is unduly exercised to prevent the emergence of work that portrays the country negatively. Attempts to defend the academic freedom of Israeli scholars are frequently rejected outright with the claim that because Israel prevents Palestinian professors and students from attending universities, travelling to conferences and engaging in scholarship, then Israelis have no right to academic freedom themselves.

Campaigners assume that challenging the denial of fundamental human rights to Palestinians trumps academic freedom. Omar

Barghouti, a founding member of the Palestinian Campaign for Academic and Cultural Boycott of Israel, argues,

> When a prevailing and consistent denial of basic human rights is recognized, the ethical responsibility of every free person and every association of free persons, academic institutions included, to resist injustice supersedes other considerations about whether such acts of resistance may directly or indirectly injure academic freedom.
>
> (2013, p. 5)

This presents human rights and freedoms as hierarchical, mutually exclusive and their distribution as a zero-sum game. Butler follows this to its logical conclusion with her argument that the

> privileging of academic freedom as a value above all other freedoms is antithetical to the very foundation of human rights. The right to live, and freedom from subjugation and colonial rule, to name a few, must be of more import than academic freedom. If the latter contributes in any way to suppression of the former, more fundamental rights, it must give way. If the struggle to attain the former necessitates a level of restraint on the latter, then so be it.
>
> (2006b, p. 9)

This falsely assumes that academic freedom competes with, rather than complements, other rights. It suggests that academic freedom for some prevents basic rights for others.

BDS proponents argue that restricting the academic freedom of Israeli scholars as a result of political and military decisions that most did not instigate, and many may not actually support, is justified when seen in comparison to the scale of human rights abuses conducted against the Palestinians. However, imposing constraints on Israeli academics as a punishment for the sins of the nation introduces political conditions upon academic freedom. What should be, within the academy at least, a universal right to further the pursuit of knowledge comes to be defined politically and selectively, applicable only to those who share the 'correct' views or live in the 'correct' part of the world. Butler's desire for 'a more inclusive version of the doctrine across national borders and along egalitarian lines' (2006b) uses equality and inclusivity to argue for some speech to be silenced so the voices of others can be heard. Ultimately, academic freedom is criticized for being too 'academic', or narrowly focused and essentially trivial. To engage in a meaningful power struggle, academics are urged to have concerns that go beyond academic freedom and encompass political positions on a range of issues.

Qualifying academic freedom with caveats of political judgement negates all that is universal and progressive about the demand. As Fish indicates, it brings about a complete reversal in the definition of academic freedom, 'from a doctrine insulating the academy from politics into a doctrine that demands of academics blatantly political actions' (2013). BDS supporters ask fellow academics to make judgements about who gets to speak, whose research gets published and what students are taught, not on the basis of what is considered most useful in advancing knowledge and arriving closer to a (still contestable) truth, but on the national identity of the speakers and the political views they espouse. Not only is this antithetical to the pursuit of knowledge it is also inherently undemocratic. Questions as to whose view of justice should prevail and which views are unacceptable are rarely raised when a prevailing political consensus is assumed.

A fundamental tenet of academic freedom is that all truth claims are contestable and nothing should be beyond question. It is only correct that this principle is turned on academic freedom and that scholars consider the political assumptions inherent within the concept itself. As has been noted throughout this book, the notion of academic freedom to have emerged within the academy over a century ago was built upon a particular view of scholarship that assumed an aspiration towards objectivity in the knowledge pursued. It is always useful to shine a light on these assumptions and question whether knowledge is, or indeed ever can be, objective in its truth claims. Likewise, it is important to question whether the traditional notion of academic freedom supports a particular political perspective and prevents other views from being heard.

Central to the demand that academic justice should dominate higher education is a critique of the principles that have shaped scholarship in general and academic freedom in particular. Butler is one of many within universities now asking, 'how are freedom of movement and communication circumscribed and defined by a particular conception of academic freedom?' (2013). Such questions encourage scholars to consider the limits of traditional notions of academic freedom. Likewise, Chatterjee and Maira suggest that the 'liberal discourse of academic freedom' is 'generally bounded by the nation and individual rights' (2014, p. 8). They are critical of the traditional concept of academic freedom as being 'a notion that is deeply bound up with academic containment' (2014, p. 23). They want to move away from a concept of academic freedom grounded in disciplinary structures that, although far from perfect, led to judgements being made about the worth of knowledge based on merit. Instead they seek a more explicitly political notion of academic justice that is reconceptualized around a particular values framework; 'the university must be reimagined as a site of solidarity with those engaged in struggles against neoliberal capitalism and organizing for the abolition of the academic-MPIC' [military–prison–industrial complex] (2014, p. 20). Scholarship and political campaigning come to be seen as one and the same.

In a number of academic disciplines, research and teaching have become so inherently bound up with the promotion of a particular political outlook that it becomes difficult to determine where scholarship ends and campaigning begins. A 2013 report by Harvard University, *Mapping the Future,* acknowledges that the humanities, 'serve only the critical function of unmasking the operations of power in language largely impenetrable to a wider public. Or even where they are intelligible, they fail to communicate their value to a wider public. They serve no constructive public function.' Nonetheless, its authors remain wedded to the view that, 'one of the major contributions of the Humanities over the past thirty years has been [...] revealing the extent to which culture serves power, the way domination and imperialism underwrite cultural production, and the ways the products of culture rehearse and even produce injustice.'

Those who argue for academic justice play a useful role in pointing out that the assumed objectivity of scholarship inherent in the concept of academic freedom can mask work that is not politically neutral but instead confirms existing power relations. However, the sleight of hand they criticize, using the neutrality of academic freedom to mask a political position, is one they then reproduce themselves. Chatterjee and Maira suggest the BDS campaign, in arguing for the human rights of Palestinians, is 'in support of and produces academic freedom' (2014, p. 40), while at the same time they impose their own politically motivated definition upon the concept and ask scholars to 'recraft our notion of "academic freedom" by focusing unflinchingly on the larger structural forces and deeper alliances between the MPIC and the academy' (2014, p. 43).

The aim to be more critical, to challenge better existing norms and to arrive at superior understandings is to be welcomed. Indeed it must drive academic work, and questioning the assumptions that underpin what counts as scholarship is a crucial part of this process. However, arguing for academic justice is not arguing for better, more objective knowledge that brings us closer to truth. It is a call on scholars to abandon any aspiration towards objectivity in favour of taking a political position. Certainly it is true that the assumption of objectivity inherent in the concept of academic freedom was not always met and did provide a veneer of neutrality for work that was not always politically neutral. Beginning by abandoning objectivity and establishing a political position, however, not only prevents academics from aspiring towards contestable truth claims, it also enforces a consensus and encourages political conformity in a way that curtails questioning and criticality from the outset. This is entirely detrimental to higher education, the pursuit of knowledge and future generations of students.

The inclusive university

Arguments for academic freedom to be replaced by or redefined as academic justice are most visible with campaigns for BDS against Israeli universities. However, the notion of academic justice stretches back further than such recent political initiatives. The second half of the twentieth century witnessed the expansion of higher education across the Western world. In the decades immediately following the Second World War, there was growth in student numbers as returning veterans sought to take up places denied them by the war. Later, increasing prosperity and burgeoning population rates led to a further increase in the number of students. From the 1960s onwards, people outside of academia began to question not just how many students should go to university but who should have access to such opportunities. In part this was a reaction to governments pushing to increase the skills of the populace in an attempt to bring about economic growth, but it was also led by campaigners who argued for greater access to higher education for previously under-represented groups.

There was a political drive, premised upon fundamental notions of justice and equality of opportunity, to make the student body more diverse and representative of the national population as whole. The under-representation of female students became an issue in both the US and the UK, although more specific discussions have focused upon race in the US and social class in the UK. On university campuses, what began as the free speech movement morphed into campaigns for affirmative action and a demand for greater representation of the student voice. It was no longer considered enough for universities simply to admit a more diverse student body. Campaigners argued for a definition of equality that went beyond just the elimination of barriers to access and sought change in the organizational culture of the university, in the guise of academic justice, that would 'affect the traditional power structure of the institution' (Hornosty, 2000, p. 40).

Some institutions and academics were slow to accept such changes and at various times panics have ensued about the 'dumbing down' of educational standards as a result of allowing too many students, and too many non-traditional entrants in particular, in to the Ivory Towers. Nonetheless, in the final decades of the twentieth century a changed higher education landscape and an influx of younger scholars less wedded to traditional academic values lent further support to universities becoming more educationally and socially diverse institutions. Nowadays universities are, for a variety of reasons, a very far cry from the white, male, middle-class preserves they were prior to the 1950s.

As we have seen in previous chapters, students began to question the representativeness of curricular content and academics, having already begun to lose confidence in the overriding significance of any particular body of subject knowledge, were often ready to capitulate to such demands. Alongside the slow abandonment of the pursuit of knowledge as a search for truth, a new and seemingly far nicer project emerged for academics to engage with. Jennie Hornosty points out that those who considered reality, and especially notions of truth, to be at best, multiple, shaped by perspectives, and subject to interpretation, were 'more likely to be proponents of the inclusive university' (2000, p. 43).

Higher education's commitment to inclusion primarily involved recruiting and supporting 'non-traditional' entrants, such as students with physical or learning disabilities, students who were the first in their family to enter higher education or from a minority social group. From the late 1990s onwards, the educational project of enacting justice by making the student body more representative of the population and the curriculum more representative of the student body, met and became increasingly integrated with 'the values and processes of the state' (Pavlich, 2000, p. x). This led to universities promoting the skills for employability that would enable students to enter the labour market and open up opportunities for social mobility.

In the UK, the Labour government elected in 1997 made 'social inclusion', or the creation of a more cohesive society, a key policy objective. Education, at all levels, became a major site for the promotion of a concept of social inclusion that rapidly moved beyond integration to encompass a broader values-driven framework. The importance of community, participation, engagement and respect for the environment became associated with social inclusion. In this way, inclusion within higher education came to be about more than just student diversity. Universities began to market themselves as inclusive institutions that not only had a diverse academic community but, more significantly, had an ethos that encompassed tolerance and respect for others irrespective of ethnicity, gender, age, disability, social class or sexuality.

Today, universities around the world are keen to promote their inclusive credentials. The University of Leicester claims to be 'the most inclusive of Britain's top-20 leading universities with the greatest proportions of students from under-represented groups'. In Canada, Queen's University describes itself as 'an inclusive community' in which 'each person feels safe to be themselves and to explore differences, where diverse views and ideas are met with openness and curiosity, and where we can approach our commonalities and differences with mutual respect'. The University of New Hampshire is 'committed to supporting and sustaining an educational community that is inclusive, diverse and equitable'.

Fish notes that inclusive higher education is marked by a 'celebration of the therapeutic where feelings trump facts'. In such a context, 'Truth is a secondary goal and is usurped by sensitivity, particularly sensitivity for the "other" ' (2015, p. 374). Academics and administrators, often pitched against each other in polarized debates about 'managerialism', 'marketization' or tuition fees come together, as Alan Charles Kors and Harvey A. Silverglate indicate in their important book, *The Shadow University*, under a shared belief 'that universities not only may but should suspend the rights of some in order to transform students, the culture and the nation according to their ideological vision and desire' (1998, p. 3). University managers, supported by academics and students, have introduced equality and diversity policies, anti-harassment initiatives and speech codes in a bid to eliminate prejudice, regulate behaviour and create an atmosphere of respect and sensitivity. Such policies also restrict free speech on campus and censor words, images and behaviour based on a perception of offence. Rather than such policies being perceived as an infringement upon free speech and students' individual rights, they are instead often portrayed as necessary to create a climate free from offence and to protect students perceived as vulnerable.

The drive to bring about inclusivity within higher education contributes to a reappraisal of academic freedom. The rhetorically correct acknowledgement that: 'Academic freedom is an important ideal' is now followed by asking,

> what does it really mean when universities have been dominated by white male elites who define knowledge, curriculum, ways of being, and the organizational culture in their image? What does it mean to talk of academic freedom in a class society with multiple layers of inequality?
>
> (Hornosty, 2000, p. 41)

The logical answer to such questions appears to be that old-fashioned notions of freedom should give way to seemingly more progressive notions of inclusivity.

Despite relatively little dissent to these changes from within the academy, the transition from the liberal to the inclusive university represents a fundamental battle of ideas between different notions of equality, freedom and justice. The lack of any real dispute accompanying this shift illustrates the extent to which higher education had already embarked upon a wholesale rejection of liberal academic principles, creating a moral vacuum for politicized values of inclusion, equality and justice to fill. Victory for the inclusive university both emerges out of and further consolidates changed understandings of the purpose of the university and what it means to be a student. The university has gone from being an organized marketplace of ideas responsible for the preservation and intergenerational transmission of knowledge and culture to a community seemingly held together by a shared commitment to sensitivity and respect for one another. In conjunction with this shift, the sense of what it means to be a student has moved from an autonomous individual capable of mastering and contributing to a body of knowledge to that of a vulnerable and stressed-out consumer in need of looking after.

Tensions between the principles of academic freedom and inclusivity are inescapable. The concept of the 'inclusive' university comes into conflict with traditional and vital elements of university life, like the practice of excluding applicants without the necessary exam results and the academic elitism of rewarding achievement. Universities cannot at the same time support free expression and respect for personal identity, academic freedom and the promotion of particular values, and free speech and sensitivity towards the feelings of others. The drive of universities to be 'inclusive' by promoting equality, diversity, sensitivity and respect, is pitched against the freedom of individual students and academics to debate and engage with topics that threaten rather than respect the identity of particular social groups.

The replacement of a clash of competing views with a focus on sensitivity and respect prevents the exercise of academic freedom as it has traditionally been understood. Worse, it often serves to enforce an intolerance of dissent. Throughout history, ideas that have most fundamentally challenged existing understandings have been considered offensive to the sensitivities of others. The battle for academic freedom began in earnest with evolutionists offending creationists. The entire history of scientific progress has been premised upon the proponents of new ideas challenging and rejecting older understandings. Such clashes have never been uncontroversial or without hurt feelings. In physics, Thomas Kuhn, writing in *The Structure of Scientific Revolutions,* points out that, 'Those who rejected Newtonianism proclaimed that its reliance upon innate forces would return science to the Dark Ages' (2012, p. 162). In the social sciences and humanities likewise, every controversial new idea – from the introduction of qualitative research methods, Critical Theory and social constructionism – has upset scholars firmly wedded to older paradigms.

Creating a climate intolerant to offence draws assumptions about personal morality, opinions and behaviour into the terrain of scholarship. Unfortunately, we do not need to look too far back in time to be reminded of an era when the presence of female, black or homosexual students on university campuses was considered offensive. Russell reminds us that, 'the days when divorce could be seen as grounds for losing an Oxford fellowship are within living memory' (1993, pp. 24/25). What may be considered offensive to one generation is not to the next; placing a premium upon sensitivity and the prevention of offence would set universities in aspic and, ironically, prevent social as well as intellectual progress.

Champions of the inclusive university assume that 'those with power, even relative power, experience reality in a different way than those with less power'. This leads to the belief that academic freedom 'should not be about freedom to say anything you please, no matter who is hurt' (Rebick, 2000, p. 58) and needs to be limited. Some have gone so far as to suggest that the inclusive university be renamed 'the "intrusive university" for its disruptive influence on academic freedom' (Fekete in Pavlich, 2000, p. xv). The inclusive university demands intrusion because 'hurt', 'emotional harm' and 'offence' are entirely subjective notions. Different people will interpret identical incidents as either offensive or simply part of the cut and thrust of university life. This lack of objectivity in defining offence contributes towards a climate of self-censorship where people police their own speech and behaviour to avoid the risk that something they utter may perhaps despite their intentions, be deemed offensive to others.

Identity politics

The traditional concept of academic freedom emerged and thrived in an era in which politics outside of the academy was marked by a clash of competing views. Debates between the political 'left' and 'right', communism and capitalism, revolutionaries and conservatives played out on the world stage throughout much of the twentieth century. Since at least the late 1980s, however, such political battles have given way to the idea that it is possible to move 'beyond left and right', to establish a 'third way' (Giddens, 1998) and that 'there is no alternative' to the market. As a commitment to particular principles has been replaced by a culture of managerialism, the terrain of political debate has moved from collective or social class concerns to demands for greater representation for the views of disparate groups. Such groups coalesce around key biological or cultural factors that the members share such as gender, ethnicity or sexuality. Whereas politics once represented a battle between the interests of capital and labour, between bourgeoisie and proletariat, today it is a clamour for different communities to have their voices heard and their identities confirmed. This is reflected in the research of some academics which is intended to 'give voice' to marginalized groups. The shift from academic freedom to academic justice within universities has emerged alongside the broader political shift away from competing grand narratives to identity politics.

The influence of identity politics within higher education can be seen most clearly with the popularity of courses in area studies, gender studies and queer studies, as well as the more general credence given to standpoint theory and the notion of truth as a matter of perspective. Identity politics rejects a belief in 'the universal category of humanity' in favour of 'specific categories of identity' (Good, 23/09/13). Individuals come to be seen as representatives of their group, speaking only on behalf of, and from the perspective of, group members. Where once the academy saw emotion as detrimental to scholarship, now the focus on identity privileges subjectivity over objectivity and places feelings at the heart of the university. The focus on identity appears to offer a radical challenge to the staid norms of academic work and the historical dominance of white males. It appears to empower groups who have traditionally not been represented or had their views heard in academia. However, it does so in a way that through a 'consciousness of the self' rejects any aspiration towards universal values. This is ultimately a 'conservative sensibility' (Furedi, 2014, p. 171) that prevents people from transgressing the limits of their own biology or narrow range of experiences. As Furedi explains, 'People whose identity is defined by their biology, emotional disposition, history and culture have as their focus what they are rather than what they could be' (2014, p. 172).

Identity politics encourages a focus on a concept of the self that is far removed from the rational, autonomous individual that had traditionally been assumed to be both the creator of, and audience for, academic work. Instead, identity politics emphasizes the emotional self and acknowledges the influence of feelings in academic work. Older methods for the pursuit of knowledge are criticized for failing to take account of such subjective factors (see Bloch, 2012; Merrill and West, 2009). A problem with bringing individual feelings into academic work is that it leaves little distance between the individual researcher and the knowledge pursued.

This trend can perhaps be seen most clearly in the demand that knowledge covered as part of the university curriculum should contain trigger warnings. The assumption behind such warnings is that students are too sensitive and vulnerable to be able to cope with the content covered and need to be warned in advance so they can either prepare themselves emotionally or avoid the triggering topics altogether. Lecturers driven by the pursuit of student satisfaction may well choose to self-censor and leave controversial topics out of the curriculum altogether to prevent potential upset. Lori Horvitz, an academic critical of the use of trigger warnings in literature classes nonetheless acknowledges, 'Last year, when revising the curriculum for a gender-studies related course I teach, I omitted books with sexually violent material to protect my students from responding negatively' (18/05/15).

The use of trigger warnings speaks to an assumption that students cannot distance themselves emotionally from the subject content under investigation and that lecturers should not expect them to do so. Without such emotional distance, criticism of the research or topic pursued is more likely to be taken personally and interpreted as criticism of the researcher; likewise, criticism of an opinion is considered to be criticism of its proponent. The more the inclusive university prioritizes sensitivity to feelings and respect for individuals, the more difficult the formulation of criticism becomes. Criticism is either avoided altogether, couched in provisos or presented as just a different understanding from a member of an alternative identity group. The prevention of offence requires the silencing of critics and potential offenders. It requires that dissenting voices be suppressed. The effect of this is to make existing understandings of the world more difficult to challenge. Without criticism it is simply impossible for knowledge to advance; as Kors and Silverglate indicate, 'no belief is so clearly certain or correct that it justifies suppressing those who question it' (1998, p. 41).

The promotion of the inclusive university, and the ascendancy of identity politics within society more broadly and within the academy in particular, creates the conditions for the shift from academic freedom to academic justice. Although the powerful legacy and positive connotations of academic freedom make it a concept scholars are reluctant to abandon altogether, attempts to redefine it as encompassing a notion of justice succeed only in rendering it hollow. Ultimately, academic freedom and academic justice are incompatible. Where academic freedom demands distance, objectivity and competition, justice demands respect, sensitivity and collaboration. As Rauch notes,

> Self-esteem, sensitivity, respect for others' beliefs, renunciation of prejudice are all good as far as they go. But as primary social goals they are incompatible with the peaceful and productive advancement of human knowledge. To advance knowledge, we must all sometimes suffer. Worse than that, we must inflict suffering on others.
>
> (2014, p. 19)

The politicization of the academy

Scholars driven by a desire to promote academic or social justice have often bought into a number of key assumptions about the purpose of higher education and the relationship between the university and wider society. This can lead to individuals blurring the boundaries between scholarship and activism and result in the politicization of the academy more broadly. This denies the fact that the goals of scholarship and the aims of political activism are fundamentally opposed to one another; 'political activists tend to have a very different attitude to alternatives to their own convictions: they must be defeated' (NAS, 2012, p. 6). When the aim of scholarship becomes the fulfilment of a political objective, rather than a search for truth, it is tempting for academics to use research to prove the conclusions that support their particular cause. This lends itself to 'advocacy research' or academic investigations carried out in order to provide the evidence needed to support a particular perspective. The desire to provide evidence to support a particular idea or cause determined in advance can also result in faculty teaching students what to think rather than how to think. There is an implicit concern that students left to make their own intellectual judgements may reach the 'wrong' conclusions. Instead of rigorous critical engagement with a range of different ideas, lecturers who are seeking to use higher education to promote justice 'demand correct attitudes and beliefs of students more than they require independent reading and thought' (NAS, 2012, p. 2).

Demonstrating attitudes and beliefs rarely requires sustained intellectual work; rather, the inculcation of values can best be observed through their demonstration in practice. New forms of teaching and assessment have entered the university in recent years that move beyond traditional expectations that students will attend lectures and seminars, read, conduct and write up experiments, or write essays and sit exams. In their place, students might be asked to undertake a group work presentation which, as well as being assessed on content, also judges their ability to work cooperatively with others; a skill considered important for employability but which also promotes inclusive values. Sometimes students are asked to record their subjective responses to an issue in the form of a reflective log or journal. What is actually being assessed in such instances is difficult to determine; it can often seem to be students' thoughts, feelings and emotions. At many British and American universities, students can gain academic credit for undertaking voluntary work, for example with a local school or charity. Again, this meets goals of both employability and inclusivity.

Other forms of assessment are both more unusual and more explicitly political. In 2008, several American universities offered students academic credit for canvassing in the presidential campaign (Wood, 2008). In 2014, a student at Columbia University, Emma Sulkhowitz, was awarded academic credit for a senior year art project entitled 'Mattress Performance' or 'Carry That Weight'. Sulkhowitz claimed to have been raped by a fellow student and launched a campaign against the university for not removing her alleged attacker from campus. The protest against the university incorporated Sulkhowitz's art project in which she carried her mattress around with her everywhere she went on campus, arguing that the mattress 'represents her specific rape, since she was attacked in her dorm room' and that the weight of the mattress symbolized how she continued to feel 'haunted' by the experience (Collman, 02/09/14).

The issue here is not the merits or otherwise of this performance as a particular art project but more the difficulties of providing objective academic assessments when the demonstration of values replaces critical engagement. Would a criticism of this performance art be interpreted as a denial of Sulkhowitz's experiences? Could a male student protesting a false allegation of rape expect his work to be judged according to the same standards? As Koppelman suggests, one impact of the demand on students to demonstrate values is the undermining of the aims of education 'by shutting down discussion and thought and turning inquiry into moral one-upmanship' (2015, p. 203). If students are not exposed to a body of knowledge, taught to engage critically with new ideas and allowed to reach their own conclusions, then the notion of intellectual and personal autonomy is called into question and students risk becoming siphons for the opinions and beliefs of their lecturers. For those academics who consider freedom to be 'merely a disguise adopted by the system, an illusion or an "effect" of bourgeois ideology' (Good, 2001, p. 42) then the loss of autonomy in academic work will provide little concern. Ironically for those so concerned with social justice, the people who have most to lose by this denial of autonomy are those who are in the least powerful positions to begin with.

Silencing dissent

The shift from academic freedom to academic justice imposes an explicitly political agenda upon higher education. Critics of traditional forms of academic practice and the teaching of a white, Western canon, such as Steven Salaita, argue that there is no such thing as objective knowledge and that all scholarship is political. With this in mind, the temptation for radical scholars to construct a concept of justice in line with their own particular outlook on the world and to seek to enact this belief system through the academy is understandable. Academic justice appears politically progressive in its support for the marginalized over the powerful, its assumption of the moral high ground and its explicit demand for political commitment. However, whereas academic freedom allowed for an (albeit sometimes limited) challenge to received wisdom, the principles of academic justice are marked by an inability to permit criticism and a silencing of dissent. Asking students to demonstrate values rather than engagement with a body of knowledge, censoring academics on the basis of their nationality, legislating for offensive views to be kept out of the classroom and off campus, all contribute towards the creation of a political consensus within higher education.

Korn's view that research or teaching that supports oppression should not be allowed to continue provoked outrage but it has come to dominate academia. Oppression, in this context, is defined sufficiently broadly to encompass any negative perception of a group not traditionally considered either politically dominant or represented within higher education. The desire to rid universities of oppression leads to existing subject content and new scholarship being judged on its political message or on the identity of its creator rather than on the basis of its intrinsic worth. Salih identifies this ideological shift as having taken shape in the West since the 1970s and being driven by the 'centrality of Western guilt' (2015, p. 143). He argues that the best criticisms of Western culture today are made by Western culture itself, as scholars routinely seek to ridicule the achievements of the Enlightenment (2015, p. 145).

How such sentiment plays out on campus can be seen in the UK National Union of Students' *Race for Equality* report, which argues that a multicultural curriculum is needed in order to promote the academic achievement of black students. The report claims that 'teachings based on unfamiliar cultural norms, histories and points of reference may have the potential to affect the educational attainment of certain minority-ethnic groups' (2011). This erroneously assumes that students can only really engage with subject matter that reflects their own cultural background. According to this logic, black, female or minority-ethnic students are excluded from a university curriculum that does not include people who look like them. Further, it suggests that academics promoting a traditional curriculum encourage students to imbibe knowledge entirely uncritically and that, regardless of whether students are taught Marx or Keynes, Nietzsche or Aristotle, they are incapable of thinking for themselves.

It is not impossible for students and lecturers to puncture the consensus created by the promotion of inclusivity and academic justice. However, a number of factors come together to make such challenges more difficult. If an academic uses the lecture theatre as pulpit or soapbox then a particular view of the topic under discussion is presented. If such a view assumes the moral high ground and appears to be shared by the majority, then it takes a very brave student indeed to publicly challenge this consensus. The American authors of the National Association of Scholars report *A Crisis of Confidence* note that 'the fixed quality of a political belief will stifle intellectual curiosity and freedom of thought when it dominates a classroom' (2012, p. 6). If a student's assessed mark explicitly depends upon them reproducing this political standpoint then they would be not only brave but potentially foolish to question the status quo. Additionally, if students are rarely presented with knowledge that runs counter to the dominant consensus then framing a challenge in suitably intellectual terms is difficult. Similar pressures to subdue criticism and to conform to a dominant view may also impact upon the work of academics subject to processes of peer review.

In the AAUP's 1915 *Declaration of Principles*, academics were warned against,

> taking unfair advantage of the student's immaturity by indoctrinating him with the teacher's own opinions before the student has had an opportunity fairly to examine other opinions upon the matters in question, and before he has sufficient knowledge and ripeness of judgement to be entitled to form any definitive opinion of his own.

If principles of academic freedom are to be extended to students (*Lehrfreiheit* as well as *Lernfreiheit*), then students need the right 'to be free from the coercive shaping of his or her mind'. Cary Nelson criticizes the AAUP's 1915 stance for presenting an outdated and unduly naïve view of students. However, it is arguably the case that nowadays students enter university having read fewer books than in the past and are therefore even more lacking in sufficient knowledge to reach independent judgements (see for example Arum and Roksa, 2011; Bloom, 1987). This would leave them less likely to have formed educated opinions of their own. Kors and Silverglate remind us that the AAUP 1967 *Joint Statement on Rights and Freedoms of Students* 'brought to the fore the students' right to seek his or her own truth' and advised professors to 'encourage free discussion, inquiry, and expression' in the classroom (1998, p. 52). The *Statement* suggests that 'In exchange for paying attention to their prescribed studies, "students should be free to take reasoned exception to the data or views offered in any course of study and to reserve judgement about matters of opinion"' (Kors and Silverglate, 1998, p. 53).

The demand for academic justice is often underpinned by an assumption that social groups under-represented within the academy need to be protected from ideas that other people deem they will find offensive. This presumes that some people have a lower level of tolerance to offence than others and are not capable of dealing with free speech or challenging views they disagree with for themselves. Kors and Silverglate describe as 'patronising paternalism' and 'yet another prejudicial stereotype' the view that 'blacks could not live with the First Amendment' (1998, p. 24). In this way, some people within the academy, and some students in particular, are permanently cast as vulnerable. The drive to protect students from offence in the classroom occurs alongside the emergence of a broader institutional view of students as 'not quite adults'. A duty of care to student–customers has replaced the *in loco parentis* legislation of a previous era. Student support services flourish as the perception of students as autonomous adults in control of their own lives has diminished. Ironically, the view of students as vulnerable has gone hand in hand with the view that it is acceptable to teach students what to think rather than simply how to think. It appears as if some scholar-activists are fearful that students may reach the wrong conclusions if left to their own devices.

All too often, it seems that students buy into this perception of themselves as unable to cope with conflicting views. It can often appear as if students, far from championing free speech, are at the forefront of campaigns to restrict what can be debated on campus. In Britain in 2014, students successfully prevented speakers from anti-abortion groups, members of the UK Independence Party and Muslim clerics from speaking on campus. One student, having successfully campaigned against a debate on abortion, argued 'I did not stifle free speech. As a student, I asserted that it would make me feel threatened in my own university; as a woman, I objected to men telling me what I should be allowed to do with my own body' (McIntyre, 18/11/14). Here we see how academic freedom, and free speech more broadly, are redefined to mean preventing debate in the name of safeguarding feelings, and the assumed feelings of others. We also see how the private nature of the university campus is misunderstood as equivalent to the domestic sphere rather than a private place dedicated to a public purpose.

Some academics are now looking on in dismay and confusion at a new generation of illiberal and censorious student activists. It is as easy, and tempting, to blame students for the collapse of academic freedom as it is to blame government legislation or the influence of big business. But to do so would be a cowardly denial of the role that scholars themselves have played in persistently undermining the fundamental principles of academic freedom. From the first day they arrive on campus, students are taught that words and images are powerful and can hurt or corrupt; that as students they are too vulnerable, and their peers too easily led, to be exposed to potentially harmful ideas; and that the way to deal with anything that makes them feel uncomfortable is either to avoid it or, even better, to ban it. More observant students see their lecturers acting in this way themselves by removing contentious material from the syllabus, organizing boycotts of Israeli academics and universities and actively campaigning against the presence on campus of controversial scholars.

Students should be challenged and held to account for their role in creating a climate of prurience and conformity that is anathema to debate. However, university lecturers need to be far more honest about their role in instigating, legitimizing and encouraging such restrictions. As the schematic view of the history of academic freedom presented in this book has shown, scholars themselves have often had too little regard for the values of scholarship and the pursuit of knowledge that underpinned academic freedom. Today the biggest threats to academic freedom come not from students, business or government but from scholars who, in seeking to promote academic justice over academic freedom, encourage self-censorship, close down debate and create a culture of conformity.

Defenders of intellectual liberty must resist current trends either to criticize academic freedom as serving only already-powerful interests within the academy, or to see it redefined as a matter of academic justice. It is all too easy to succumb to such temptations when academic freedom is separated from any intellectual mission in relation to the pursuit of knowledge.

Conclusions

Over a century on from the AAUP's *Declaration of Principles,* the rhetoric of academic freedom continues to resonate with scholars around the world. In a period when academics are expected to meet the demands of funding bodies, student–customers and institutional regulations, the legacy of academic freedom recalls a bygone era of professional autonomy few wish to jettison entirely. Issues such as the introduction of national anti-terrorism legislation provide a useful rallying point for those keen to remember past principles.

Increasingly, however, the rhetoric of academic freedom is employed by people uncertain as to what exactly the term means, or with some degree of unease as to its assumed elitism and association with dead, white men. This ambiguity means that protesters against government legislation, or the influence of private benefactors, often ignore the threats to academic freedom that originate from within universities themselves.

Restrictions on academic freedom that emerge from within universities are more insidious than externally imposed legislation. They are less easily recognizable and often stem from well-intentioned students or colleagues rather than heavy-handed managers. Such restrictions can take the form of speech codes, anti-harassment policies, codes of conduct, safe space initiatives, equality and diversity statements or even, ironically, policies on academic freedom. Individual scholars may find themselves unintentionally in breach of such regulations.

Only some academics gain media attention when they face sanctions for having spoken out of turn; others are never hired in the first place, find their employment contract is not renewed or that they are overlooked for promotion. Whether or not such cases garner the support of colleagues can appear fairly arbitrary. Even if sympathy does lie with the accused, the partial and one-sided definitions of academic freedom that are usually employed in such cases can never challenge the broader climate of censoriousness that has come to define universities.

Despite the publicity given to some high-profile individuals, most scholars do little to test the boundaries of academic freedom, preferring instead to self-censor and fall in line with regulations. Some on campus welcome this as a victory for civility and inclusion; others are unaware of the erosion of academic freedom until they come up against restrictions for themselves.

Recently, attention has focused upon the role of students in demanding that universities become a 'safe space' free from intellectual conflict or offence. Students have banned songs, newspapers, art works and speakers from campus. They have demanded 'trigger warnings' if potentially controversial material is to be covered in the classroom. It is tempting to blame students for curtailing free speech on campus but this ignores the extent to which they have learnt intolerance of dissent at the feet of their lecturers.

Scholars who campaign for academic freedom in one arena are often at the forefront of calling for restrictions on debate in another. Some argue that particular issues are 'settled' and that further discussion is unhelpful. In other instances, political judgements are employed to determine who has the right to speak and who does not. Supposedly radical academics argue academic freedom is an outdated concept because it provides a platform for dominant social groups and makes no allowances for those considered marginalized or under-represented within the academy.

This limits academic freedom for everyone by placing some ideas beyond discussion. It also assumes historically disadvantaged groups are unable to cope with free speech and to win debates on the merit of their arguments. When political conditions are placed upon academic freedom it stops being a meaningful concept for anyone in universities.

Academic freedom comes to be a loosely held principle when it is separated from broader goals relating to the pursuit of knowledge. Academic freedom arose from the need for scholars to challenge established orthodoxies with new knowledge. In this way, it epitomized the liberal academic project of advancing knowledge through competing and always-contestable truth claims in a 'marketplace of ideas'. In the second half of the twentieth century, concepts of truth and objectivity were increasingly derided by academics as providing a veneer of neutrality to mask white, male, heterosexual interests and reinforcing society's existing power relationships.

What began as a useful questioning of entrenched beliefs about the nature of knowledge and the methods for its pursuit ultimately led to the widespread abandonment of all claims to truth and objectivity. For many academics, knowledge is relativized as little more than perspectives and few works are considered more worth passing on to a new generation of students than any others. Instead, ideas are judged on their political merit or on the identity of their proposer. This challenge to objectivity leads criticism of scholarship to be interpreted as criticism of the individual. In the inclusive university, such criticisms are often deemed offensive. Students take their lead from their lecturers in demanding that higher education becomes a zone free from criticism and offence.

Rejecting the liberal project of advancing knowledge through competing truth claims has left universities without a purpose. This has been filled either by teaching employability skills or, what is to many, a more appealing promotion of inclusive values. Both skills and values demand that students demonstrate obedience rather than critical thinking. The promotion of particular values and the tendency to judge the worth of ideas not objectively but on the perspective they represent leads to the emergence of a dominant consensus within the academy. Academics who blur the boundaries between scholarship and campaigning squash dissent and enforce new orthodoxies in the name of mounting a radical critique of the status quo. For many scholars, particularly those worried about job security, the temptation is to fall in line with dominant ideas.

When scholarship is politicized in this way, the concept of academic freedom is either criticized for privileging already dominant voices or reconceived as academic justice and defined as giving a voice to less powerful groups. It is applied selectively to protect some people but not others. This partial, patronizing and anti-democratic view is the opposite of academic freedom.

Without academic freedom, there is no point to higher education. Knowledge advances through the freedom to provoke, cause offence and upset tradition. Without academic freedom, universities risk returning to the status of medieval institutions, only rather than paying homage to the church, many scholars today choose to worship at the altar of liberal opinion. The principles that underpin academic freedom are far too important to be abandoned with such little debate.

Academic freedom goes hand in hand with the broader scholarly project of the pursuit of knowledge and any serious debate about its future needs to be placed in this context. Academic freedom implies a concept of knowledge that is neither fixed for all time, nor reducible to ideology, but takes objectivity from its social composition. This in turn assumes individuals with a capacity to reason and test out ideas.

To breathe life back into academic freedom, those working in universities need to see students and members of the public alike as intelligent, rational and autonomous individuals, capable of engaging in reasoned debate. Academics need to encourage the free exchange of ideas rather than looking to close down discussion. The prevention of offence must not be placed above the right to debate. The pursuit of knowledge, rather than the promotion of values, skills or personal codes of behaviour, must lie at the heart of the university.

Most importantly of all, academic freedom can only survive through being continually exercised in the classroom, in writing and in the public square. If not exercised, academic freedom quickly becomes reduced to rhetoric or dead dogma.

Bibliography

AAUP. (1915) *Declaration of Principles*. http://www.aaup-tnconf.org/Documents_PDF/1915_Declaration_of_Principles.pdf (accessed 5/04/15).

AAUP. (1940) *Statement of Principles on Academic Freedom and Tenure*. http://www.aaup.org/report/1940-statement-principles-academic-freedom-and-tenure (accessed 5/04/15).

Abbas, A. and McLean, M. (2010) 'Tackling Inequality through Quality: A Comparative Case Study Using Bernsteinian Concepts' (pp. 241–267) in E. Unterhalter and V. Carpentier (eds.) *Global Inequalities and Higher Education: Whose Interests Are We Serving?* London: Palgrave Macmillan.

Adler, J. H. (2014) 'University of Illinois Trustees Vote against Appointment of Salaita' in *The Washington Post* (9/11/14).

Ali, T. (2014) 'Stuart Hall's Message to Those Who Want Change: Think, Debate – and Get Off Your Backside' in *The Guardian* (10/01/14).

Althusser, L. (1971) 'Ideology and Ideological State Apparatuses' in *Lenin and Philosophy and Other Essays*. Translated by A. Blunden. New York and London: Monthly Review Press.

Annas, J. (2000) *Ancient Philosophy: A Very Short Introduction*. Oxford: Oxford University Press.

Arendt, H. (1954) *Between Past and Future*. London: Penguin.

Arendt, H. (1973) *Remarks by Hannah Arendt*. Advisory Council, Princeton: Princeton University.

Arnold, M. (2009) *Culture and Anarchy*. Oxford: Oxford World Classics.

Arts and Humanities Research Council. (2013) *Strategy 2013–2018*. http://www.ahrc.ac.uk/News-and-Events/News/Documents/AHRC-Strategy-2013-18.pdf (accessed 30/4/15).

Arum, R. and Roksa, J. (2011) *Academically Adrift*. Chicago: The University of Chicago Press.

Bailey, R. (2001) 'Overcoming Veriphobia – Learning to Love Truth Again' in *British Journal of Educational Studies*, 49 (2) pp. 159–172.

Barendt, E. (2010) *Academic Freedom and the Law: A Comparative Study*. Oxford: Hart Publishing.

Barghouti, O. (2013) 'Boycott, Moral Responsibility and the Moral Responsibility to Uphold Human Rights' in *Journal of Academic Freedom*, 4 pp. 1–8.

Barnett, C. (2010) 'Publics and Markets, What's Wrong with Neoliberalism' in S. Smith, S. Marston, R. Pain, and J. P. Jones III (eds.) *The Handbook of Social Geography*. London and New York: Sage.

Barnett, R. (2009) 'Knowing and Becoming in the Higher Education Curriculum' in *Studies in Higher Education*, 34 (4) pp. 429–440.

Barrow, R. (2009) 'Academic Freedom: Its Nature, Extent and Value' in *British Journal of Educational Studies*, 57 (2) pp. 178–190.

Barthes, R. (1977) *The Death of the Author Image – Music – Text*. S. Heath (ed. and trans.). London: Fontana.

Bartky, S. L. (1975) 'Towards a Phenomenology of Feminist Consciousness' in *Social Theory and Practice*, 3 (4) pp. 425–439.

Bauman, Z. (1991) *Modernity and the Holocaust*. Cambridge: Polity Press.

BBC News. (2003) 'Clarke Criticised Over Classics' in *BBC News* (31/01/2003). http://news.bbc.co.uk/1/hi/education/2712833.stm (accessed 07/04/15).

Beck, J. (2010) 'Promoting Official Pedagogic Identities: The Sacred and the Profane' (pp. 81–92) in K. Maton and R. Moore (eds.) *Social Realism, Knowledge and the Sociology of Education*. London: Continuum.

Belsey, C. (2002) *Critical Practice*. London: Routledge.

Berger, P. and Luckmann, T. (1991) *The Social Construction of Reality*. New York: Anchor Books.

Bernstein, B. (1971) 'On the Classification and Framing of Educational Knowledge' (pp. 47–69) in M. F. D. Young (ed.) *Knowledge and Control, New Directions for the Sociology of Education*. London: Collier Macmillan.

Bernstein, B. (1996) *Pedagogy, Symbolic Control and Identity: Theory, Research and Critique*. London: Taylor and Francis.

Bernstein, B. (2000) *Pedagogy, Symbolic Control and Identity: Theory, Research and Critique*. Maryland: Rowman & Littlefield.

Bloch, C. (2012) *Passion and Paranoia: Emotions and the Culture of Emotion in Academia*. Surrey: Ashgate.

Bloom, A. (1987) *The Closing of the American Mind*. New York: Simon and Schuster.

Boghossian, P. (2006) *Fear of Knowledge, against Relativism and Social Constructivism*. Oxford: Clarendon Press.

Bok, D. (2003) *Universities in the Marketplace: The Commercialisation of Higher Education*. New Jersey: Princeton University Press.

Bourdieu, P. and Passeron, J.-C.(2000) *Reproduction in Education, Society and Culture*. London: Sage Publications.

Bristow, J. (2015) *Baby Boomers and Generational Conflict*. London: Palgrave Macmillan.

Brooker, P. (1999) *A Concise Glossary of Cultural Theory*. London: Hodder Education.

Bronner, S. E. (2011) *Critical Theory: A Very Short Introduction*. Oxford: Oxford University Press.

Brown, R. with Carasso, H. (2013) *Everything for Sale? The Marketisation of UK Higher Education*. London: Routledge and SRHE.

Butcher, J. and Smith, P. (2015) *Volunteer Tourism: The Lifestyle Politics of International Development*. London: Routledge.

Butler, J. (1988) 'Performative Acts and Gender Constitution: An Essay in Phenomenology and Feminist Theory' in *Theatre Journal*, 40 (4) pp. 519–531.

Butler, J. (2006a) 'Academic Norms, Contemporary Challenges: A Reply to Robert Post on Academic Freedom' in B. Doumani (ed.) *Academic Freedom after September 11*. New York: Zone Books.

Butler, J. (2006b) 'Israel/Palestine and the Paradoxes of Academic Freedom' in *Radical Philosophy*, 135 pp. 8–17.

Burke and Crozier. (2012) *Teaching Inclusively Resource Pack*. https://www.heacademy.ac.uk/sites/default/files/projects/Teaching%20Inclusively%20Resource%20Pack%20Final%20Version_opt.pdf (accessed 3/05/15).

Carey, J. (1992) *The Intellectuals and the Masses*. London: Faber and Faber.

Carr, D. (2009) 'Revisiting the Liberal and Vocational Dimensions of University Education' in *British Journal of Educational Studies*, 57 (1) pp. 1–17.

Chatterjee, P. and Maira, S. (2014) 'The Imperial University: Race, War, and the Nation-State' (pp. 1–52) in P. Chatterjee and S. Maira (eds.) *The Imperial University*. Minneapolis: University of Minnesota Press.

Colgate University, *Colgate for All*. http://colgate.edu/about/people-of-colgate/president-jeffrey-herbst/colgate-for-all (accessed 26/04/15).

Collman, A. (2014) 'Columbia Student Carrying Mattress with Her Everywhere She Goes for as Long as Her Alleged Rapist Remains on Campus' in *The Daily Mail* (02/09/14).

Committee on Higher Education. (1963) *Higher Education: Report of the Committee Appointed by the Prime Minister under the Chairmanship of Lord Robbins 1961–1963*. London: HMSO.

Cooper, D. (2013) 'Question Everything? Rape Law/Free Speech' in *Critical Legal Thinking*. http://criticallegalthinking.com/2013/11/28/question-everything-rape-law-free-speech/ (accessed 03/04/15).

Corbyn, Z. (2009) 'UCL Provost: Libel Law Is Stifling Academic Freedom' in *Times Higher Education* (10/12/09).

Court, F. E. (1992) *Institutionalising English Literature: The Culture and Politics of Literary Study, 1750–1900*. California: Stanford University Press.

Crowley, H. and Himmelweit, S. (1992) *Knowing Women: Feminism and Knowledge*. Cambridge: Polity Press.

David, M. (2004) 'Feminist Sociology and Feminist Knowledges: Contributions to Higher Education Pedagogies and Professional Practices in the Knowledge Economy' in *International Studies in Sociology of Education*, 14 (2) pp. 99–123.

Delanty, G. (2001) *Challenging Knowledge: The University in the Knowledge Society*. Buckingham: SRHE and Open University Press.

Derrida, J. (1997) *Of Grammatology*. Trans. G. C. Spivak. Baltimore: John Hopkins University Press.

Desai, M. (2003) 'Public Goods: A Historical Perspective' (pp. 63–77) in I. Kaul (ed.) *Providing Global Public Goods*. Oxford: Oxford University Press.

Descartes, R. (1999) *Discourse on Method and Related Writings*. London: Penguin Classics.

Docherty, T. (2014) 'Thomas Docherty on Academic Freedom' in *Times Higher Education* (04/12/14).

Downing, L. (2013) 'Identity Crisis for Women's Studies' in *Times Higher Education* (20/06/13).

Duarte, J. L., Crawford, J. T., Stern, C., Haidt, J., Jussim, L., Tetlock, P. E. (2014) 'Political Diversity Will Improve Social Psychological Science' in *Behavioral and Brain Sciences*. Cambridge University Press.

Durkheim, E. (1956) *Education and Sociology*. New York: The Free Press.

Durkheim, E. (2001) *The Elementary Forms of Religious Life*. Oxford: Oxford University Press.

Eagleton, T. (2008) *Literary Theory: An Introduction*. Oxford: Blackwell Publishing.

Ecclestone, K. and Hayes, D. (2008) *The Dangerous Rise of Therapeutic Education*. London: Routledge.

Editors. (2013) 'Editorial: A Response to the LSE Event "Is Rape Different?" ' in *Feminists@Law*, 3 (2). https://journals.kent.ac.uk/index.php/feministsatlaw/article/view/80 (accessed 03/04/15).

Einstein, A. (1933) *Science and Civilisation*. London: Speech Given to the Academic Assistance Council. http://www.cara1933.org/downloads/Science%20and%20Civilisation%20transcript.pdf (accessed 5/4/15).

Fanghanel, J. (2009) 'The Role of Ideology in Shaping Academics' Conceptions of Their Discipline' in *Teaching in Higher Education*, 5 (14) pp. 565–577.

Fish, S. (2001) 'What's Sauce for One Goose: The Logic of Academic Freedom' (pp. 3–12) in S. Kahn and D. Pavlich (eds.) *Academic Freedom and the Inclusive University*. Vancouver: University of British Columbia Press.

Fish, S. (2013) 'Academic Freedom against Itself: Boycotting Israeli Universities' in *The New York Times* (28/10/13).

Fish, S. (2014) *Versions of Academic Freedom from Professionalism to Revolution*. Chicago and London: The University of Chicago Press.

Foucault, M. (1980)*Power/Knowledge*. New York: Vintage Books.

Foucault, M. (1989) *The Archaeology of Knowledge*. London: Routledge Classics.

Fraser, N. and Nicholson, L. (1990) 'Social Criticism without Philosophy: An Encounter between Feminism and Postmodernism' (pp. 19–39) in L. Nicholson (ed.) *Feminism/Postmodernism*. London: Routledge.

Furedi, F. (2004) *Where Have All the Intellectuals Gone?* London: Continuum.

Furedi, F. (2013) *Authority: A Sociological History*. Cambridge: Cambridge University Press.

Furedi, F. (2014) *First World War: Still No End in Sight*. London: Bloomsbury.

Gibbs, P. (2013) 'Role Virtue Ethics and Academic Ethics: A Consideration of Academic Freedom' in *International Journal of Educational Management*, 27 (7) pp. 720–729.

Giddens, A. (1998) *The Third Way: The Renewal of Social Democracy*. London: Polity Press.

Gobry, P. E. (2014) 'How Academia's Liberal Bias Is Killing Social Science' in *The Week* (17/12/14). http://theweek.com/articles/441474/how-academias-liberal-bias-killing-social-science (accessed 6/4/15).

Good, G. (2001) *Humanism Betrayed: Theory, Ideology and Culture in the Contemporary University*. Montreal: McGill-Queen's University Press.

Good, G. (2013) 'Identity Politics Is Killing College Life' in *Spiked* (23/09/13). http://www.spiked-online.com/newsite/article/identity_politics_is_killing_college_life/14066#.VV8nRrlViko (accessed 22/05/15).

Gordon, J. (1997) 'John Stuart Mill and the "Marketplace of Ideas"' in *Social Theory and Practice*, 23 (2) pp. 235–249.

Graham, C. (2014) 'The Transcripts: The Partial Works of Professor Barry Spurr. Poet.Racist. Misogynist' in *newmatilda.com* (19/10/14). https://newmatilda.com/2014/10/19/transcripts-partial-works-professor-barry-spurr-poet-racist-misogynist (accessed 3/4/15).

Gregor, M. (1979) 'Translator's Introduction' in I. Kant (ed.) *The Conflict of the Faculties*. New York: Abaris Books.

Griffin, A. (1997) 'Knowledge under Attack: Consumption, Diversity and the Need for Values' (pp. 2–13) in R. Barnett and A. Griffin (eds.) *The End of Knowledge in Higher Education*. London: Cassell.

Grundmann, R. and Stehr, N. (2012) *The Power of Scientific Knowledge from Research to Public Policy*. Cambridge: Cambridge University Press.

Guardian Music (2013) 'Robin Thicke's Blurred Lines Gets Banned at Another University' in *The Guardian* (12/11/13).

Habermas, J. (1985) *The Theory of Communicative Action*. Boston: Beacon Press.

Hall, S. (1990) 'The Emergence of Cultural Studies and the Crisis of the Humanities' in *The Humanities as Social Technology*, 53 pp. 11–23.

Halsey, A. H. (2004) *A History of Sociology in Britain*. Oxford: Oxford University Press.

Harvard (2013) Mapping the Future: The Teaching of the Arts and Humanities at Harvard College. http://artsandhumanities.fas.harvard.edu/files/humanities/files/mapping_the_future_31_may_2013.pdf (accessed 22/05/15).

Haskell T. L. (1996) 'Justifying the Rights of Academic Freedom in the Era of "Power/Knowledge"' (pp. 43–93) in L. Menand (ed.) *The Future of Academic Freedom*. Chicago: The University of Chicago Press.

Hayes, D. (2009) 'Editorial: Academic Freedom' in *British Journal of Educational Studies*, 57 (2) pp. 107–110.

HEFCE (2014) *Sustainable Development in Higher Education*. http://www.hefce.ac.uk/media/hefce/content/pubs/2014/201430/HEFCE2014_30.pdf (accessed 7/4/15).

Hoff Sommers, C. (1994) *Who Stole Feminism?* New York: Simon and Schuster.

Hofstadter, R. (1996) *Academic Freedom in the Age of the College*. New Jersey: Transaction Publishers.

Hohendorf, G. (1993) 'Wilhelm Von Humboldt' in *Prospects: The Quarterly Review of Comparative Education*, XIII (3/4) pp. 665–676.

Horkheimer, M. and Adorno, T. (2002) *Dialectic of Enlightenment*. Stanford: Stanford University Press.

Hornosty, J. (2000) 'Academic Freedom in a Social Context' (pp. 36–48) in S. E. Kahn and D. Pavlich (eds.) *Academic Freedom and the Inclusive University*. Vancouver: University of British Columbia Press.

Horowitz, D. (2007) *Indoctrination U. The Left's War against Academic Freedom.* New York: Encounter Books.

Horvitz, L. (2015) 'Life Doesn't Come with Trigger Warnings. Why Should Books?' in *The Guardian* (18/05/15).

Husbands, C. T. (2007) 'German Academics in British Universities during the First World War: The Case of Karl Wichmann' in *German Life and Letters*, 60 (4) pp. 493–517.

Jabour, B. (2014) 'Barry Spurr Drops Legal Action to force New Matilda to Reveal Source of Emails' in *Guardian Australia* (23/10/14).

Jacobs, J. A. (2013) *In Defense of Disciplines.* London: The University of Chicago Press.

Jarvie, J. (2014) 'Trigger Happy' in *New Republic* (03/03/14).

Jaschik, S. (2014) 'Censoring Art and History' in *Inside Higher Ed* (03/03/14).

Jaschik, S. (2015) 'A Mixed Report on Salaita Controversy' in *Inside Higher Ed* (2/1/15).

Jeory, T. (2013) 'College Head Suspended over Rant about "gayism", Elton John and Ku Klux Klan' in *The Daily Express* (27/11/13).

Kaminer, W. (2015) 'The Progressive Ideas Behind the Lack of Free Speech on Campus' in *The Washington Post* (20/02/15).

Kamler, B. (2001) *Relocating the Personal: A Critical Writing Pedagogy.* Albany: State University of New York Press.

Kant, I. (1979) *The Conflict of the Faculties.* New York: Abaris Books.

Kant, I. (2009) *An Answer to the Question: What Is Enlightenment?* London: Penguin Books.

Kennedy, A. (2014) *Being Cultured: In Defence of Discrimination.* Exeter: Imprint Academic.

Kennedy, J. F. (1956) Speech at Harvard University (14/6/1956). http://www.jfklibrary.org/Research/Research-Aids/Ready-Reference/JFK-Quotations/Harvard-University-Speech.aspx (accessed 7/4/15).

Kissel, A. (2014) 'Revisiting the Classics: Joan and Peter by H. G. Wells' *NAS Article* (08/09/14). http://www.nas.org/articles/revisiting_the_classics_joan_and_peter_by_h._g._wells (accessed 18/05/15).

Koppelman, N. (2015) ' "When you want to do something join us!" The Limits of the Social Justice Mandate in Higher Education' (pp. 202–218) in C. Nelson and G. N. Brahm (eds.) *The Case against Academic Boycotts of Israel.* Chicago: Wayne State University Press.

Korn, S. Y. L. (2014) 'The Doctrine of Academic Freedom' in *The Harvard Crimson* (18/02/14).

Kors, A. C. and Silverglate, H. (1998) *The Shadow University: The Betrayal of Liberty on America's Campuses.* New York: HarperPerennial.

Kristeva, J. (1982) *Powers of Horror: An Essay on Abjection.* Trans. L. S. Roudiez. New York: Colombia University Press.

Kuhn, T. S. (2012) *The Structure of Scientific Revolutions* (Fourth Edition). London: The University of Chicago Press.

Kumar, K. (2001) 'Sociology and the Englishness of English Social Theory' in *Sociological Theory*, 19 (1) pp. 41–64.

Lacan, J. (2004) 'The Function and Field of Speech and Language' in *Écrites*. Trans. B. Fink. New York: W.W. Norton & Company.

Leathwood, C. and O'Connell, P. (2003) ' "It's a Struggle": The Construction of the "New Student" in Higher Education" ' in *Journal of Education Policy*, 18 (6) pp. 597–615.

Leavis, F. R. (1979) *Education and the University*. Cambridge: Cambridge University Press.

Lessing, D. (1962) *The Golden Notebook*. London: Fourth Estate.

Levinson, R. (2007) 'Academic Freedom and the First Amendment' *Presentation to the AAUP Summer Institute*. http://www.aaup.org/our-work/protecting-academic-freedom/academic-freedom-and-first-amendment-2007 (accessed 05/04/15).

Liptak, A. (2008) 'Hate Speech or Free Speech? What Much of West Bans Is Protectedin US' in *The New York Times* (11/06/08).

Lowe, P. (2014) 'Why UK Universities Must Steer Clear of Trigger Warnings' in *The New Statesman* (24/10/14).

Lukianoff, G. (2012) *Unlearning Liberty Campus Censorship and the End of American Debate*. New York: Encounter Books.

Lukianoff, G. (2014) *Freedom from Speech*. New York: Encounter Books.

Mahmood, S. (2014) 'Why Wellesley Should Remove Life like Statue of a Man in His Underwear' (02/06/14). http://www.huffingtonpost.com/sarah-mahmood/why-wellesley-should-remove-lifelike-statue-of-a-man-in-his-underwear_b_4732982.html (accessed 27/4/15).

Mair, J. (2003) 'The Agitators' in *The Guardian* (10/07/03).

Maira, S. (2014) 'The BDS Movement and the Front Lines of the War on Academic Freedom' (09/04/14). http://www.uminnpressblog.com/2014/04/the-bds-movement-and-front-lines-of-war.html (accessed 27/04/15).

Marcuse, H. (1991) *One Dimensional Man*. Abingdon: Routledge.

Marginson, S. (2011) 'Higher Education and Public Good' in *Higher Education Quarterly*, 65 (4) pp. 411–433.

Markle, G. E. (1995) *Meditations of a Holocaust Traveler*. New York: Albany.

Martin, J. (Ed.) (2002) *Antonio Gramsci: Critical Assessments of Leading Political Philosophers*. London: Routledge.

Marx, K. (1977) *Capital: A Critique of Political Economy*. Vol. 1. London: Lawrence and Wishart.

Marx, K. and Engels, F. (2011) *The German Ideology Including Theses on Feuerbach*. London: Prometheus Books.

Massie, A. (2014) 'Study for Its Own Sake Can Lead Down a Glorious Path – It's Never Useless' in *The Daily Telegraph* (09/10/14).

Mathiesen, K. (2014) 'Brian Cox: Scientists Giving False Sense of Debate on Climate Change' in *The Guardian* (03/09/14).

Matthews, D. (2014) 'Docherty to Face Insubordination Charge in Tribunal' in *Times Higher Education* (24/07/14).

McLean, M. (2008) *Pedagogy and the University*. Continuum: London.

McIntyre, N. (2014) 'I Helped Shut Down an Abortion Debate between Two Men Because My Uterus Isn't up for Their Discussion' in *The Independent* (18/11/14).

Menand, L. (1996) 'The Limits of Academic Freedom' (pp. 3–21) in L. Menand (ed.) *The Future of Academic Freedom*. Chicago: The University of Chicago Press.

Merrill, B. and West, L. (2009) *Using Biographical Methods in Social Research*. London: Sage.

Metzger, W. P. (1961) *Academic Freedom in the Age of the University*. Columbia: Columbia University Press.

Metzger, W. P. (1990) 'The 1940 Statement of Principles on Academic Freedom and Tenure' in *Law and Contemporary Problems*, 53 (3) pp. 3–77.

Mill, J. S. (1867) *Inaugural Address: Delivered to the University of St Andrews*. https://archive.org/details/inauguraladdres00millgoog (accessed 04/05/15).

Mill, J. S. (2005) *On Liberty*. New York: Cosimo Classics.

Miller, T. (2006) *A Companion to Cultural Studies*. New York: John Wiley and Sons.

Moberly, W. (1949) *The Crisis in the University*. London: SCM Press Ltd.

Moi, T. (1989) 'Feminist, Female, Feminine' in C. Belsey and J. Moore (eds.) *The Feminist Reader Essays in Gender and the Politics of Literary Criticism*. New York: Basil Blackwell.

Morgan, J. (2014) 'Warwick's Thomas Docherty Could Face £50,000 Legal Bill' in *Times Higher Education* (30/10/14).

Morley, L. (2001) 'Producing New Workers: Quality, Equality and Employability in Higher Education' in *Quality in Higher Education*, 7 (2) pp. 131–138.

Muller, J. and Young, M. (2014) 'Disciplines, Skills and the University' in *Higher Education*, 67 (2) pp. 127–140.

NAS. (2012) *A Crisis of Competence: The Corrupting Effect of Political Activism in the University of California* (April 2012).

NAS. (2015) *Sustainability: Higher Education's New Fundamentalism* (March 2015).

Nelson, C. (2010) *No University Is an Island*. New York: New York University Press.

Nelson, C. (2015) 'The Fragility of Academic Freedom' (pp. 60–75) in C. Nelson and G. N. Brahm (eds.) *The Case against Academic Boycotts of Israel*. Chicago and New York: Wayne State University Press.

Newman, Cardinal, J. H. (1959) *The Idea of a University*. New York: Image Books.

Nicholson, L. J. (1990) *Feminism/Postmodernism*. London: Routledge.

Nixon, J. (2011) *Higher Education and the Public Good*. Continuum: London.

O'Brien, G. D. (1998) *All the Essential Half-Truths about Higher Education*. London: University of Chicago Press.

O'Neill, B. (2014) 'Free Speech Is so Last Century. Today's Students Want the "Right to Be Comfortable"' in *The Spectator* (22/11/14).

Oparah, J. C. (2014) 'Challenging Complicity: The Neoliberal University and the Prison–Industrial Complex' in P. Chatterjee and S. Maira (eds.) *The Imperial University*. Minneapolis: University of Minnesota Press.

Patai, D. and Koertge, N. (2003) *Professing Feminism, Education and Indoctrination in Women's Studies*. Maryland: Lexington Books.

Papadimitriou, A. (2011) 'Academic Freedom and Student Grading in Greek Higher Education' in *Quality in Higher Education*, 17 (1) pp. 105–109.

Parr, C. (2014) 'University of Leeds Lectures Legal Scholar over "Political" Tweets' in *Times Higher Education* (21/08/14).

Pavlich, D. (2000) 'Academic Freedom and Inclusivity: A Perspective' (pp. vi–xvi) in S. E. Kahn and D. Pavlich (eds.) *Academic Freedom and the Inclusive University*. Vancouver: Columbia University Press.

Pinker, S. (2014) 'Three Reasons to Affirm Free Speech' in *Minding the Campus*. http://www.mindingthecampus.com/2014/10/three-reasons-to-affirm-free-speech/ (accessed 27/04/15).

Prickard, O. A. (2010) *New College Oxford*. Cambridge: Cambridge University Press.

Rauch, J. (2014) *Kindly Inquisitors: The New Attacks on Free Thought*. Chicago: University of Chicago Press.

Raunig, G. (2013) *Factories of Knowledge, Industries of Creativity*. Los Angeles: Semiotexte.

Readfearn, G. (2015) 'Australian Taxpayers Funding Climate Contrarian's Methods with $4m Bjorn Lomborg Centre' in *The Guardian* (23/04/15).

Readings, B. (1996) *The University in Ruins*. Cambridge, MA: Harvard University Press.

Rebick, J. (2000) 'Inclusion and the Academy: Debating a Good Idea Freely' (pp. 57–64) in S. E. Kahn and D. Pavlich (eds.) *Academic Freedom and the Inclusive University*. Vancouver: University of British Columbia Press.

Reece, H. (2013) 'Rape Myths: Is Elite Opinion Right and Popular Opinion Wrong?' in *Oxford Journal of Legal Studies*, 33 (3) pp. 445–473.

Rees, E. (2015) 'Self-Reflective Study: The Rise of "Mesearch"' in *Times Higher Education* (19/03/15).

Robbins, D. (1993) 'The Practical Importance of Bourdieu's Analyses of Higher Education' in *Studies in Higher Education*, 18 (2) pp. 151–163.

Robbins, L. (1966) 'Of Academic Freedom' in *Higher Education Quarterly* 20 pp. 420–435.

Robinson, J. (2010) *Bluestockings*. London: Penguin.

Rorty, R. (1996) 'Does Academic Freedom Have Philosophical Presuppositions?' (pp. 21–43) in L. Menand (ed.) *The Future of Academic Freedom*. Chicago: The University of Chicago Press.

Rose, J. (2001) *The Intellectual Life of the British Working Classes*. New Haven and London: Yale University Press.

Russell, C. (1993) *Academic Freedom*. London: Routledge.

Russia Today (2014) 'Well-"Red": MI5 Spied on Prominent Academics "for Decades", Secret Docs Show'. http://rt.com/uk/199008-mi6-spy-uk-academic/ (24/10/14) (accessed 22/05/15).

Salaita, S. (2014a) 'Normatizing State Power: Uncritical Ethical Praxis and Zionism' in P. Chatterjee and S. Maira (eds.) *The Imperial University*. Minneapolis: University of Minnesota Press.

Salaita, S. (2014b) 'The Definition of Academic Freedom, for Many, Does not Accommodate Dissent'. http://www.uminnpressblog.com/2014/04/the-definition-of-academic-freedom-for.html (accessed 27/04/15).

Schaefer, K. (2015) 'The Black Panther Party in Seattle 1968–1970' in *Seattle Civil Rights and Labor History Project*. http://depts.washington.edu/civilr/Panthers1_schaefer.htm (accessed 5/4/15).

Scott, J. W. (1996) 'Academic Freedom as an Ethical Practice' (pp. 163–187) in L. Menand (ed.) *The Future of Academic Freedom*. Chicago: The University of Chicago Press.

Scruton, R. (2001) *Kant: A Very Short Introduction*. Oxford: Oxford University Press.

Scruton, R. (2013) 'Scientism in the Arts and Humanities', in *The New Atlantis*, Fall 2013.

Schrecker, E. W. (1986) *No Ivory Tower: McCarthyism and the Universities*. Oxford: Oxford University Press.

Schrecker, E. W. (1994) *The Age of McCarthyism: A Brief History with Documents*. Boston: St. Martin's Press.

Salih, S. A. (2015) 'Islam, BDS, and the West' (pp. 141–156) in C. Nelson and G. N. Brahm (eds.) *The Case against Academic Boycotts of Israel*. Chicago: Wayne State University Press.

Shattock, M. (2012) *Making Policy in British Higher Education 1945–2011*. Buckingham: Open University Press.

Sherriff, L. (2014) 'UEA Students Stop UKIP from Speaking on Campus Following Petition' (28/11/14). http://www.huffingtonpost.co.uk/2014/11/28/uea-students-stop-ukip-speaking-campus-petition_n_6235312.html (accessed 27/4/15).

Shukman, H. (2014) 'NUS Send DJ Home for Playing Banned Hit Blurred Lines' in *The Tab* (04/11/14). http://tab.co.uk/2014/11/04/nus-boot-out-classic-dj-for-playing-blurred-lines/ (accessed 27/04/15).

Sinfield, A. (1997) *Literature, Politics and Culture in Post-War Britain*. London: The Athlone Press.

Slater, T. (2014) 'When Students Believed in Liberty' in *Spiked* (26/09/14). http://www.spiked-online.com/freespeechnow/fsn_article/when-students-believed-in-liberty#.VTzrMFU4nTZ (accessed 27/4/15).

Small, H. (2013) *The Value of the Humanities*. Oxford: Oxford University Press.

Solomon, B. M. (1985) *In the Company of Educated Women: A History of Women and Higher Education in America*. New Haven: Yale University Press.

Sontag, S. (2013) *Against Interpretation and Other Essays*. London: Penguin.

Staff Reporter. (2007) 'Push for EU Holocaust Denial Ban' in *BBC News* (15/01/07). http://news.bbc.co.uk/1/hi/world/europe/6263103.stm (accessed 03/04/15).

Staff Reporter. (2013) 'University of Kansas Suspends Controversial Journalism Professor Over Vile Tweets Calling for the Murder of NRA Members' Children' in *The Daily Mail* (21/09/13).

Standish, A. (2012) *The False Promise of Global Learning: Why Education Needs Boundaries*. London: Continuum.

Stanford University. 'Why Do the Humanities Matter?' http://humanexperience.stanford.edu/why (accessed 4/05/15).

Steedman, C. (1986) *Landscape for a Good Woman*. London: Virago Press.

Streb, M. (2006) 'The Reemergence of the Academic Freedom Debate' in E. Gerstmann and M. Streb (eds.) *Academic Freedom at the Dawn of a New Century*. Stanford: Stanford University Press.

Such, C. (2014) 'Art School Rejects Demands to Censor "Dolphin Rape" Photo as "Triggering"' in *The College Fix* (24/9/14), http://www.thecollegefix.com/post/19417/ (accessed 27/04/15).

Tallis, R. (1988) *Not Saussure*. London: Palgrave Macmillan.

Thompson, P. (2013) 'The Frankfurt School, Part Seven: What's Left?' in *The Guardian* (06/05/13).

Thompson, P. (2013) 'The Frankfurt School, Part Eight: Where Do We Go from Here?' in *The Guardian* (13/05/15).

Tiede, H-J. (2014) '"To Make Collective Action Possible": The Founding of the AAUP' in *Journal of Academic Freedom* (5) pp. 1–29.

Tilbury, C. (2014) '"The Sun Has Contributed to Rape Culture": Page 3 Banned' in *The Tab* (18/03/14), http://leicester.tab.co.uk/2014/03/18/the-sun-has-contributed-to-rape-culture-page-3-banned/ (accessed 27/4/15).

Toensing, G. C. (2014) 'Salaita awarded $5,000 AAUP Foundation Academic Freedom Grant' in *Indian Country Today Media Network* (17/10/14).

Travis, A. (2015) 'Anti-Terror Bill a Threat to Academic Freedom, MPs tell Theresa May' in *The Guardian* (12/01/15).

Victor, G. (2000) *Hitler: The Pathology of Evil*. Virginia: Potomac Books.

Williams, J. (2005) 'Skill as Metaphor: An Analysis of Terminology Used in Success For All and 21st Century Skills' in *Journal of Further and Higher Education*, 29 (2) pp. 181–190.

Williams, J. (2013) *Consuming Higher Education: Why Learning Can't Be Bought*. London: Bloomsbury.

Williams, J. (2014) 'A Critical Exploration of Changing Definitions of Public Good in Relation to Higher Education' in *Studies in Higher Education*. DOI: 10.1080/03075079.2014.942270

Williams, R. (1977) *Marxism and Literature*. Oxford: Oxford Paperbacks.

Williams, R. (1983) *Keywords*. London: Fontana Press.

Wilson, J. K. (2014) 'Fighting the Twitter Police' in *Inside Higher Ed* (08/08/14).

Winch, C. (2002) 'The Economic Aims of Education' in *Journal of Philosophy of Education* (36) pp. 101–117.

Wood. P. (2008) 'College Credit for Campaign Volunteers' NAS Article (22/09/08). http://www.nas.org/articles/College_Credit_for_Campaign_Volunteers (accessed 21/05/15).

Wright E. (1993) 'Book Review: Institutionalising English Literature' in *History of Education*, 22 pp. 227–229.

Young, M. F. D. (1971). 'An Approach to the Study of Curricula as Socially Organised Knowledge' (pp. 19–47) in M. F. D. Young (ed.) *Knowledge and Control, New Directions for the Sociology of Education*. London: Collier Macmillan.

Young, M. F. D. (2008) *Bringing Knowledge Back In*. London: Routledge.

Index

CPSIA information can be obtained
at www.ICGtesting.com
Printed in the USA
LVOW13s0414080817
544214LV00029B/1308/P